Inside the Church of Flannery O'Connor

MERCER
UNIVERSITY PRESS

Endowed by
TOM WATSON BROWN
and
THE WATSON-BROWN FOUNDATION, INC.

Inside the Church of

Flannery O'Connor

Sacrament, Sacramental, and the Sacred

in Her Fiction

Edited by

Joanne Halleran McMullen

and

Jon Parrish Peede

MERCER UNIVERSITY PRESS
MACON, GEORGIA

MUP/P384

© 2007 Mercer University Press
1400 Coleman Avenue
Macon, Georgia 31207
All rights reserved

First Paperback Edition 2008.

Books published by Mercer University Press are printed on acid free
paper that meets the requirements of American National Standard for
Information Sciences—Permanence of Paper for Printed Library
Materials.

Mercer University Press is a member of Green Press initiative (greenpressinitiative.org),
a nonprofit organization working to help publishers and printers increase their use of
recycled paper and decrease their use of fiber derived from endangered forests. This book
is printed on recycled paper.

Library of Congress Cataloging-in-Publication Data

Inside the church of Flannery O'Connor : sacrament, sacramental, and the sacred in her
fiction / edited by Joanne Halleran McMullen and Jon Parrish Peede.
1st ed.
Macon, Ga. : Mercer University Press, c2007.
McMullen, Joanne Halleran. Peede, Jon Parrish.
231 p. : ill. ; 24 cm.
9780881460551 (hardback : acid free paper)
0881460559 (hardback : acid free paper)
9780881461381 (paperback: acid free paper)
Includes bibliographical references and index.
1. O'Connor, Flannery—Criticism and interpretation.2. O'Connor, Flannery—Religion.
3. Christianity in literature. 4, Sacraments in literature. 5.Theology in literature.
6. Christianity and literature—Southern States.
PS3565.C57 Z715 2007
2007012272

For Bob, Rob, and Bridget
With love
—J.H.M.

For Mary Ann, Nancy, and Somerset
All my love
—J.P.P.

Abbreviations

The abbreviations of O'Connor's works commonly cited in the text refer to the following editions:

CS — *The Complete Stories*. Introduced by Robert Giroux. New York: Farrar, Straus, and Giroux, 1986.

CW — *Flannery O'Connor: Collected Works*. Edited by Sally Fitzgerald. New York: Library of America, 1988.

GM—*A Good Man is Hard to Find, and Other Stories*. New York: Harcourt, Brace, 1955.

HB — *The Habit of Being: Letters of Flannery O'Connor*. Edited by Sally Fitzgerald. New York: Farrar, Straus, and Giroux, 1979.

MM — *Mystery and Manners: Occasional Prose*. Edited by Sally and Robert Fitzgerald. New York: Farrar, Straus, and Giroux, 1969.

VBIA—*The Violent Bear it Away*. New York: Farrar, Straus, and Cudahy, 1960.

Contents

Inside the Church of Flannery O'Connor: An Introduction

Jon Parrish Peede

I.

Though she was a cradle-to-the-grave Catholic orthodox in her faith, in her afterlife Flannery O'Connor has come to resemble the rural evangelists she so often contemplated in her fiction. With *Wise Blood* she climbed into the pulpit as a pious young handmaiden and left it twelve years later as an immutable voice through which a creator God powerfully spoke. When examining O'Connor's journey to literary sainthood, one should not be surprised that a certain infallibility has been projected not only onto the Word, but onto her word. Such transference is common enough with fundamentalist preachers but is rare among Catholics, whether priest or parishioner. In this recomposition of the body, and by extension the body politic, one might well imagine the pale and fiery O'Connor holding forth in a sagging, clapboarded church in the Deep South, with parishioners in sunlit pews following the litany with the clear, confident voice common to the believers, while their younger brethren—the self-described skeptics— speak in the dimly lit pews across the center aisle in a cacophony of voices but not, significantly, in tongues. There she is in their unwashed memory, bent forward on her arm braces, drawing large and startling figures in the air and shouting to the hard of hearing. The believers recollect in their late priestess the workings of a faithful servant; their brethren, a gifted but self-negating master scribe. This is a house increasingly divided against itself, with the congregation meditating on an empty pulpit that speaks of mystery in a manner that only a long absence can provoke.

From the earliest appearance of her haunting dialectic stories, O'Connor cultivated a circle of steadfast advocates, many of whom exerted tremendous influence on her literary reception throughout her career, including Katherine Anne Porter, Caroline Gordon, Allen Tate, Robert Penn Warren, John Crowe Ransom, Robert and Sally Fitzgerald, and others. Of course, there were dissenting voices even among her most ardent early admirers, such as John Hawkes who found the demonic had the upper hand page after page. Others were decidedly in her camp—they just could not discern from her writing exactly where her camp was. When interviewed about Catholic literature, Walker Percy replied, "I think a lot of novels, so-called Catholic novels, American-Catholic novels, are usually Irish Catholic. Some of them are very well done indeed. Like Edwin O'Connor. And then there's Flannery—although she's a Georgia fundamentalist." The bivouacking Percy not excepted, when O'Connor said she wrote as a Roman Catholic and from a Roman Catholic worldview, her supporters not only believed her, but they helped to spread the gospel. Within her lifetime and the early decades of her afterlife, O'Connor was studied through a proscribed master text: as a religious writer who used a rural Southern, Protestant fictional backdrop as a setting to express the core tenets of not only Christianity, but of pre-Vatican II Roman Catholicism in particular.

This collection offers significant new essays by leading scholars—W. A. (William) Sessions, John F. Desmond, Jill Peláez Baumgaertner, Ralph C. Wood, and John R. May—who have advanced the codification of O'Connor as a writer preoccupied with religious, and particularly Catholic, themes. Of course, to lump these scholars together as a monolithic group does them an injustice by seeming to reduce their perceptive studies into mere broadsides from "her camp." This is not the case with their submissions here, or elsewhere for that matter. Rather, their readings share affinity with O'Connor's own views of her work.

In counterbalance, the collection presents voices of sharp dissent—chiefly Joanne Halleran McMullen and Timothy P. Caron.

These scholars find themselves at odds with O'Connor's own interpretations and with much of the existing scholarship concerning her work. They are the minority within this collection but join Michael Kreyling and others in a large and growing subset of O'Connor scholars. Contributors Helen R. Andretta, Stephen C. Behrendt, and Robert Donahoo explore theological, philosophical, and scholarly issues completely outside this believer/skeptic dichotomy, such as comparative literature and the influence of consumer culture on her writing.

Regardless of their individual positions, all ten contributors to this collection share a deep knowledge of O'Connor and her work. Indeed, seven of them have published at least one book each on her, and collectively they have invested some two centuries discussing, teaching, and writing about her work. The promise of such a diverse collection rests in the dialogues between and among their essays. One will not find consensus within these pages, nor even a settled path for the future of O'Connor studies. Rather, the collection puts on record the state of affairs during this period of transition, when those scholars who knew O'Connor personally are declining in number and canonical authority, and those who know her as a field of study as opposed to a flesh-and-blood human being are in ascension. Both groups have much to learn from the other.

II.

We chose W. A. Sessions to open this collection because of his unique authority in the field as an O'Conner friend, scholar, and advisor to her literary estate. Consider the most basic fact: for Sessions, she was a close friend named Flannery, not the vague, malleable authorial presence to which she is often reduced in order to reconcile her work with the latest continental theorist. Such carping is not against theory per se, but rather against its "one-size-fits-all" excesses in the academy over the past several decades. The benefit of a sound critical apparatus is readily apparent in the three essays forming the first section of this collection, "The Church: Sacrament and Sacramental in O'Connor's Fiction." Exploring the respective influences of Newman, Aquinas, and medieval

Church doctrine, these essays underscore the essential importance of Catholic philosophy to O'Connor's creative aesthetic and also hint at the tremendous depth of ecclesiastical learning at the heart of her fictional oeuvre.

In "Real Presence: Flannery O'Connor and the Saints," exegete exemplar W. A. Sessions demonstrates that "O'Connor is at pains to dramatize a real world of evil" and "the possibility of the good or transcendent" in response to such evil. Though O'Connor used fiction to confront these matters, Sessions states that how "the sacred operates in her texts can be defined in actuality." He provides the example of the cancer-ridden child memorialized by O'Connor in her introduction to *A Memoir of Mary Ann*, as well as O'Connor's own devout life. The difficulty for O'Connor as an artist, he argues, was manifesting an evil so well as to convince a secular world of its existence. She succeeded, but at a cost. Faulting scholars for "confus[ing] the message with the messenger," Sessions laments, "[t]hey have assumed the evil O'Connor so powerfully and mysteriously 'renders' in her texts must spring from her own 'evil,' i.e., meaning in a modern context, her personal neurosis as Catholic virgin and her cultural neurosis as one living in a South backward, race-ridden, ...and 'third-world.'" He forcefully rejects readings that spring from what Hans Georg Gadamer called the "hermeneutics of suspicion." Instead, Sessions takes O'Connor at her word: she believed we are pilgrims who must pass by the dragon on the roadside, and she wrote from that central belief. In his careful analysis of how she put that belief into practice, Sessions illustrates the influence of Cardinal John Henry Newman's *Apologia pro Vita Sua* on the structure of her fiction, especially her use of counterpoints where the diabolical and sacred intersect within her dialectics. Having "rendered" what Newman termed "aboriginal calamity," O'Connor moves the reader into the Real Presence where the existence of God is no longer a quaint archaic idea but transcendent reality.

In her essay "The Hylomorphic Sacramentalism of 'Parker's Back,'" Helen R. Andretta provides fresh insight into how aptly O'Connor—a self-described "hillbilly Thomist"—adapted Thomas Aquinas's foundational theological treatise *Summa Theologica* for her fictional world. Andretta argues that O'Connor made particular use of Aquinas's hylomorphic doctrine—the philosophical position that "all natural things are essentially constituted of 'prime matter' (Greek *hyle*) and 'substantial form' (Greek *morphe*)." In a refinement of Aristotle, Aquinas posited that we are composed of a physical body and rational soul, and that a natural tension often exists within us between these two co-principles of human substance. O'Connor internalized this philosophical argument in her nightly reading of the *Summa Theologia*, and Andretta clearly establishes its influence on her literary works. "The hylomorphic elements of 'Parker's Back' are apparent," explains Andretta, "in the imagery of various levels of life alluded to: the vegetative fruits of courtship, the sentient insects, the appetitive and locomotive representations in the tattoos, and the examined intellectual soul of Obadiah Elihue Parker." Drawing upon her research in the areas of philosophical, theological, and psychological influences on literature, Andretta concludes that "Parker's Back" is a successful attempt by the gravely ill O'Connor to create a work that brings *body* (Parker) and *soul* (Sarah Ruth) into a state of sacramental unity.

To understand the struggle of O'Connor as a writer of faith confronting a secular audience, John F. Desmond directs us to the words of her fellow Catholic writer of the South, Walker Percy, who wrote, "The question is not whether the Good News is no longer relevant, but rather whether it is possible that man is presently undergoing a tempestuous restructuring of his consciousness that does not presently allow him to take account of the Good News." Percy continued: "Such a man could not take account of God, the devil, and the angels if they were standing before him, because he has already peopled the universe with his own hierarchies." In his new essay "Flannery O'Connor and the Displaced Sacrament," Desmond delves into O'Connor's fiction with special emphasis on the rapid demystification of the Eucharist that continues in our day with what George Steiner terms the "flight from [I]ncarnation" by "thinkers and artists." Desmond names several culprits among us: Hulga Hopewell with her pseudo-nihilism, Asbury Fox with his idolatrous worship of art, and George Rayber with his perverse imitation of Christian sacramental vision. Focusing on *The Violent Bear It*

Away, Desmond identifies Rayber as a fugitive from eucharistic transubstantiation. In his reading, Rayber is not merely the modern secular humanist that other scholars have labeled him, but rather he has become "anti-human" in his disassociation from his own body and the *Corpus Christi*. "In Rayber's painless collapse," writes Desmond, "O'Connor seems to dramatize the fate of the abstract man *in extremis*, a spiritual suicide committed by one who renounces the body and the created world that she found validated and spiritualized through the sacrament of the Eucharist." However, Desmond notes that her linguistic construction holds open the possibility that Rayber's "dying" may signal the death of the self and a new openness to receive "the transformed bread and wine."

III.

Nature or nurture? That fundamental question has been at the center of Western thought for centuries. The four essays in the second section—"The Congregation: Cultural and Artistic Influences on O'Connor's Fiction"—address this question in terms of O'Connor's work. These essays explore where and to what extent her writing reflects the preoccupations and viewpoints of her cultural milieu. Did her regional culture and religious environment limit her with its rigid boundaries? Or did it provide an invaluable framing context? Or both? Whether negative and restrictive or positive and enriching, did she break free of her confinement personally and artistically?

To address such matters properly, Robert Donahoo argues that first we must be more discerning in our understanding of O'Connor's cultural context, especially how it relates to the portrayal of women in her fiction. In his essay "Beholding the Handmaids: Catholic Womanhood and 'The Comforts of Home,'" he cautions scholars against hagiographic or debunking approaches that devolve into fictive criticism rather than criticism of fiction. On the other hand, he calls for a corrective approach that does not declare "O'Connor, if not St. Flannery, at least a bold bearer of light into the literary darkness." Donahoo focuses on the emerging consensus from leading scholars such as Sarah Gordon and Katherine Hemple Prown that O'Connor revised her manuscripts—"suppressing their initial feminist tendencies"—to align them more closely with Church doctrine concerning the familial role and societal responsibilities of women. After an extensive review of Catholic publications from the 1940s and 1950s, Donahoo concludes that they were generally restrictive about the role of women in the workforce and similar subjects but were in no way homogenous. Further, their conservatism was consistent with that of popular secular magazines of that era. For example, in a 1956 *New York Times* magazine article, Sloan Wilson pronounced that "maybe...the place for women is in the home." Stressing that the Church was no more antifeminist than the culture at large was, Donahoo repositions "The Comforts of Home" as a story of a powerful woman that has been *mis*read by scholars due to their "expectation that questioning male domination, the rule of the phallus, is out of place in O'Connor's religious world." Such views, he argues, paint a less independent artist—and less independent woman—than was the case.

In the accessible language praised by reviewers of her study *Flannery O'Connor: A Proper Scaring* (1999), Jill Peláez Baumgaertner's perceptive new essay "Flannery O'Connor and the Cartoon Catechism" outlines the popularity of illustrated catechetical supplements during O'Connor's youth and links specific images from those publications to many of the author's later stories. While O'Connor's thoroughly Catholic upbringing and education were proudly acknowledged by the author and have been confirmed by researchers, scholars have penned few speculative essays regarding her early religious influences. Baumgaertner's essay serves a curative role by exploring four stories in which the *Baltimore Catechism* itself or catechetical exchanges occur at pivotal moments from a theological and narrative point of view. After outlining the verbal and structural presence of catechetical elements in "The Enduring Chill," "The Displaced Person," "The Artificial Nigger," and "The Life You Save May Be Your Own," Baumgaertner argues that O'Connor's texts also "may contain other, submerged references that are primarily visual." Focusing on eight illustrations from *Father McGuire's The New Baltimore Catechism* and *The Saint Joseph Baltimore Catechism*, Baumgaertner finds numerous images—the dangerous automobile, the tainted milk bottle, the feverish child, the blasphemous invoking of God's name—at operation in O'Connor's fiction. She concludes that catechetical books consciously or unconsciously "provided [O'Connor] with images which were subject to her relentless irony and which infused and informed her imagination as she wrote."

In "Partaking of the Sacraments with Blake and O'Connor: A Reading," Stephen C. Behrendt confronts the difficulty of reading and interpreting O'Connor texts due to the "unfamiliar ways in which [her] stories operate." Citing the model of W. A. Sessions, Behrendt calls for a contemplative *explication de texte*, a scholarly approach not unlike that required to enter the imaginative world of William Blake. Indeed, Behrendt finds an "intellectual and spiritual kinship" between the two writers. He makes no bold claims that Blake had an influence on O'Connor—Blake's books are not included in her library, discussed in *The Habit of Being*, or referenced in Jean Cash's O'Connor biography. But rather Behrendt argues that the two authors' highly idiosyncratic creative and expository writings possess remarkable similarities in terms of apocalyptic language and thematic preoccupations. He outlines four shared characteristics: (1) the carefully delineated detail in their work, (2) their similar views regarding the prophet and prophetic art, (3) their denunciation of the public's desire for the merely fashionable over the visionary or sublime, and (4) the sacramental aspect of their art. For these and other reasons, they are not artists easily summarized or explicated after a few surface readings. Rather, Behrendt concludes that "the reading process they require of us is inherently 'sacramental' in the sense in which these two devoutly Christian writers understood it—that the text becomes the mediating agency in a transfigurative and transubstantiative transaction between an eternal creative genius (whether O'Connor's very Catholic 'God' or Blake's 'Human Imagination Divine,' both operating through the artist) and a mortal, temporal reader." For those readers who move beyond merely unpacking symbols and who expose themselves as true communicants to the text, Behrendt holds out the potential of mystery unfolding "within the space of that expanded human consciousness."

In his provocative essay, "'The Bottom Rail Is on the Top': Race and 'Theological Whiteness' in Flannery O'Connor's Short Fiction," Timothy P. Caron takes exception to those scholars he terms True Believers who, following O'Connor's lead, argue that we live in "a fallen world where 'evil' is a mystery that must be endured and social justice will do little, if anything at all, to change significantly and substantially the fundamental evils with which the world is beset." Caron identifies himself as an Apostate—a believer who is concerned as much with earthly injustice as heavenly rewards. As such, he finds O'Connor wanting on the matter of race in her personal correspondence and public writing. He builds upon the central thesis of Toni Morrison's *Playing in the Dark: Whiteness and the Literary Imagination* (1993), which examines the extent to which prominent American writers such as Hemingway focus so narrowly on white characters that their oeuvres suffer from "literary whiteness." Though African Americans frequently appear in O'Connor's stories, Caron argues that her fiction is plagued by a pervasive sense of what he terms "theological whiteness"; that is to say, her fiction is preoccupied with the spiritual lives of white characters. Excepting Ralph C. Wood and a few others, Caron believes that the True Believers have ignored the issue of race by "focusing instead on the 'conversions' of the central white characters, or consider[ing] African Americans only as a sort of spiritual catalyst for Southern whites who need help in understanding God's salvational plan." Thus these scholars fail to observe how closely O'Connor's stories replicate and reinforce the dominant cultural values of the then-segregated South. In his careful explication of "Everything That Rises Must Converge," "Revelation," and "The Artificial Nigger," Caron contends that black characters are present to authenticate the setting and serve as mere "spiritual Step-n-fetchits" who are never granted their own transformative religious experiences. Caron's essay reminds us that O'Connor studies are destined to contemplate race (along with gender) in the future.

Taken as a whole, these four essays suggest that O'Connor was very much a product of her societal and religious environment and further that this environment shaped her more profoundly as a writer than did later literary mentors or historic changes unfolding in the nation in her final years. For better or worse, she emerged into adulthood with "her mind made up." Indeed, when a potential publisher could not come to terms with *Wise Blood* and less still its young author, O'Connor provided him with the phrase he was looking for—she called herself "prematurely arrogant." No matter how much she grew in her craft, O'Connor developed her artistic vision early in life; this has largely been seen as a virtue, but, as Caron cautions, it is a matter of perspective.

IV.

In *Mystery and Manners*, Flannery O'Conner lamented that in twentieth-century fiction "author and character seldom now go out to explore and penetrate a world in which the sacred is respected" (*MM*, 158). She strived to right this imbalance in her stories and novels, and the consensus of scholars has been that she succeeded in the main. However, certain stories, such as "The River," have provoked widely divergent readings on what constitutes the sacred and its attendant rites. By presenting three contradictory scholarly opinions on this single canonical story, the final section of this collection—"The Word: Denominational Doctrine in O'Connor's Fiction"—underscores the textual complexity at the heart of O'Connor's seemingly simple parables.

In her book *Writing against God: Language as Message in the Literature of Flannery O'Connor* (1998), Joanne Halleran McMullen used reader-response and linguistic analysis to build a convincing case that O'Connor's grammatical negation often placed her fictional texts in direct opposition to her intentions as expressed in her letters and essays. McMullen continues in this contrarian vein with a new essay, "Christian But Not Catholic: Baptism in Flannery O'Connor's 'The River.'" Here she argues that the story does not conform to Church doctrine concerning the sacrament of baptism, and further that critics have overlooked this fact because of their overreliance upon the author for interpretation. McMullen applies to the text the Church's definition of baptism of water, desire, and blood, as well as conditional baptism, and concludes that the necessary conditions are not met. "Her treatment of baptism is foreign to the teachings of the *Baltimore Catechism* and the Council of Trent, both of which defined all that was Catholic in O'Connor's day," McMullen writes, "yet traditional O'Connor critics repeatedly ignore the nuances in her text that assign contradictions with orthodox pre-ecumenical Catholicism." While conceding that others might reasonably perceive a *Christian* baptism in "The River," McMullen concludes that young Harry Ashfield "abandons O'Connor's Church and drowns himself in search of a God he barely knows," leaving this life unbaptized by Catholic standards.

In sharp contrast with McMullen's interpretation, Ralph C. Wood celebrates Harry Ashfield's escape from the nihilistic world of his parents into "temporal and eternal salvation." In his suasive essay, Wood recalls teaching "The River" to undergraduates, one of whom argued quite logically that Preacher Bevel and Mrs. Connin should have been charged with child abuse for leading the innocent boy to his bodily death. From a secular point of view where "survival is the ultimate good and death is the ultimate evil," the student made a reasonable argument. However, O'Connor was not working from a secular point of view, nor was she predisposed to make concessions to those who do. In her personal life and fictional world, she was firm: either one believes in Christ, or one does not. Either one embraces salvation, or one does not. According to Wood, O'Connor made "Harry Ashfield's altered allegiance as scandalous and objectionable as possible, so the readers will be compelled to make a dire decision about the boy's baptism and death—whether they are fraudulent and enslaving or truthful and freeing." Framing the story within Christian tradition, Wood shares O'Connor's conviction that for Harry the drowning was an essential rite of initiation into the kingdom of God: "As the public event that incorporates believers into the visible church, baptism is the sacrament of transferred citizenship from the *civitas terrena* to the *civitas dei*: from a realm that is perishing to another that is eternal." Wood makes a provocative parting statement about young Harry's fateful decision: "His death thus makes for a supremely happy ending to a supremely happy story." In making such a strong pronouncement, Wood follows the lead of O'Connor, who wrote famously that "to the hard of hearing you shout, and for the almost blind you draw large and startling figures" (*CW*, 806).

In the final essay of this collection, "Flannery O'Connor and the Discernment of Catholic Fiction," John R. May explores the difference between a Catholic writer and a writer of Catholic fiction. Like Wood, he also challenges McMullen's conclusions about "The River," especially the absence of Catholic sacrament in the story. May argues that scholars should focus on the fiction itself and whether it is open to a Catholic interpretation, as opposed to the author's adherence to Church dogma in her personal life or expository writing. Adopting Richard P. McBrien's identification of "sacramentality, mediation, and communion as significant dimensions of the Catholic worldview," May finds these very characteristics embedded in "The River" and *The Violent Bear It Away*. Citing mischaracterizations of Percy, O'Connor, and other religious writers, May argues for scholars to move beyond denominational labels:

> Nonetheless, I am fully aware that there will always be a reasonable, though at times unnecessarily parochial, desire on the part of critics to deal with the specifically Jewish or Protestant or Catholic in arts and fiction; on those occasions, we must take a cue from the Puritan woman Emerson referred to and "hold on hard to the huckleberry bushes," so that our discernment of Judaism, Protestantism, and Catholicism begins not from biography and explicit creedal or sacramental references but from the evidence of a particular faith's literary and artistic analogues or, as Paul Giles puts it, from the unconscious sediments of belief.

Speaking for many readers, May finds such belief at work in O'Connor's fiction.

V.

In the four decades since her death, we have witnessed no new O'Connor on the horizon. As Faulkner was to the novel, Welty to the story, Warren to the poem, and Tate to the essay, Flannery O'Connor remains a singular literary artist unequalled in her time and region. She is, to be sure, an industry as well. Such is the reward of literary success—and the curse. As each generation discovers O'Connor, the dialectic plays out anew: Was she a pious visionary or trapped in the old catechism? Did she break free of her regionalism or conform to its more ignoble beliefs? Was she a brilliant writer because of her Catholicism or in spite of it? Was she great for the reasons we suspected or for reasons only now becoming clear? As we file out from the shadow of her church into the Christ-haunted land, we are closer to these answers than when our journey began, but we aren't there yet and cannot be there yet, as is often the way with knowledge worth having.

I.

The Church:
Sacrament and Sacramental in
O'Connor's Fiction

Real Presence:
Flannery O'Connor and the Saints

W. A. Sessions

Recently a young O'Connor scholar asked to see books of mine that Flannery O'Connor had read. Looking through these books, she discovered one that startled her. "She liked that?" she asked. It was a book on Satan, a collection of essays compiled in 1951 by French Carmelites in that wonderful reflorescence of European Christian culture right after the Second World War.[1] I laughed. "Well, she wrote me she thought the book terrific, but the original cover a mess." The cover showed a kind of 1950s monster-movie Satan still popular today—a curving snake with distorted face and one horrible eye. Further, I pointed out, one of the essays, "The Devil in Contemporary Literature," was by a French writer to whom she had referred in her letters, Mme. Claude-Edmonde Magny, whose ideas had been seminal in helping O'Connor understand the nature of evil. "And read the first line of the epigraph to the book," I went on, "NON DRACO SIT MIHI DUX. Does that sound familiar?" And I added at once, in a sudden flow of memory to that time of friendship more than forty years ago, "I believe it was after this book that she first used the dragon image she loved."

I had met Flannery O'Connor in May 1956. I was in my mid-twenties, and she had invited me down from the college town where I

---

[1] *Satan: A Collection of Essays*, trans. Malachy Carroll, A. C. Downes, George R. Lamb, Christine Pietrkiewicz, Hester Whitlock et al. from unspecified volume in *Collection de Psychologie Religieuse* ETUDES CARMELITAINES (New York: Sheed & Ward, 1952). See especially the essay by Claude-Edmonde Magny, "The Devil in Contemporary Literature," 432–66. Madame Magny is referred to in *The Habit of Being*, and Flannery discussed the essay with me on the porch at Andalusia.

was teaching because she had read a review I had written of Romano Guardini's *The Lord*, which she had liked very much. I saw her last in Piedmont Hospital in Atlanta in June 1964, where, with my wife, I introduced her to my two-year-old son, the godchild of her mother, Regina. In the intervening years, I visited Andalusia many times, knowing her family well, especially her mother, uncle, and aunts. In fact, I spent Thanksgiving there for a number of consecutive years. Flannery O'Connor and her family were there as crucial supports at key moments of my life, and in those brief years, I knew her less as an author and more as a friend with whom I discussed ideas and books and made jokes about the world in which we lived in the 1950s. These conversations led us to borrow books from one another, like the volume of French essays on Satan the young scholar was examining. Such books and ideas were, in fact, the basis of our relationship, and I now remember the conversations about them as well as anything else about Flannery O'Connor.

In the following essay, I want to continue one of those conversations about the problem not of evil but of good in the modern world—specifically, how to make it real and believable in a narrative. I want to take essentially two steps in my proof: first, to demonstrate how O'Connor is at pains to dramatize a real world of evil, and then, following a dialectical structure for her stories (a strategy with sources in her immense reading), how she takes even greater pains to dramatize the possibility of the good or the transcendent within her fiction. Finally, I want to examine just how this dialectic by which the sacred operates in her texts can be defined in actuality, that is, what constitutes a living saint in the world of Flannery O'Connor.

I.

I don't know if I convinced the scholar of the two points I wanted to make. First, O'Connor did recognize that an actual devil exists, and second, just as important, she knew that recognition of total evil is only the first step. This first step before the harder task of actualizing total good was to represent such a force of evil—that is, the devil—in her own work. The problem was creative, not personal. She knew quite well diabolic energies exist, as she discussed them many times in correspondence with her novelist friend John Hawkes. It was a matter of writing well about them, an objective dilemma in representing evil, not her personality disorder. But just how could she—so certain of these realities—actualize these realities in the method Carolina Gordon taught us both, that is, in Henry James's phrase that O'Connor often quoted, not to "report" but to "render"? How could she dramatize a kind of total evil incarnate in a Satan figure, for example, within the concrete realism modern fiction demands?

She could only begin, as she must have seen immediately, with rejection. She could not accept most inherited traditions of depicting evil. They were too sensational. As O'Connor knew well, the whole Dracula world was a flashy offshoot of the far more serious concept of evil developed in Romanticism and implicit in Western cultural representation at least since Milton's Satan in *Paradise Lost*. What had passed for evil had become thrills as in teenage movies and television, where everyone has kicks and some male-hero figure—cowboy or super-cop or super-lawyer (now, some Xena-figure)—cleans it all up. The wicked are punished, but they are a lot of fun in the process. Not surprisingly, O'Connor rejected this kind of Satan, and a look at her strategy of actualizing evil is to see it's far from fun.

The Misfit, for example, may or may not be hilarious to readers, but he kills, as Dracula bites, with deadly accuracy. Both Dracula and The Misfit are essentially variants of the Romantic hero, with the originating Miltonic Satan—the quintessential "Misfit"—as generic model (as Milton's Satan would be for Hawthorne and Melville). The difference of O'Connor's Misfit from these earlier intertextual figurations illustrates her special depth and sheer wit in inverting a popular Satan figure. This Misfit kills with the absolute—in this case, theological—justification that dispassionate human beings generally seem to give themselves if they are to kill. Theological justification is especially necessary if thinking killers destroy the innocent or those who do not deserve to die, whether the killers be individual suicide bombers or a *Wehrmacht* murdering unarmed civilians or simply supreme seducers. The Misfit too is punished, of course. At least in the narrative O'Connor gives us, he

seems set to have forever the same self-doubt and puzzlement. He
cannot escape the single fact he accepts as certainty, and he broods over
it: "He [Jesus] thown everything off balance" (*CW*, 152). But must
everyone die because of The Misfit's painful doubting and wonder? As
O'Connor knew, modern human history abounds with such abstract
cases of homicide and genocide. In fact, one may argue that in the world
of "A Good Man Is Hard to Find," we find what A. C. Bradley said
about Shakespeare's universe of *King Lear*, itself inhabited by thinking
killers: "In the end the wicked are punished, and the good are not
rewarded."[2]

Indeed, in O'Connor's entire canon, there is only one story with a
relatively happy ending. Its difference and significance illustrate the
argument I hope to make about the dialectic of good and evil in her
work. "A Temple of the Holy Ghost" builds on defining the place of the
human body as young adolescent women consider what their own might
be. Surprisingly, an almost domestic story leads to a textual definition (as
nowhere else in her fiction) of the Real Presence, the Catholic Eucharist
that O'Connor devoutly believed was the actual body and blood of Jesus
Christ, as reenacted on an altar or kept in a tabernacle for reverence (or
in a monstrance for exaltation, as in the liturgy of the Blessed Sacrament
that ends the story). Ironically the narrative rises from comic
eccentricity, adolescent jokes, and carnival distortion toward this sacred
presence—out of a negative, then, certainly a trivial presence, to a
sublime positive that reaffirms and supports the innocence of the
adolescent women. By no accident, this story becomes far more realistic
and less parabolic than almost any other. It is as though, in framing the
sacred as the main operative element in the story, O'Connor understood
that this positive could only be accepted by realistic inversion. A moment
of innocence is defined by a narrative of oddities in a carnival and new
possibilities the young women discover for their bodies, both in terms of
"boys" and the Real Presence.

Choosing a model for this story, O'Connor appears deliberately to
have chosen to imitate an American Southern master. One of the great

---

[2] A.C. Bradley, *Shakespearean Tragedy: Lectures on Hamlet, Othello, King Lear, and Macbeth* (Second edition. London: MacMillan and Co., 1905) 312.

stylists in modern literature, Eudora Welty was a writer no one could ever accuse of having an interest in, or devotion to, the Real Presence. Thus, O'Connor's distancing and yet ironic and admiring parody of the Welty world allows for a unique strategy in "A Temple of the Holy Ghost": Welty's wonderfully comic world of Southern life is reinvented to become, through similes and the delight of any children's story, one of O'Connor's most theologically complex stories. It defines emblematically the human body moving from its obverse or counterpoint in a carnival oddity as the monstrous hermaphrodite to the exalted body of Jesus Christ in the Eucharist of her ideology. The plot may play within this spectrum of the "distortion" of the human body from carnival oddity to exalted Blessed Sacrament, but it is focused as an initiation story. Innocent now, the young protagonists will inevitably enter their own distortions and discover, one way or another, the doomed and murderous universe of the self-hating Hulga, the wandering Hazel Motes, and the abstracting Rayber. For that moment, however, in what I would call a Welty moment, these young women (and men) discover the presence and possibility of a real innocence within themselves. Quite literally, at the end of the text, the young women pray before the exalted Real Presence of Jesus Christ, about whose accessible innocence the young girls have earlier sung a Latin hymn. As a kind of competing joke, the boys rejoin with a Georgia country Protestant hymn about an innocent Jesus to tease them.

As this story makes clear, innocence, even the most exalted, exists in a Misfit universe. As O'Connor herself pointed out in her humorous explication of the meeting of St. Francis of Assisi and the wolf of Gubbio, the wolf remained a wolf. Human reality remains displaced. O'Connor understood such displacement from the start, with her child's literary sketches and wonderful early cartoons and satiric drawings that ridicule so much of her Savannah world. Flannery discovered displacement of human existence, whether in Georgia or antebellum Milledgeville in mid-twentieth century or in the worlds of Atlanta and New York. Rewards in such a displaced world had become increasingly irrelevant as a concept, as she knew. Iris Murdoch, a fellow novelist hardly hostile to religion (she prayed the Rosary at one time), was much closer to the truth about her culture in *Sovereignty of the Good*: "In the case of morality, although there are sometimes rewards, the idea of a reward is out of place."[3]

So, for O'Connor's fiction to have any credibility in the modern world, she had to undertake, from the beginning, a strategy without rewards, at least within the plot of the story. This was O'Connor's first step as a writer of narrative. In fact, like Pascal, she had early recognized *la rèalitè des choses* in the modern world. The rigorous honesty Caroline Gordon had taught her demanded, first, dramatizing the negative world of The Misfit. She had, in this sense, to pass by the dragon—to use her adaptation of the saying of St. Cyril of Jerusalem—not only in her own encountering of a universe of evil but in composing her own texts. Above all, the truth of the story must pass by the threatening dragon before it can discover its own freedom and reality.

II.

O'Connor succeeded quite well in the first part of her writing strategy. It is no surprise that, from fellow novelists such as John Hawkes, Walker Percy, and Truman Capote, to a multitude of scholars, critics, and fascinated readers, her audience had the sense that Flannery was playing for keeps. In fact, for many, O'Connor's universe appears bereft not only of rewards but of any transcendence at all—that is, any awareness of a presence beyond the immanence of human history—an absence of grace, as so many of her critics lament. One reason for this success in "rendering" the negative is that her stories, no matter how naturalistic in detail, quickly become parables. Even the casual reader finds her fictions loaded, like an aimed automatic. The cosmic is at work, most readers feel; something larger than what the script is saying operates—if not overtly, then indirectly. This is what O'Connor calls "the added dimension" of her writing that looks, at least at one end of the spectrum, to the sacred, another kind of presence. It could only operate within, however, and be added on to, that fragmented Los-Angelized reality

---

[3] Iris Murdoch, *The Sovereignty of Good* (London: Chatto and Windus, 1970) 95.

prophetically "rendered" by her Jewish literary ancestor, Nathanael West. As O'Connor saw less than twenty years later, that particular landscape was rapidly becoming the Southern landscape in the 1950s and early 1960s.

So, although never at any moment in her life did she not accept a cosmic frame for human existence, the much harder process was to add it into her Misfit text. This became her technical challenge. She knew well the undivine comedy of modern existence from, among other things, her own local sense of displacement—a Catholic woman in a Protestant South ruled by Herman Talmadge and dangerous segregationists (one of the Ks in KKK stood for Catholics). From her adolescence, she had lived, like her country, in a perpetual state of war, with the terror of attack like December 7, 1941, always at hand. She also spent almost fifteen of her few years of life with the knowledge that her own body was collapsing and she would soon die. These personal experiences told her any moment of harmony or transcendence could only begin in displacement: her own and that of the history unfolding around her. Enlightenment, secularism, and liberal metaphysics with their theories of fulfilled immanence (monological, without transcendence) never seemed to have meaning for her; on the contrary, she admired the attacks on them by the pioneering neo-conservative Russell Kirk. Displacement, as her ancestors and her body were telling her, had to lead to survival, not illusion.

Her reading of the German historian Eric Vögelin also told her of a breakdown and shift in human history—Pascal's *rèalitè des choses* refers actually to the huge psychological shift brought about by the Copernican revolution made possible by the breakdown of the Middle Ages, the historical period that most developed O'Connor's theology. Beyond this recognition of universal displacement, O'Connor went a step further. She followed the corollary Pascal also made in his *Pensèes*: in such a radical break that all Western culture shared, what must also be radical is any representation of human existence, if like Pascal, it was to be viewed *sub specie aeternitate*. That is, if O'Connor wanted her writing to actualize a living cosmic frame (as opposed to an agnostic or deist static framing of an absolute), she would have to be radical. In short, representations had to be—or at least appear to be—almost self-originating in a free-flowing universe, whether the author did or did not believe in an absolute frame. Discourse, therefore, must seek new forms—and the more radical the disconnect with one's own world, the more violent and shocking the artisitic form for showing this negative reality might have to be. But how to find the truthful discourse that would "render" O'Connor's communal world with so few certainties and "where ignorant armies clash by night," in Matthew Arnold's famous description of the displaced Victorian world?

Ironically, then, for O'Connor the believer, the devout language of saints, holy men and women, and the Virgin Mary would no longer do for "rendering" her world. But it was still, of course, a world in which she kept continuous company with the saints and prayed often at the end of her life, for example, to the holy Archangel St. Raphael. Indeed she was, for much of her life, a daily communicant of the Catholic Eucharist, all of the Masses in Latin. She completely believed, as she once witnessed before three of the most renowned literary figures of the twentieth century (two of them ex-Catholics), in that most sacred of the Catholic Christian dogmas, the Real Presence of the Jesus Christ in the Catholic and Orthodox liturgies.   Questions of holiness, therefore, concerned her more deeply than one might think, but for any kind of holiness she knew an original language would have to be found.

It is probable, then, that O'Connor knew the cost of leaving behind the old language that had defined her being for so many years and of having now, in a new world, to invent another. Using her personal library that has been called one of the finest private theological libraries in America, she read and contemplated the texts of saints—for example, of two other young women, St. Catherine of Genoa, especially her writing on purgatory, and St. Catherine of Siena, to whom Christ had said in a vision, "Know, daughter, that I am He who is, and thou art that which is not." The excellent catalogues of these books on religion and philosophy and a myriad of subjects show not only O'Connor's range but her depth. In her library, works on Christology and the nature of the Real Presence deal especially with modern and contemporary interpretations by Baron von Hügel, Romano Guardini, and other

British, German, and French theologians as well as significant texts from modern philosophy and psychology. What all this reading suggests—and the letters from *The Habit of Being* confirm—is that O'Connor herself sought a holy life and, above all, a language that would express her own sense of holiness but in a Misfit world.

Such a language would need to have, therefore, its validity in Pascal's post-Copernican reality of things. The old language of the saints held no such external truth. The old presence of grace had once been set in its most beautiful dialectical form—at least for O'Connor—in Dante's *Divine Comedy*, about which she wrote her friend "A." (Betty Hester): "For my money Dante is about as great as you can get" (*HB*, 116). Closer to the actual universe O'Connor saw around her, however, was a universe of Misfits with distorted ambitious Hulgas and preacher-prophets seemingly wandering in circles and being raped by other men or themselves murdering. A divine intervening Beatrice with an announced hope of redeeming love would be absurd. Where then, to represent her strong sense of the sacred, could she find the proper language for her own parabolic fiction? To use the old language of saints would deny the very purpose of what she wanted most as a writer, to reach an audience lost in a secular age, as she discusses in "The Nature and Aim of Fiction."

Thus, without such a language that would reach her audience, O'Connor could never effect "a willing suspension of disbelief," as she wanted to use the Romantic poet Samuel Taylor Coleridge's famous definition for reading a text. Coleridge's was a negative definition, one may note, using the rhetorical figure of speech of *litotes* to describe something quite simple but intellectually forbidden (at least in his post-Copernican modern Europe): an act of *faith*, in this case in what one is reading. Looking back at the world Pascal described and predicted, in which faith of any kind would be redefined and often through the negative, a contemporary reader of O'Connor might say "the narrow way that leads to salvation" often appears to turn, in her twentieth century, into a vague track that leads to nowhere in particular, and the "pearl of great price," to transfer to O'Connor in 1960, has the value of a trinket that the Bible salesman might have given Hulga for her wooden leg.

Not everyone has been satisfied with O'Connor's solutions to the problem of modern life as she saw it. Many readers see no problem at all. The problem they see elsewhere. What, for example, are *her* intentions with so much negation?[4] What is she really after? Is she a Manichean, for whom evil is an absolute in itself, not just less good as in St. Augustine's definition of evil, and therefore Flannery's evil total in itself and incapable of any dialectic with the sacred? Or is her technique of deliberate denigration of the human being simply a game, her own and her culture's? That is, is O'Connor's Jesus only one more mockery of the props of Western culture especially encouraged since the Romantics and epitomized in Baudelaire's phrase *èpater le bourgeois* (still the ideological subtext for rock bands and MTV acts and considerable media communication)?

In the 1840s, the French symbolist poet Charles Baudelaire had already offered, in fact, the standard definition of the modern Satanic figure as moral. This French symbolist poet wrote that he could not be moral as defined by his European culture; he would not be amoral like the Belgians he despised, and so he would affirm his morality by being immoral. For Flannery's master, Faulkner, or such writers as Gordon, Tate, Eliot, and even her earlier special hero, Leon Bloy, Baudelaire was heroic in originating such a strategy of evil. And there is always, it seems, a more sinister question: is this strategy of actualizing diabolic energies merely another form of masochistic solipsism coming from the violence the author herself felt about her unhappy existence? Can her fiction be explained as a means to release her personal aggression and anger as her own body and being were being violated and, in terms of her innocence and seeming lack of sexual activity, unfulfilled, her dying body even raped by death?

By no surprise, such readers and critics have confused the message with the messenger. They have assumed the evil that O'Connor so

---

[4] On the topic of O'Connor's grammatical negation, see Joanne Halleran McMullen, *Writing against God: Language as Message in the Literature of Flannery O'Connor* (Macon GA: Mercer University Press, 1996).

powerfully and mysteriously "renders" in her texts as springing from her own "evil." That means in a modern context, that she does not escape what has been assumed to be her personal neurosis as Catholic virgin and her cultural neurosis as one living in a South backward, race-ridden and, according to Gabriel García Márquez traveling through it in the 1950s, as run-down as any other "third-world." In other words, such a reader does not appear to grasp the meaning of the more objective world of O'Connor's texts. This reader must find a monological interpretation based on the author's personal failures or her physical or mental disabilities or on the sickness of her region or on her hopelessly outdated ideological training.

This kind of reading is in itself, of course, one more Romantic critical fallacy. It reflects what Wimsatt calls "the intentional fallacy" and "the generic fallacy." Its resultant critical method of "I gotcha ya!" is endemic in the modern world and named by Paul Ricoeur, the French theorist and philosopher, and the German philosopher Hans Georg Gadamer as "a hermeneutics of suspicion." Thus, while such negative critical strategy may be valuable as a tool of exploration and contextual interpretation, a reading based only on this strategy obviates the elementary fact existing in the text—the story or the novel itself provides the *only* instrument by which we know these "neuroses," and it is fiction.

Such a focus on the text is exactly what O'Connor herself called for in all her discourses on the craft of fiction, especially in her letters to "A." and Erik Langkjaer. Without the objective text, then, that Flannery expected us to read, our readings may be reduced as she understood, to to demonizing or hagiography, both essentially forms of sentimentality. Good reading starts with the author's *invention*. It provides the objective evidence. The text may originate in personal biography or other life-situations, but can we know these beyond the most fragmentary generalizations? Flannery underlined a crucial sentence in her readings of the Swiss Protestant Denis de Rougement's *The Christian Opportunity*: "Sincerity has scarcely any significance in art."[5]

---

[5] Denis De Rougement, *The Christian Opportunity*, trans. Donald Lehmkuhl (New York: Holt, Rinehart, and Winston, 1963) 84.

III.

But can we start with an actualization of evil—hardly "sincere" in the modern sense—in these invented fictional texts of O'Connor? Her "rendering" of evil is quite relentless and, at times, as charged as anything in Dante (whose *Inferno* is the only part of the *Comedy*, incidentally, she did mark in her copy). A further irony is that, however "neurotic" the origins or whatever the reason, the violent texts work—and not just because of their calculated shock and wild laughter. Surely, the enormous popularity of "A Good Man Is Hard to Find" among students into the twenty-first century cannot be merely because of its negative energies. They see considerably more violence on MTV, I-Pods, the Internet, and in video games every hour. What such readers must instinctively recognize is that, even if O'Connor's play of fiction is carried out with the Irish Protestant Samuel Beckett's circularity of language, high humor, sexual violence, and seemingly lack of direction (his waiting metaphor), the effect is not Beckett's. And it is the same in almost every work by O'Connor: a grim judgment awaits human nature. There is a destiny at work amid it all, O'Connor is saying, or in the twentieth-century French poet Paul Claudel's observation, "God writes straight with crooked lines."[6]

Such surprised readers are often like the little boy Harry Ashfield in "The River" finally facing some force he cannot comprehend with the result that he is so excited he heads out to drown himself in it. In O'Connor, some excited readers see an absolute judgment as a "relief" beyond the endless deceptions of television, the Internet, and the Enlightenment mentality that runs societies with its fallacy that solutions are always possible in history (and if they don't work, still must be required as solutions). Is it any wonder that the film director Quentin Tarantino would borrow from O'Connor's texts for his postmodern *Pulp Fiction* set literally in Los Angeles and that its ending, if any exists in this circular film, reverts to the language of O'Connor? This continuous

---

[6] Paul Claudel, epigraph to his play *Le Soulier de Satin* (*The Satin Slipper*).

influence attests to the success O'Connor has achieved by her actualization of evil in her fictional texts.

But is it negation alone that inspires such imitation? If the old language of the sacred is ridiculous, if there is no longer any mountain of purgatory to be climbed and certainly no heaven with fixed stars, to what has O'Connor reverted? The strategy by which O'Connor set up her world of evil began, as I shall now show, as she discovered how to "render" the sacred. It was a technical strategy that involved establishing a counterpointing between her two worlds, the negative as well as the positive, the sacred as well as the Satanic. This counterpointing or dialectic in the text provides the tension that gives her fiction its dramatic intensity. But how could she develop a technique that would so attract a Tarantino and a remarkably diverse international audience? Where could she find that much harder term of her dialectic to be "rendered" the sacred?

The answer may finally remain as much a mystery as the reality of O'Connor's own life. We may be able to trace some kind of answer through the intertextuality of her reading, as profound as it was wide. Whether she knew it firsthand or not, her literary antecedents such as the Tates, Ransom, and the masters at Iowa knew that from Petrarch and certainly the Romantics on, another tradition had developed to describe a technique used by generations of poets, novelists, and artists. This technique can be succinctly encapsulated in Wordsworth's famous phrase to describe a growing poet's sensibility: "intimations of immortality." That is, in the midst of a negative universe, a character (or speaking poet) discovers another "universe" speaking to this character or poet. This "universal" speaks with a radically different voice and juxtaposes itself in a kind of counterpoint to the negative world dominating the text. Thus, in the midst of the Los Angeles of *Pulp Fiction*, for example, the African-American lead actor, Samuel Jackson, recalls a Bible passage of prophecy. Such moments of transcendence appear as a kind of counterpoint or dialectic, outside of the more normative sex, violence, and drugs. They appear in what the Catholic-bred James Joyce named his version of these "intimations" in his own text—"epiphanies."

Joyce chooses this word deliberately out of the Catholic liturgy, the ritual of saints' and holy days. His term "epiphanies" describes important structures within the symbolic realism of his stories in *Dubliners* and the play *Exiles,* and they focus the magnificent renderings of *Ulysses* and become the very threads of *Finnegan's Wake.* Joyce was a master for O'Connor, and she appropriated this technique in which she could technically bring her narrative the closest to Dante and to the perception of a moment of transcendence within the text. Such a technique involves a sudden perception by a character in graphically realistic time, but the perception is only momentary, as in the gross Ruby Turpin's vision beyond her history. This character looks at the Georgia sunset from the midst of her hog pen. Like the epiphany of the falling snow scene that concludes James Joyce's long story "The Dead," on which O'Connor's "Revelation" is modeled, Ruby has her "intimation of eternity." But it is just a moment, no more. Ruby must wait without clear direction, at least as O'Connor has developed her text. At the end she can only hear the highway in the distance, turn off the water faucet that has been running during her "epiphany," and walk home in the dark to the sound of the crickets. More resolved because of her "intimation," Ruby still returns like the wolf Gubbio to the still broken world of The Misfit.

IV.

There is thus a framing in O'Connor's texts that allows a system of counterpoints to exist, an interaction of presences, diabolical and sacred. It usually works or comes into play when, as in Tarantino, a character is under stress, even facing annihilation, perhaps physical, perhaps deeper, perhaps both. Such stress defines both the grandmother and The Misfit in the parable of "A Good Man Is Hard to Find" when an outside force is violently entering the old woman's world and causing The Misfit to define his own. The sacred may not save anyone in such a world, but it does redefine Pascal's *rèalitè des choses* as it existed in The Misfit's Georgia landscape of the 1950s. Nothing can ever be the same again. A more formal structure operates in the language of an O'Connor text in order to allow the interaction—in the poet Hopkins's term, "counterpointing"—of these two worlds of the diabolic and the sacred. A quotation from Cardinal John Henry Newman may be helpful here to focus this pervasive framing in O'Connor's works. It comes from a text she knew well and marked, Newman's *Apologia pro Vita Sua*: "And so I argue about the world;—*if* there be a God, *since* there is a God, the human race is implicated in some terrible aboriginal calamity. It is out of joint with the purposes of its Creator. This is a fact…almost as certain as that the world exists, and as the existence of God."[7]

Newman is setting up two terms in his definition of his own quite modern Victorian world. In fact, what Newman is describing cannot be stated logically without such a dialectical definition. He starts with the simplest recognition about human existence, whether in twenty-first-century Los Angeles or nineteenth-century London, to set his first term. It establishes the basic negative condition of human existence. For Newman, an evidential "fact" is as real as anything his contemporary Darwin might have found in Galapagos Islands: human life and human history are "implicated in some terrible aboriginal calamity," a *devolution* of disaster. The origin of this continuing disaster may be, in fact, as mysterious as Darwin's origins—the first premise of Darwin's logical inductive proof is one, in fact, Darwin himself never fully explains. For Newman, this "calamity" also exists as "fact" as much as any evolutionary species—"almost as certain as that the world exists." Such an "aboriginal calamity" defines therefore human existence at any time, whether it be, in terms O'Connor used in an interview with Granville Hicks to describe the perennial relevance of a text, "in 1950, 2050, or 50-50."[8] Needless to say, not even Quentin Tarantino or the masters of our media appear to deny this "fact" of essential "calamity." In point of fact, media masters make their cash on reminding audiences just how implicated or lost they are.

---

[7] John Henry Cardinal Newman, *Apologia Pro Vita Sua* (Boston: Houghton Mifflin Company, 1956) 23.

[8] Rosemary M. Magee, ed., *Conversations with Flannery O'Connor* (Jackson: University Press of Mississippi, 1987) 81.

Newman is saying something else here. He is setting up terms for a definition, and they form a dialectic.[9] For Newman, the first term is the obvious negative of an ongoing "calamity" revealed in universal human history and in the specific London of Dickens, Newman, Karl Marx, and Oscar Wilde. This logical force of Newman's second term—what amounts to a positive framing for human existence—is centered, in his definition, on the word "*since*." The word implies a condition of total belief as the logical base for the assertion and climax in his definition of "Creator," the ultimate term for this part of the dialectic. There is an important context here for this second part of Newman's definition. Just before the Victorian died in 1890, Newman himself noted that the real religious problems in the West are no longer about which form of religion to choose. Modern Europe and the West, he argued, have serious doubts about the existence of a God at all, a question Newman's European contemporary Nietzsche was just then answering with the announcement of God's death. This second corollary thus becomes the more treacherous to assert and certainly to "render" for a modern Nietzschean audience—O'Connor's targeted audience.

V.

Flannery O'Connor uses the terms of Newman's dialectic, but she recalibrates them each time in her fiction for special purposes. Like St. Francis, she has to aim her message at a special kind of wolf. In these texts themselves, O'Connor reveals her concept of sanctity as well as anywhere else. Her letters, essays, and book reviews also disclose her ideas about saints and the question of sanctity, but nothing is more revealing than her fictional texts. Given the limits of this essay, I can only refer to selected texts to demonstrate the parabolic dimension of the whole canon.

---

[9] I am using this term *dialectic* as Gadamer does, and, for our specific purposes, I mean precisely dialectic as counterpoint, an interaction of contrasting relationships within an O'Connor text, or, if you want, the larger framing in her work of the cosmic dialectic the Chinese call *ying* and *yang*.

I want to emphasize the obvious that O'Connor's dialectical strategy is an old literary strategy, especially suited for satire and comedy. As logic itself and modern scientific method have taught us, negatives cannot exist without positives. Absence can perform only where a positive exists as "fact." In literary genre, this interplay of the negative and the positive forms the very structure of satire and good comedy, whether mock-heroic or parody or Oscar Wilde's larger dialectical triumph in *The Importance of Being Earnest.* In the classic eighteenth-century satire of Alexander Pope, "The Rape of the Lock," critics have long remarked that, without a castigating moralistic Clarissa, there can be no laughter and mocking of the beautiful but silly Belinda.

Such a dichotomous literary structure was there from the start. The great Roman master of satire, Juvenal, the violent mocker of another kind of Los Angeles, followed precisely this dialectical structure. Against the scenes of debauchery, corruption, and political and social breakdown under Nero, Juvenal establishes a simple authorial voice that recalls the old Roman Stoic ideals. The negative and hilarious and comic absurd exist, then, but only because of this dialectical framing set by a positive in interaction with the negative.

So we come back to a fundamental problem in trying to understand O'Connor's concept of the saints: how does an artist "render" a universe in which not only a fallen archangel exists and controls but another archangel Raphael is operative, an angel who will not seduce but lead and guide as long ago this angel did Tobias? More crucially, how could O'Connor actualize a cosmic and quite local dialectic operating at the same time in human existence? The answer appears to be simple in theory. Images and language and events in the narratives, however marginal, perform as counterpoints to the continuing "aboriginal calamity" that, in most cases, defines the plot. O'Connor places these counterpoints at crucial moments, often at end of a narrative but also at the beginning, as though both parts of the dialectic were endemic to the universe she is trying to dramatize and must be seen to contain it at its heart.

The opening of O'Connor's story "The Displaced Person" "renders" such a dialectic. The dialectic is immediately designated. Newman's first term ("aboriginal calamity") is given at once:

> The peacock was following Mrs. Shortley up the road to the hill where she meant to stand. Moving one behind the other, they looked like a complete procession. Her arms were folded and as she mounted the prominence, she might have been the giant wife of the countryside, come out at some sign of danger to see what the trouble was. ...She ignored the white afternoon sun which was creeping behind a ragged wall of cloud as if it pretended to be an intruder and cast her gaze down the red clay road that turned off from the highway. (*CW*, 285)

Then O'Connor gives the second and positive term ("existence of God") of Newman's dialectic that will now resonate throughout the plot: "The peacock stopped just behind her, his tail—glittering green-gold and blue in the sunlight—lifted just enough so that it would not touch the ground. It flowed out on either side like a floating train and his head on the long blue reed-like neck was drawn back as if his attention were fixed in the distance on something no one else could see" (*CW*, 285).

Two forces are colliding; each is looking a different direction. It is not that "grace" or more technically an "intimation" of transcendence is not working in Mrs. Shortley—she is not the diabolic Bible salesman—but the magnificent peacock that in the O'Connor parable embodies the force of transcendence is behind her. Mrs. Shortley ignores it. This bird-creature is like the winged Raphael and performs as an instrument leading to a meeting of two realms or an "intimation" of a reality beyond the history of this particular Georgia world. The countrywoman is no doubt aware of the peacock, but its presence is meaningless for her. In the plot—the only place where either the peacock or Mrs. Shortley exists in any actuality—neither is free of The Misfit's world. The peacock, certainly as O'Connor sets the creature up, can only operate as a tangent of transcendence. It becomes a *momentary* presence in a world that is largely absent of recognition of what is stalking it. Ironically, what Mrs. Shortley and the peacock (stalking her like Hazel Motes's shadow) have in common is their dual representation of a moment in which, at least in O'Connor's plot, the absolute intervenes in a local Georgia world.

For O'Connor, such intervention can only happen within the plot—exactly what Aristotle predicated. The wolf of Gubbio remains a wolf. To succeed in "converting" that wolf, O'Connor used the concrete, specific method of St. Francis (which in the legend appears almost desultory like the remarkable often is in a Buddhist parable). Such narration for a modern wolf of Gubbio must also include the indirect, the tangential, the marginal, even the odd, if the action is be believed by a modern audience. Even the violence in the plot must arise from a carefully crafted method. The next step is the reader's, and, if meditation or contemplation of the event by characters in the story—Ruby's, for example—can open for them the cosmic framing, so with a modern audience.

Thus, as in the repetitive recapitulation process in yoga meditation, the story demands an accurate "breathing" or concrete reading, perhaps several times, before the cosmic appears. This is the nature of the parable and reading a parable. Thus, the Holocaust in Europe can be abstracted and generalized, but to see it enacted on a farm in "The Displaced Person" in Georgia in the 1950s in vivid concrete language is to make, if not the actual person of Satan tangible, at least the effects of a new Holocaust alive. In fact, the more times we read and think about the various strands of the plot coming together in this story by O'Connor, the more the larger meaning in the parable story hits us. Such reading makes a local diabolic catastrophe so credible it can be believed—"a willing suspension of disbelief"—by modern audiences all over the world.

The parable has to begin and end, however, as a specific plot, not an abstraction. Before any dialectical meaning can be found, the writer must follow a technique of specificity or what Gerard Manley Hopkins, a favorite poet of O'Connor's, calls "thing-ness." Hopkins meant the inherent nature of specific local reality, and it was a term, as O'Connor knew, translated from the term *quidditas*, which St. Thomas adapted from the Aristotelian dialectical emphasis on the essential metaphysical nature of our specific material reality. Thus, for O'Connor, the sacred—the Real Presence itself—enters a mixed universe. It can never be revealed in art or anywhere else. Even visions, like St. Francis's or St. Catherine of Siena's, are quite local, as she knew. Through this technique of specific "thing-ness," O'Connor wanted to "render" in her stories a larger frame. Heaven as well as a hell may be capable of being glimpsed, however briefly. The French twentieth-century novelist François Mauriac, one of O'Connor's important sources as a writer, went a step further about human existence: we have already begun our heaven and hell.

VI.

Finally, we know how Flannery O'Connor saw the face of a saint or, more exactly, a human being she considered holy. It was, in fact, a very specific local face. It defined once more for her the ongoing counterpoint of the positive and negative. Although she knew the face only by photograph, she saw the distorted face of a child—half of it eaten away (the left side, as I recall), the eye hooded, the other half of the face quite bright, the glowing skin of a girl of six, with one large bright alert eye that moved constantly, happy at seeing everything, the bangs of her hair bouncing across her unmarked forehead. By accident, I did see her once—Flannery's only friend who came in contact with Mary Ann. The little girl was swinging on a gate at the Trappist Monastery near Atlanta and surrounded by lively nuns in long habits in black, in those days before another world-shift (one Flannery never knew) of the Second Vatican Council. The little girl might have been an oddity such as the two adolescent girls saw at the carnival in "A Temple of the Holy Ghost."

She was not, however. She was quite real, not fictional. Flannery saw enough in the little girl's photograph to write the preface to a book telling the story of her short life. Flannery had written to me immediately when she had first received the letter of request from the Dominican Sisters in Atlanta who care for incurable cases of cancer.

Flannery thought I could write a popular book the nuns wanted on the girl Mary Ann, whose Baptist parents had left her as a child with the nuns who then watched over her for years and then had watched her die. I could not, and she knew she could not, but she decided on the strategy I suggested: ask the nuns themselves to write on the impossible subject of a pious child and, if they did, O'Connor would edit and help and we would hope for the miracle of its being accepted by a publisher. It was, and then the book elicited another kind of miracle—O'Connor's extraordinary preface with her subtle interweaving of the story of the order's founder, Rose Hawthorne, the daughter of the American writer Nathaniel Hawthorne, who had influenced O'Connor so powerfully.[10]

O'Connor's preface can help us reach some conclusions about how she viewed the saints and the whole concept of sanctity. First, it tells us saints or holy people are always local, never abstract, and are involved in specific acts. O'Connor wrote me after my own First Communion when I was discussing my "experiences" a story about Gerard Manley Hopkins. Hopkins said to the poet Robert Bridges, who had contemplated entering the Catholic Church, that he should quit thinking about it and "give alms." In other words, he should act and not think. Secondly, because of its specific reality, sanctity is always partial. It remains to be "rendered" in the actuality of our wolf-ness. In her preface, O'Connor explains that the story of Mary Ann, whose supposed piety had seemed so repugnant at first, opened her to "a new perspective on the grotesque." Most of us, Flannery says, have learned to endure the terrible evil around us, and when we "look it in the face," we "find, as often as not, our own grinning reflections with which we do not argue" (*HB*, 164). Flannery continued this image of the mirror and the face. She declares her concept of the positive to this negative, the functioning of the transcendent within this very immanent universe. She reveals the dialectic of the two sides of the child's cancerous face. "Good," she

---

[10] After her divorce in the late nineteenth century and a wandering lonely life, Rose Hawthorne entered the Catholic Church and soon began working with incurable and abandoned cases of cancer in the lower east side of Manhattan. She founded an order that has flourished and endured and is herself now a woman in the process of canonization by the Catholic Church.

writes, "is another matter. Few have stared at that [the face of good itself] long enough to accept the fact that its face too is grotesque, that in us the good is something under construction" (*CW*, 830).

"Something under construction": we have now come to Flannery O'Connor's concept of the good. It also defines the action or person of the saint, even the Real Presence itself as it is being actualized in our time and place. Furthermore, if, as O'Connor's ideology had taught her and she believed totally, "the Word of God is like a two-edged sword," then heaven itself can only be a challenge, "something under construction" also, at least in our perception of it from a double-edged world. Heaven in this sense is like that large right eye of the little girl I saw swinging on the gate and that O'Connor saw in the photograph or Rose Hawthorne searching out the cancerous in the slums of the modern city or O'Connor in every word she wrote. Even Dante's great beatific vision—the sight of God at the end of his epic—is only described in images of motion, of looking.

So, if saints do exist in O'Connor's fiction, they exist in terms of their seeking. They exist in terms of their awful ongoing discoveries, most of all about themselves as living between both ends of the spectrum of their universe—Hazel Motes moving farther and farther into darkness but as "a pin-point of light"; Francis Marion Tarwater by the burning tree before heading out for the dark city, conscious of the new fire within himself; Ruby moving back from her vision to her world to wait; Parker, conscious at last of his complete loneliness, except for the Byzantine Christ on his back, and weeping with the burden he now will carry forever. In each the Real Presence itself is being actualized and in each there is "something under construction."

VII.

Saints are then quite possible in the dialectic of human existence, and they do exist in a community like the moving rose Dante describes in the *Paradiso*, but in our world it is a community of love they must actively seek. This constant looking and listening to find community can lead O'Connor seekers into violence and pain, a world without love.

O'Connor marked a passage in a text by the Swiss Protestant Karl Barth: "It is a terrible thing when God keeps silence, and by keeping silence speaks."[11] This silence, this loneliness, is the negative, whether in the red clay hills of Parker's world or the Georgia trees of Ruby's vision or the city maze Hazel Motes wandered or the crowded traffic of Rose Hawthorne's streets. It is there, often in a speaking silence, that every saint must start.

Did Flannery O'Connor consider herself such a seeker in silence? No one can know, but I do remember a conversation in the 1950s on the front porch of her Andalusia. "Have you ever thought about what it would mean to be a saint yourself?" I must have asked. I remember distinctly the reaction to this Enoch-like question I was always prone to ask. It was a surprise. Flannery suddenly smiled, her round face and blue eyes lit up. "Oh yes," she laughed, "and the price to pay." Flannery O'Connor had underlined another passage about this waiting and the dark night of the soul described by all saints. Cardinal Newman led O'Connor to the full dimension of the two-edged sword of the Bible, a text. Faith—interpretation of an ultimate text—is a matter for Newman also of two realms. Faith exists in a waiting pattern between a diabolical world and a sacred. This kind of interpretation may cut in either direction. What is certain in this waiting between two worlds is one fact: the self is not alone. In another passage from Newman's *Apologia*, O'Connor specifically marked lines that conclude the passage: "It is face to face, 'solus cum solo,' in all matters between man and his God. He alone creates; He also has redeemed; before His awful eyes we go in death; in the vision of Him is our eternal beatitude."[12]

Waiting then is active, a meeting that always lies before us. This process of anticipation was a process O'Connor would have read in Simone Weil's deeply personal transformation of the Hebraic prophets and their waiting and then in Samuel Beckett's great parody of Weil in *Waiting for Godot*. Waiting with hope defines precisely the meaning of the prayer to St. Raphael that O'Connor adapts from a French text by

---

[11] Karl Barth, *Evangelical Theology: and Introduction*, trans. Grover Foley (New York: Rhinehardt and Winston, 1963) 136.

[12] Newman, *Apologia*, 203.

Ernest Hello, a precursor of Leon Bloy, one of her key influences: "O
Raphael, lead us toward those we are waiting for, those who are waiting
for us: Raphael, Angel of happy meeting, lead us by the hand toward
those we are looking for." Such hope of ultimate "meeting" drives
O'Connor's seekers in their fictional worlds from Hazel Motes to
Tarwater to Ruby to Parker to, even in their inverted ways, The Misfit
and Hulga.

Further, as the images of motion in the Raphael prayer dramatize
more concretely than Newman's "beatitude," heaven or the saints
themselves are defined by another kind of walking and waiting and
meeting. O'Connor knew another passage that more exactly describes
the condition of waiting as a definition of heaven, and it too is a story of
walking and of meeting—the hope that drives all of O'Connor's seekers
through all the mazes of their existence.

After the lonely walkers to Emmaus have met the mysterious
stranger and heard him expound on the necessity for the sufferings and
death of their beloved leader the event that has left the walkers so broken
and in search of meaning, they suddenly recognize the leader himself. It
is in the breaking of the bread. He blesses this bread and offers it to
them. Their eyes are opened for the first time, and they see the Real
Presence that has been with them all along. Then the two say to each
other, in a condition that describes not only O'Connor's heaven but her
saints: "Were not our hearts burning within us when he spoke to us on
the road?"

The Hylomorphic Sacramentalism of "Parker's Back"

Helen R. Andretta

The terms "sacrament" and "sacramental" have separate meanings as nouns and are inclusive and exclusive of each other when applied with particular religious meaning. Both are external signs and communicate grace. The former is "a sensibly perceptible rite" instituted "by Christ the God-man during his visible stay on earth" to confer "the supernatural grace it symbolizes," and the variety of the latter "spans the whole range of times and places, words and actions, objects and gestures that, on the Church's authority, draw not only on the personal dispositions of the individual but on the merits and prayers of the whole Mystical Body of Christ."[1] The sacraments in the Roman Catholic faith are seven in number: Baptism, Confirmation, Penance, Holy Eucharist, Holy Orders, Matrimony, and Anointing of the Sick (formerly Extreme Unction). The sacramentals by nature of their definition are innumerable. The distinctions between the "sacrament" and "sacramental" would have mattered to Flannery O'Connor as a practicing Roman Catholic, but the distinctions probably did not matter to her as a writer. For her, the "sacrament" and "sacramental" exemplify the basic truth of her faith belief in the Incarnation of Christ. Her writings contain elements alluding to both. One of O'Connor's last stories, "Parker's Back," seems to evidence the significance of the "sacramentalized" unity of body and soul.

Before I focus on this late work of O'Connor, I shall review some of her statements about being a Catholic fiction writer and comment on

---

[1] John A. Hardon, *Modern Catholic Dictionary* (Garden City NY: Doubleday, 1980) 477.

their relevance to my thesis that the "sacramentalism" in "Parker's Back" is based on the hylomorphic doctrine of theologian-philosopher Thomas Aquinas (1225–1274). In "The Nature and Aim of Fiction," O'Connor defines the art of a writer as "writing something that is valuable in itself and that works in itself. The basis of art is truth, both in matter and in mode. The person who aims after art in his work aims after truth in an imaginative sense, no more and no less." She continues, "St. Thomas said that the artist is concerned with the good of that which is made" (*MM*, 65). This good she makes through her writing, she admits, is influenced by her Catholicism. In her first letter to "A." (20 July 1955), a frequent correspondent later revealed to be Elizabeth Hester, O'Connor asserted, "I write the way I do because (not though) I am a Catholic. This is a fact and nothing covers it like the bald statement. However, I am a Catholic peculiarly possessed of the modern consciousness, that thing Jung describes as unhistorical, solitary, and guilty" (*HB*, 90). This admission to "A." was followed by many more regarding the connection of her faith and Thomistic philosophy to her writing. As I indicated in a close study of O'Connor's letters to "A.," "The letters from Flannery O'Connor to 'A' are more numerous than other exchanges collected by Sally Fitzgerald in *The Habit of Being*. They cover a novena of years, July 1955 to July 1964."[2] Seventeen of twenty-three collected letters with references to St. Thomas Aquinas are to "A."

O'Connor's relating the truth of an artist's work to the good of the work comes from Aquinas's discussion of the question "Whether the Intellectual Habit, Art, Is a Virtue." Aquinas defines art as "the right reason about certain works to be made." The good of the work depends not on the will of the craftsman "but on the goodness of the work done." The good of a craftsman "is commendable, not for the will with which he does a work, but for the quality of the work."[3] This synthesis of truth and goodness is not only religious but also philosophical and expressive of both sacramentalism and hylomorphism in O'Connor's writings.

---

[2] Helen R. Andretta, "A Thomist's Letters to 'A,'" *The Flannery O'Connor Bulletin* 26–27 (1998–2000): 52.

[3] Thomas Aquinas, *Summa Theologica*, trans. Fathers of the English Dominican Province, 3 vols. (New York: Benziger, 1947) vol. 1, I-II, q. 57, art. 3.

Hylomorphism is the philosophical doctrine that all natural things are essentially constituted of "prime matter" (Greek *hyle*) and "substantial form" (Greek *morphe*). This doctrine, developed from Aristotle's definition of change in *De anima* and *Physica*, was a view of reality expanded by Thomas Aquinas into an understanding of human nature as composed of co-principles of physical body and rational soul. "The Treatise on Man," a large section in Aquinas's monumental work, the *Summa Theologica*, discusses in twenty-eight questions the unity of these co-principles in the human substance.[4] Additional questions in the *Summa* relate to the nature of man.[5]

The extant holdings of O'Connor's personal library in the Ina Dillard Russell Library at Georgia State College and University Center in Milledgeville have numerous markings and annotations that relate to an interest in religious, philosophical, and psychological aspects of human nature. Many of her reviews in diocesan papers are of books relating to the human condition. Notable examples are her reviews of Romano Guardini's *Freedom, Grace, and Destiny* (1961), Jacques Maritain's *The Range of Reason* (1961), Teilhard de Chardin's *The Phenomenon of Man* (1959) and *The Divine Milieu* (1960), Gustave Weigel's *The Modern God: Faith in a Secular Culture* (1963), and Victor White's *Soul And Psyche: An Enquiry into the Relationship of Psychotherapy and Religion* (1960).[6] The basis for her understanding and critical approach lies in her familiarity with the thought of Thomas Aquinas.

In another letter to "A." in 1955, O'Connor wrote, "I read it [the *Summa Theologica*] for about twenty minutes every night before I go to bed" (*HB*, 93). In a letter to John Hawkes in 1961, O'Connor asserted, "I am a Thomist three times removed and live amongst many distinctions" (*HB*, 439). It was inevitable that O'Connor should be influenced by the most all-pervasive principle of Thomistic philosophy with relation to humanity—hylomorphism, the essential unity of body and soul. This doctrine is related to the "sacramentalism" of human existence. Since all

---

[4] Ibid., I, qq. 75–102.

[5] Ibid., I-II, qq. 1–114.

[6] See Lorine M. Getz, *Flannery O'Connor: Her Life, Library and Book Reviews* (New York: Edward Mellon Press, 1980) 165, 175, 179, 161, 199, 158.

humankind has been redeemed by the salvational act of Christ's death and resurrection, its very nature has been sanctified.

In "The Church and the Fiction Writer," one of many essays collected by Sally and Robert Fitzgerald in *Mystery and Manners* (1969), O'Connor admits that "belief in a fixed dogma" does "add a dimension to the writer's observation" and that "the added dimension will be judged in a work of fiction by the truthfulness and wholeness of the natural events presented" (*MM*, 150). Yet this regional Southern writer revealed mystery and grace with such grotesquery that one questions "the truthfulness and wholeness of the natural events presented." On consideration of some of the events in her stories, one wonders even about their naturalness. The question and wonder, however, are resolved perhaps by recognizing the concern of O'Connor "with the good of that which is made," giving her stories a value of the sacrament and the sacramental with the imaginative sense of a Roman Catholic artist who was also a Thomist. Just as Aquinas synthesized faith and reason into an acceptable understanding of who we are, from where we have come, where we are going, and how we will get there, so O'Connor synthesized her religious belief and Thomistic leanings into an acceptable understanding of who she was as an artist and incorporated in her writings the mystery of the human condition.

The mystery of human existence as a theme of plot and character depends on O'Connor's vision as related in "The Fiction Writer & His Country": "I am no disbeliever in spiritual purpose and no vague believer. I see from the standpoint of Christian orthodoxy. This means that for me the meaning of life is centered in our redemption by Christ and what I see in the world I see in its relationship to that" (*MM*, 32). Sally Fitzgerald states that the young O'Connor recognized her vocation as having "three components—the personal, the religious, and the literary—[and they] were not only inextricably bound together and interactive but were in themselves profoundly Catholic, not only by reason of a lifelong personal and religious formation, but by her own will and intent, and ensuing deep commitment to excellence in all three areas, as she approached and reached adulthood."[7] In "The Fiction Writer & His Country," O'Connor expresses that commitment in her explanation of "mystery" in fiction:

> In the greatest fiction, the writer's moral sense coincides with his dramatic sense, and I see no way for it to do this unless his moral judgment is part of the very art of seeing, and he is free to use it. I have heard it said that belief in Christian dogma is a hindrance to the writer, but I myself have found nothing further from the truth. Actually, it frees the storyteller to observe. It is not a set of rules which fixes what he sees in the world. It affects his writing primarily by guaranteeing his respect for mystery. (*MM*, 31)

Since her faith comprised various elements of mystery, the communication of mystery in her art came naturally to O'Connor. However, she admitted that what she viewed as natural in real life were distorted depictions. These sometimes violent distortions had a shock value, which she found necessary for a hostile audience: "[T]o the hard of hearing you shout, and for the almost-blind you draw large and startling figures" (*MM*, 34). O'Connor depicts violence as a means to effect a revelatory end. Her violent, sometimes grotesque, stories concern mysterious passages past or into the jaws of St. Cyril of Jerusalem's dragon who "sits by the side of the road" ready to devour us as "[w]e go to the Father of Souls" (*MM*, 35). Passing the dragon, a symbolic grotesque creature of evil, is often the journey her characters make in her stories.

The grotesque elements of the passage through life of her characters are deliberate, for in "Some Aspects of the Grotesque in Southern Fiction," O'Connor defines the grotesque as "a directed intention...on the part of the author," yet she tells us that despite our unaccustomed experience of grotesque actions, her "characters have an inner coherence, if not always a coherence to their social framework.

---

[7] Sally Fitzgerald, "Sources and Resources: The Catholic Imagination of Flannery O'Connor," *Logos: A Journal of Catholic Thought and Culture* 1/1 (1997): 79.

Their fictional qualities lean away from typical social patterns, toward mystery and the unexpected" (*MM*, 40). The "mystery and the unexpected" are often sacramental, for O'Connor desires to have her fiction push "its own limits outward toward the limits of mystery" (*MM*, 41). She uses vivid images, which shock the senses but communicate messages of grace, for she explains, "Fiction begins where human knowledge begins—with the senses—and every fiction writer is bound by this fundamental aspect of his medium. I do believe, however, that the kind of writer I am describing will use the concrete in a more drastic way. His way will much more obviously be the way of distortion" (*MM*, 42). That knowledge begins with the senses is an aspect of Thomistic thought discussed in the *Summa Theologica*: "[O]ur intellect, which takes cognizance of the essence of a thing as its proper object, gains knowledge from sense, of which the proper objects are external accidents. Hence from external appearances we come to the knowledge of the essence of things."[8] By using images that distort the concrete, O'Connor forces her audience to encounter mystery. For her, the writer of grotesque fiction looks "for one image that will connect or combine or embody two points; one is a point in the concrete, and the other is a point not visible to the naked eye, but believed in by him firmly, just as real to him, really, as the one that everybody sees" (*MM*, 42). That invisible point is the mystery of life itself, the "sacramentalism" of human existence and the redeemed journey of particular humanity to a place outside the temporal order.

For O'Connor the movement of fiction "toward the limits of mystery" means the novelist faces the problem of distorting without destroying. She tells us he must descend within himself to reach "those underground springs that give life to his work" for the beginning of vision (*MM*, 50). O'Connor imposes this quest for vision upon her characters, who often reside in the country. Their environment has an expansion of meaning for O'Connor. In "The Fiction Writer & His Country," she defines "country" as being

---

[8] Aquinas, *Summa Theologica*, vol. 1, I, q. 18, art. 2.

everything from the actual countryside...on to and through the peculiar characteristic of his [the writer's] region and his nation, and on, through, and under all of these to his true country, which the writer with Christian convictions will consider to be what is eternal and absolute. This covers considerable territory, and if one were talking of any other kind of writing than the writing of fiction, one would perhaps say "countries," but it is the peculiar burden of the fiction writer that he has to make one country do for all and that he has to evoke that one country through the concrete particulars of a life that he can make believable. (*MM*, 27)

"[T]hat one country" is for O'Connor the Ultimate Reality, the Alpha and Omega. That the word "country" can suggest both the concrete and the abstract relates to Thomas Aquinas's discussion of how words and names can have concrete and abstract meanings. Aquinas tells us that "all names used by us to signify a complete subsisting thing must have a concrete meaning as applicable to compound things; whereas names given to signify simple forms, signify a thing not as subsisting, but as that whereby a thing is; as for instance, whiteness signifies that whereby a thing is white. And as God is simple, and subsisting, we attribute to Him abstract names to signify His simplicity, and concrete names to signify His substance and perfection[.]"[9]

In both the *Summa Theologica*[10] and the *Summa Contra Gentiles*,[11] Aquinas speaks of the names of God and creatures being predicated neither univocally nor equivocally but analogically, concluding "we come to a knowledge of God from other things, the reality in the names said of God and other things belongs by priority in God according to His mode of being, but the meaning of the name belongs to God by posteriority. And so He is said to be named from His effects."[12] The distinctions

---

[9] Ibid., I, q. 13, art. 1.

[10] Ibid., I, q. 13, arts. 5–10.

[11] Thomas Aquinas, *Summa Contra Gentiles; Book One: God*, trans. Anton C. Pegis, FRSC (Notre Dame: University of Notre Dame Press, 1975) bk. 1, chs. 32–34.

[12] Ibid., bk. 1, ch. 34.

made in the naming of things with reference to O'Connor's use of the name "country" have both concrete and abstract meanings. The geographical "country" is distinct from the eternal "country," yet O'Connor points out through her stories that traveling through the first, concrete in meaning, inevitably involves a movement toward the "true country," abstract in meaning, especially because it relates analogically to God.

In the same essay, O'Connor alludes to the hylomorphic doctrine when she states of her stories, "I find that they are, for the most part, about people who are poor, who are afflicted in both mind and body, who have little—or at best a distorted—sense of spiritual purpose, and whose actions do not apparently give the reader a great assurance of the joy of life" (*MM*, 32). For O'Connor an affliction of mind is an affliction of soul, and the symbols of physical affliction in some of her characters often relate to a spiritual one as in the wooden leg of Joy/Hulga, which she takes care of "as someone else would his soul" (*CW*, 281), and the damaged sockets of Hazel Motes, which he creates by bathing his eyes in a quicklime solution (*CW*, 119). Joy/Hulga depends on her prosthesis as a mental crutch, and Hazel blinds himself so he can see.

During the writing of "Parker's Back," O'Connor was acutely aware of affliction in body and its relationship to affliction in soul. At the age of twenty-five she was experiencing the complications of lupus erythematosus, the debilitating disease that took her father's life nine years before. The month before she succumbed to the disease's effects, she sent copies of "Parker's Back," one of three final stories she was working on, to close friends for their feedback. In a letter to "A." dated 25 July 1964, she wrote that she would ignore "a lot of advice" Caroline Carver gave her, that she was "letting it [the story] lay." She explained Carver's use of the term "heresy" for her story as not applicable to Parker's tattoos but to Sarah Ruth's being "the heretic—the notion that you can worship in pure spirit" (*HB*, 594). Such an assessment refers to gnostic thought, a heresy that challenges the hylomorphic view of humankind's co-principles of body and soul, i.e., matter and form. Thomas Pink defines Gnosticism as "dualist, distinguishing the spiritual and good world from the evil and material world. Matter was the creation of a wicked demi-urge. But a spiritual saviour had come to offer redeeming gnosis, or knowledge of our true spiritual selves. The gnostic would be released from the material world, the non-gnostic doomed to reincarnation."[13] Gnosticism is a precursor of Manichaeism, defined by Philip L. Quinn as "a radical dualism of good and evil that is metaphysically grounded in coeternal and independent cosmic powers of Light and Darkness. This world was regarded as a mixture of good and evil in which spirit represents Light and matter represents Darkness. Manichaean morality was severely ascetic."[14] As a fiction writer, O'Connor related Manichaeism to a spirit of modern times: "The Manicheans separated spirit and matter. To them all material things were evil. They sought pure spirit and tried to approach the infinite directly without any mediation of matter. This is also pretty much the modern spirit, and for the sensibility infected with it, fiction is hard if not impossible to write because fiction is so very much an incarnational art" (*MM*, 68).

To call fiction an incarnational art suggests O'Connor attributed to it not only matter and spirit (form) but also a redemptive aspect. The sacraments are incarnational in that they require proper matter and form to effect grace. O'Connor seems to focus on two sacraments in her works: Baptism, which requires water and particular formulaic words, and the Holy Eucharist, which requires bread and wine and also particular formulaic words. The formula of spoken words is a physical rendering of spirituality. Grace flows mysteriously from God to humankind through matter. As God was incarnated to redeem the fallen world, so in a sense is grace in continuing manifestations of redemption. The references in her stories to Manichaeism, Gnosticism, nihilism, or other skeptical beliefs are diametrically opposed to a Thomistic and specifically hylomorphic understanding of human nature; they reveal obstacles to redemption. The familiarity of O'Connor with these beliefs through her wide range of reading enabled her to show in her stories

---

[13] Ted Honderich, ed., *The Oxford Companion to Philosophy* (New York: Oxford University Press, 1995) 314.
[14] Ibid., 519.

how inadequate they are to understanding the human condition, thereby indirectly elucidating her own belief system.

In its elements of Manichaeism, "Parker's Back" seems to express O'Connor's understanding of the soul-body connection in the context of hylomorphism. The story suggests the absoluteness of the unity of soul and body particularly and of form and matter universally by depicting the deprivation in self when a human being becomes obsessed with either spirit or matter. The two main characters, O. E. Parker and Sarah Ruth Cates, represent these deprivations. They are introduced to the reader as unexplainably attracted to each other: "Her being against color, it was the more remarkable she had married him" (*CW*, 655). Parker is colorful in tattoos. In philosophical terms, color is an accident of substance, but the attributes of color are the result of numerous tattoos, which, ironically, are literally "accidents" in their disorganized markings of Parker's flesh. As a human being, Parker is the substance whose many colors individualize and identify him but not in a complete way. For Sarah Ruth, the attraction to Parker seems to be rebellion against her own self since she frowns upon material glorifications of the spirit. I say "seems" because O'Connor gives us, the readers, no experience of the inner workings of the mind of Sarah Ruth. We see her through the eyes of Parker, who does not understand why he is attracted to Sarah Ruth. She is "plain, plain. The skin on her face was thin and drawn as tight as the skin on an onion and her eyes were grey and sharp like the points of two icepicks" (*CW*, 655). A hylomorphic interpretation makes the attraction understandable.

Parker and Sarah Ruth are two very different beings: Parker is concerned with the outer manifestation of self, and Sarah Ruth, the daughter of a Straight Gospel preacher, is concerned with her inner spirit. Despite the difference, they contract to be man and wife after a courtship that involves Parker's giving three different gifts to Sarah Ruth: a bushel of apples the second time he sees her, a basket of peaches the third time, and two cantaloupes the fourth time. That O'Connor indicates the gifts of fruits as the initial signs of courtship is significant. If indeed this tale of dissatisfaction in marriage has hylomorphic interpretation, the flashback of courtship must begin by allusion to the lowest power of soul in matter, the vegetative power possessed by plants solely but by higher forms of living things according to their level of existence, as described by Aristotle and elucidated by Aquinas. Only the souls of rational beings possess the highest power in earthly existence, intellectual power, as well as all the powers of the lower forms: vegetative, sensitive, appetitive, and locomotive.[15] The story itself opens with the imagery of the vegetative in Sarah Ruth's onionskin, a single tall pecan tree, and a newspaper full of beans.

In his courting, Parker offers Sarah Ruth the fruits of his literal labor,[16] and Sarah Ruth accepts them. After the last gift, upon her questioning, Parker reveals in a low voice the names behind his initials O. E.: Obadiah Elihue. Obadiah literally means "worshiper of Jehovah," and Elihue means "whose God is He."[17] That O'Connor chose these particular names for her protagonist Parker is significant to his characterization. Obadiah's story is found in 1 Kings 18. Obadiah is a zealous follower of the Lord, although in service to Ahab, worshiper of Baal. He hides from Ahab's wife Jezebel a hundred prophets, fifty in each of two caves, supplying them with food and drink. Elijah calls upon him to inform Ahab that he, Elijah, is in the land. Obadiah fears for his life, but Elijah reassures him and Obadiah delivers the message to Ahab. We do sense a fear in Parker not only of Sarah Ruth's reaction to anything he does but also to the specific declaration of his name as though he is not able to live up to its meaning. He ran away from his home as a teen, shortly after his mother, a laundress, took him to a revival meeting in the hope that he would change his life of drinking, getting into fights, and

---

[15] See Aristotle, *On the Soul (De anima)*, trans. J. A. Smith, in vol. 8 of *Great Books of the Western World*, ed. Robert Maynard Hutchins, 54 vols. (Chicago: William Benton, 1952) bk. 2, ch. 3. See also Thomas Aquinas, *A Commentary on Aristotle's De Anima*, trans. Robert Pasnau (New Haven: Yale University Press, 1999) bk. 2, ch. 5.

[16] He sells apples from his truck to isolated homesteaders at the same price for which he buys them, evidence of either his altruism to his fellow man or a lack of intelligence. If the former, this is a manifest sign of goodness in Parker; if the latter, this is a sign of his inability to make good choices because of a dimming of his intellectual power. He picks the peaches and somehow comes across the cantaloupes.

[17] Miles Orvell, *Flannery O'Connor: An Introduction* (Jackson: University Press of Mississippi, 1991) 169.

pursuing girls attracted to his tattoos, actions representative of the sentient and appetitive powers in living things, feeling and desire without reason. As for the name Elihue, it is of the young man who tries to explain in Job 32–37 reasons why Job has been afflicted with suffering. I would argue that Parker refuses to acknowledge this name because again he is not able to live up to its meaning. He is not wise enough, like Elihue, to have an explanation for his predicament of dissatisfaction with life, that is, with his suffering condition.

Although Sarah Ruth appears not to appreciate Parker's body markings of colorful tattoos, they do not interfere with her willingness to marry him; although Parker considers the features of Sarah Ruth as plain and lean, they do not present an obstacle to his desiring her. Sarah Ruth is not concerned with things of the flesh, but Parker's name, when revealed to her, evokes her repetition of it "in a reverent voice" (*CW*, 662). Perhaps to her, the name Obadiah Elihue transcends the present and refers to religious emissaries of the past whose bodies have long rotted in the ground but whose names still breathe the life of their enduring spirits. Sarah Ruth's response to the name Obadiah Elihue suggests O'Connor's knowledge of Aquinas's treatment of the significance of names. In the context of discussing the intellect, Aquinas speaks of our naming "a thing in accordance with our knowledge of it…, so from external properties names are often imposed to signify essences."[18] Elsewhere, as mentioned earlier, Aquinas gives an expansive treatment of names of God and creatures neither as univocal nor equivocal but analogical "according to an order or reference to something [that is] one" since "the order according to the name and according to reality is sometimes found to be the same and sometimes not. For the order of the name follows the order of knowledge because it is the sign of an intelligible conception."[19] Applied to Sarah Ruth, her intelligible conception of Parker's name is an association with the spiritual, with the abstract form, and not with the carnal and uniquely individual Parker. Since Sarah Ruth makes it clear she will not be possessed except in marriage, she and Parker become one in the flesh

---

[18] Aquinas, *Summa Theologica*, vol. 1, I, q. 18, art. 3.

[19] Aquinas, *Summa Contra Gentiles*, bk. 1, ch. 34.

after their state-sanctioned union "in the County Ordinary's office." Sarah Ruth calls churches "idolatrous" (*CW*, 663), perhaps because churches have statues, material representations of spiritual beings.

When Sarah Ruth gets pregnant, Parker is not happy about her condition, for "pregnant women were not his favorite kind" (*CW*, 655). He attempts to lighten the gloom in his marriage by getting additional tattoos on the remaining unmarked space on his body, everywhere except his back. He bears on his body a red and blue eagle (Sarah Ruth calls it a chicken) perched on a cannon, a serpent coiled about a shield, arrowed and arrowless hearts, a spread hand of cards, anchors and crossed rifles from his five-year stint in the navy, a tiger, a panther, a cobra-coiled torch, a lion, hawks, the Buddha, peacocks, Elizabeth II and Philip, the name of Betty Jean (a concession to his mother to permit his tattooing), and a few obscenities. For Sarah Ruth these body markings probably represent material and therefore negative aspects of human existence: war, death, and sin. The images of Buddha and Elizabeth II with Philip, as objects of worship (the former) and adulation (the latter), are akin to church statuary. The tattoos of the peacocks stand out as images of the radiance of God and creation, but they are on his knees and rarely seen, even by Parker.

Parker's fascination with tattoos dates back to his adolescence when at the age of fourteen, Parker saw on the body of a small and sturdy man an "intricate design of brilliant color," which, when the man flexed his muscles, made "the arabesque of men and beasts and flowers on his skin" appear "to have a subtle motion of its own." The movement of these images moved Parker, who "was filled with emotion" at the sight (*CW*, 657). Emotion and instinct appear to be his responses to life. He is attracted emotionally and instinctively to images he wishes to have stamped on his body as though they confirm his state of existence. His marriage to Sarah Ruth appears to be an instinctive action as well, for in the deliberation about his state, he sees no reason for having been attracted to her.

The first tattoo "hurt very little, just to make it appear to Parker to be worth doing" (*CW*, 658), which is to say pain must accompany the rendering of images upon his flesh. The need for pain recalls Hazel

Motes, the protagonist in O'Connor's novel *Wise Blood*, who, though professing nonbelief in Christ, enigmatically wears stones and broken glass in his shoes and three strands of barbed wire around his chest. For Motes the suffering seems to be a desire to participate in the suffering of him who is denied. Although Parker does not say so, his reason for experiencing pain may be that expressed by Motes, who tells his inquisitive landlady, Mrs. Flood, "To pay.... It don't make any difference for what. ...I'm paying" (*CW*, 125). Parker does not publicly declare a denial of Christ as Motes does, but he is trying to escape from the strictures of religion communicated to him by his mother. The tattoos seem acts of rebellion as well as signs of affirmation of who he is. If he feels pain, he affirms his existence and the tattoos make his living worthwhile. Years later, after many tattoos and a satisfaction for each that lasted about a month, Parker sees not "one intricate arabesque of colors but something haphazard and botched" (*CW*, 659). He tries to remedy his dissatisfaction by filling up the empty space on the front of his body with more tattoos. There is no order in their distribution. Parker's body seems to reflect his soul, which is not clear to him: "himself he could not understand" (*CW*, 655).

It appears if Sarah Ruth would appreciate his outward self, Parker could understand and esteem himself better. There would be some satisfaction for him if he could rouse an appreciation by Sarah Ruth for his tattoos. He tells her "tales of the hefty girl he worked for," who he says made such remarks as "Mr. Parker,...I hired you for your brains" and "Mr. Parker,...you're a walking panner-rammer" (*CW*, 664). He neglects to tell his wife that the speaker issued the latter comment out of the side of her seventy-year-old mouth.

Desperate to please a wife who takes no pleasure in any material joy or thing in this world, tic-plagued Parker has the inspiration to have his tattoo-free back marked with a religious subject. Perhaps this will please Sarah Ruth. Marshall Bruce Gentry refers to this decision as "part of Parker's unconscious strategy for using his devotion to his wife to bring himself to Christ"; Gentry adds, however, that the decision is also

"Parker's conscious motivation."[20] This view is consistent with my thesis that there is an incompleteness to Parker's being. He hungers for a fulfillment of self. In desiring to please Sarah Ruth, Parker is longing to satisfy himself with what she "seems" to have so completely—a spirituality that if embraced by him will make him attractive to her. Of course, what he does not see in his limited vision is that Sarah Ruth is lacking in that which he possesses, a human expression of his sentient and appetitive powers.

The preoccupation of Parker with the idea of a religious tattoo leads to an accident with an old tractor while he is baling hay. He has been warned by his aged employer to be careful about doing injury to an old tree, but here he is, jolted into the air and landing "on his back while the tractor" crashes "upside-down into the tree and burst[s] into flame." Parker sees "his shoes, quickly being eaten by the fire," and scrambles backward and toward his truck, collapsing "on his knees twice" (*CW*, 665). The allusions are religious: to the Old Testament Moses in the flaming bush and to the New Testament Christ in his falls on the way of carrying the cross. The merger of scriptural images can be viewed in a broad sense as a sacramental signifier to be distinguished from "sacramental sign" as defined by John A. Hardon: "the external ritual by which a sacrament is performed and through which the distinctive graces of that sacrament are conferred. ...e.g., the pouring of water, and the Trinitarian formula in baptism."[21]

The tractor crash experience leads to the decision by barefooted Parker to have an image of God tattooed upon his back. As he thumbs through the pages of a book of pictures of Christ in a tattoo parlor, his heart dictates, "Go back," and he does, to "the haloed head of a flat stern Byzantine Christ with all-demanding eyes"; he trembles (*CW*, 667). Paul Elie tells us that in this "grotesque modern romance,"[22] the use of the image of the Byzantine Christ may have been prompted by the

---

[20] Marshall Bruce Gentry, *Flannery O'Connor's Religion of the Grotesque* (Jackson: University of Mississippi Press, 1986) 79.

[21] Hardon, *Modern Catholic Dictionary*, 478.

[22] Paul Elie, *The Life You Save May Be Your Own: An American Pilgrimage* (New York: Farrar, Strauss and Giroux, 2003) 362.

recollection of an illustration in a book O'Connor read in her twenties, André Malraux's *The Voices of Silence*, a "great mosaic Christ of Santa Sophia in Istanbul." Elie bases his speculation on the use of the word "silence" many times in O'Connor's story.[23] The attraction to an image that speaks to Parker in its silent and stern visage expresses his longing for a completeness he does not understand.

Parker insists that the artist include "all those little [mosaic] blocks" of the image (recall the earlier allusion to Moses) and not just the outline and features; it takes two long days to complete the image (Christ spent two days in the tomb before he effected redemption). After the first day, Parker spends a sleepless night on a cot at the Haven of Light Christian Mission, where he is shod in second-hand shoes and where a phosphorescent cross glows in the room (another sacramental signifier). He recalls the accident scene and envisions the tree's reaching out to grasp him, the tree's bursting into flame, the shoe's burning quietly, and the eyes in the book. Like Elie, Edward Kessler describes "an articulate silence" in this story "which ultimately overpowers both word and image, the language itself. ...Parker recollects the flaming tree and the possessive eyes of the Byzantine Christ—not as visual or auditory images, but as feeling. The eyes speak, but without sound."[24] This "silent" communication by the eyes is a voice not blaring but glaring at Parker. O'Connor does tell us Parker longs miserably for Sarah Ruth, whose eyes appear softer than those of the Byzantine Christ, whose gaze makes him feel "as transparent as the wing of a fly" (*CW*, 669). The imagery suggests Parker is feeling reduced to part of a lower level of life, the wing of an insect. The eyes of a wife who is "ugly and pregnant and no cook," who makes "him generally nervous and irritable," causing him to develop "a little tic in the side of his face" (*CW*, 664, 655), are not as demanding despite their being "grey and sharp like the points of two icepicks" (*CW*, 670). The next day as the artist completes the image, Parker tries to sleep on the table but again envisions "the tree of fire and

---

[23] Ibid., 361–62.

[24] Edward Kessler, *Flannery O'Connor and the Language of Apocalypse* (Princeton: Princeton University Press, 1986) 81.

his empty shoe burning beneath it" (*CW*, 670), repetitive imagery suggestive of a purgatorial cleansing.

On the completion of the tattoo, the pleased artist demands Parker see his work and as Parker does so, he whitens at the face reflected in the two mirrors, especially at the eyes that continue "to look at him—still, straight, all-demanding, enclosed in silence" (*CW*, 670). A visit to the pool hall after a rapid imbibing of a pint of whiskey suggests his need for a community to recognize his sacrificial act. The shocked silent response of the observers of his tattoo, followed by gibing about Parker's "witnessing for Jesus" (*CW*, 671), results in the defensive remark by Parker that he had the tattoo for laughs. When somebody yells, "Why ain't you laughing then?" Parker acts like a "whirlwind," and the raging fight leads to his being thrown out with an aftermath of calm descending "on the pool hall as nerve shattering as if the long barn-like room were the ship from which Jonah had been cast into the sea" (*CW*, 671). The mixture of scriptural images again creates what can be termed a sacramental unity of the Old and New Testaments.

Leon V. Driskell and Joan T. Brittain relate the pool hall scene to Parker's association with the Old Testament prophet Obadiah who is sent among the heathen. Parker "goes among the heathen, the blasphemers in the pool hall and 'rises up against them.'" The simile use of Jonah, Driskell and Brittain opine, "makes explicit the prophetic role which descends upon Parker because of the 'rumour from the Lord'. ...Jonah follows Obadiah and...the great storm at sea results from Jonah's disobeying the Lord."[25] Their further explication of the text of the story leads to equating the mention of Job to the scene in the book of Job in which Elihu remonstrates with Job in attempting to justify himself rather than admitting his deficiencies and accepting God's will, "an allusion paralleling the book of Obadiah."[26] We have in the revealed naming of Parker biblical associations that relate to prophecy. Like Obadiah and Job, Parker must search his spirit to know his way, fearfully (the fear of God is one of the gifts of the Holy Spirit) yet with wisdom.

---

[25] Leon V. Driskell and Joan T. Brittain, *The Eternal Crossroads: The Art of Flannery O'Connor* (Lexington: The University Press of Kentucky, 1971) 118.

[26] Ibid., 119.

Parker sits on the ground and examines his soul; he sees it as "a spider web of facts and lies that was not at all important to him which appeared to be necessary in spite of his opinion" (*CW*, 672). That the soul of Parker is to him an image of the creation of a tiny sentient creature relates to his earlier feeling of reduction to the transparent wing of a similar creature, higher in power than a vegetable. Parker appears to be engaging in an ascent to an understanding of himself. He sees he is not whole. He is a being penetrated with a gaze that comes from outside himself but is literally upon himself. He longs for Sarah Ruth to tell him what to do. David Eggenschwiler, who views the tattoos Parker bears as "symbols of demonic possession," says of Sarah Ruth that she "is a skinny, nasty, self-righteous daughter of a fundamentalist preacher. ...But he [Parker] cannot run away from her absoluteness, her judgments, her demands upon him. Although she, too, is somewhat demonic in the arrogance and animosity of her Manichean religion, she suggests something that he needs and has not been able to achieve through his botched assortment of tattoos."[27] To me, the tattoos and Sarah Ruth's attitude are not symbols of demonic possession but screens or shields from the actuality of human existence. The "something that he [Parker] needs" is some of his wife's spirituality to complement his carnality and give him an identity with which he can be satisfied. Sarah Ruth too has a need, to appreciate the physical expression of Parker's love, an intimacy that has impregnated her with a life.

Contrary to Eggenschwiler, John F. Desmond views Sarah Ruth not as a Manichaean but as a positive influence in the realizing by Parker of "his potential for real spiritual growth."[28] Such an assessment is consistent with my line of thinking that what Parker lacks Sarah Ruth has and, complementarily, what Sarah Ruth lacks Parker has. O'Connor's having them united in marriage gives each an opportunity to discover what is absent in the self but present in the other. Each is not whole because of an emphasis on either the carnal or the spiritual. Each

---

[27] David Eggenschwiler, *The Christian Humanism of Flannery O'Connor* (Detroit: Wayne State University Press, 1972) 76.

[28] John F. Desmond, *Risen Sons, Flannery O'Connor's Vision of History* (Athens: University of Georgia Press, 1987) 77.

needs the other, but it is only Parker who is revealed to us as expressing that need. He turns to Sarah Ruth to guide him in his new country; as he drives home from the pool hall encounter with its soul-searching experience afterward, he feels "a stranger to himself, driving into a new country" (*CW*, 672). The country is the spiritual country referred to earlier, and O'Connor describes it as the "true country, which the writer with Christian convictions will consider to be what is eternal and absolute" (*MM*, 27).

After parking under the pecan tree and stamping up to the locked door as though a new power is urging him on, Parker demands Sarah Ruth let him in. Four times his wife asks, "Who's there?" and three times Parker answers "O. E." Parker finally whispers "Obadiah," and "all at once he felt the light pouring through him, turning his spider web soul into a perfect arabesque of colors, a garden of trees and birds and beasts" (*CW*, 673). Momentarily, Parker seems to experience a wholeness of self within the order of creation. The garden imagery alludes to the first garden enveloping the highest level of earthly life, intelligent being, composite of body and soul in the image and likeness of God. Desmond points to this imagistic scene of revelation as Sarah Ruth's effecting "symbolically the transformation of the whole person by insisting that Parker use his own biblical name."[29] Again Parker whispers "Obadiah Elihue" and Sarah Ruth admits him, then regales him about the truth of his employer, who has come to demand reimbursement for the damaged tractor. As Desmond states, Sarah Ruth has provoked him into a realization of spiritual potentiality. She may not accept the tattoos he bears upon his skin, but he can, and he is able to associate them with his soul. If Sarah Ruth could only see the recent tattoo, he believes she would be pleased. When Parker unbuttons his shirt, his wife, thinking only of the sexual significance of his action, reacts by saying, "And you ain't going to have none of me this near morning" (*CW*, 674). He insists she look upon his back, which she does, but not with the response he expects. She calls the tattoo "trash," and his knees (covered with the images of the peacocks) go "hollow under him" as though he were going

---

[29] Ibid., 78.

to fall a third time, another sacramental signifier (recall his collapsing "on his knees twice" after the tractor accident) (*CW*, 665). Sarah Ruth accuses him of idolatry and sets to beating with the broom his unresisting body until large welts form "on the face of the tattooed Christ" (*CW*, 674). Contrary to my view, Miles Orvell considers Sarah Ruth a "pretender to the Christian mystery. ...When she denies, in the end [of the story], the tattooed Christ on Parker's back, she is denying as well the doctrine of the Incarnation, of the corporeality of God."[30]

The doctrine of the Incarnation is central to the Roman Catholic belief professed by O'Connor. Early in her writing career in a letter to "A." dated 2 August 1955, O'Connor proclaimed,

> I believe...there is only one Reality and that that is the end of it, but the term, "Christian Realism," has become necessary for me, perhaps in a purely academic way, because I find myself in a world where everybody has his compartment, puts you in yours, shuts the door and departs. One of the awful things about writing when you are a Christian is that for you the ultimate reality is the Incarnation, the present reality is the Incarnation, and nobody believes in the Incarnation; that is, nobody in your audience. My audience are the people who think God is dead. At least these are the people I am conscious of writing for. (*HB*, 92)

That O'Connor made an issue of the doctrine through the Christ image in "Parker's Back" at a time of writing "in extremis" (*HB*, 559) would be her final faith affirmation through her fiction. Although O'Connor did not explicitly identify herself with the character Parker as she did with Hulga and Tarwater,[31] had she more time to comment on her identification with Parker, she probably would have. In winter, spring, and summer of the last year of her life, she was in and out of the hospital with a questionable prognosis on the complications arising from a reactivation of lupus after surgery for a fibroid tumor. She was

---

[30] Orvell, *Flannery O'Connor: An Introduction*, 167.

[31] See *HB*, Letter to "A.," 24 August 1956, p. 170 for the former and *HB*, Letter to "A.," 14 November 1959, p. 358 for the latter.

experiencing a literal physical suffering identifiable with Parker's spiritual one.

The closing scene of Parker's rejection—indicated by Sarah Ruth's beating him—associates his suffering with that of Christ. However, we are not made privy to the thoughts of Obadiah Elihue as he flees outside to the pecan tree. The image of this tree is present at the beginning of the story with other images of the vegetative state. Its reappearance at the end of the story is symbolically and sacramentally significant in that the sweet fruit of its nut is related to the sweet fruit of the cross—the redemption. The image is elevated in our minds from the concrete vegetative state to the higher abstract state of symbolism, which embraces not only the human but also the divine. The tree is a real substance in the country in which Parker and Sarah Ruth live. It suggests a second point of meaning related to the "true country" of the eternal and absolute. Parker's embrace of the tree is the expression of the greatest desire of the human intellectual soul: the Ultimate Reality. For Parker this is a moment of grace. It is a culminating sacramental moment in the story. Parker not only knows his name but who he is, and he weeps.

Sarah Ruth, with a hardened look, sees him "crying like a baby" (CW, 675). Her look may be described as hard, but at the beginning of the story we are told Parker "had a suspicion that she actually liked everything she said she didn't" (CW, 655). Sarah Ruth is named after two great women of the Old Testament. Sarah was the wife of Abraham and at the age of ninety was blessed by God to bear Abraham a son: "[S]he shall be the mother of nations: kings of people shall descend from her. It is with Isaac her son that God will establish a covenant" (Genesis 17:15–22). Three men of God, whom Abraham invited to rest under a tree, announced the promise formally. They also ate under this tree. Sarah laughed to herself when she heard she would have a son and exclaimed, "Now that I am grown old and my husband is old, shall I have pleasure?" (Genesis 18:10–13). As a solemn woman whose disposition affects Parker so adversely, who is like Sarah in carrying a child, perhaps Sarah Ruth, like the biblical Sarah, will relate the conception of her child to the pleasure of the carnal act—and perhaps laugh at the thought.

According to the book of Ruth, Ruth was the Moabite woman who, on the death of her husband, Mahlon, did not return to her people but remained with her mother-in-law Naomi. Because of her fidelity and worthiness, she was rewarded with marriage to Boaz, a kinsman of Elimelech, the deceased husband of Naomi. She eventually bore Obed, grandfather to David of whose house is born the Christ, the Messiah. These events in Ruth's life seem to bear little relationship to that of Sarah Ruth unless we consider that she has left her home and people to marry Parker. She remains faithful to her husband despite her berating of him, and she carries a child whose destiny we cannot foresee. These interpretations are at odds with those of Orvell who, as indicated earlier, views Sarah Ruth as denying the doctrine of the Incarnation. I would argue that she may seem to express an impulsive temporary denial, but not to be forgotten is that Sarah Ruth is with child, a being whose corporeality she may not deny.

Sarah Ruth's gaze upon the weeping Parker is a human gaze. Her look may be as scourging as the blows she gave to Parker's back, but perhaps she has softened within. The question is whether she sees what Parker seems to know. She has inflicted on Parker's back greater pain than he has known with the process of tattooing. He is a participant in the suffering condition of the one whose image he bears upon his back. Can such a realization for Sarah Ruth be her sacramental moment?

The ending intimates closure and resolution for the substance of Parker and Sarah Ruth; revelation is possible for each of them. The final image of a rejected figure against the tree is real in its depiction of a dejected individual, and if the tree becomes a cross, the image is allusive in its suggestion of the dependence of Christ's both human and divine spirit on matter for the fulfillment of redemption for all humankind. The hylomorphic elements of "Parker's Back" are apparent in the imagery of various levels of life alluded to: the vegetative fruits of courtship, the sentient insects, the appetitive and locomotive representations in the tattoos, and the examined intellectual soul of Obadiah Elihue Parker. The hylomorphic interpretation lies in considering Parker and Sarah Ruth as the complementary aspects of body and soul, each in need of the other. Flannery O'Connor's concern "with the good of that which is made" (*MM*, 65) involved imaginatively rendering truths of religious belief and elements of Thomistic philosophy to produce through "Parker's Back" a work of hylomorphic sacramental significance.

Flannery O'Connor and the Displaced Sacrament

John F. Desmond

Any discussion of the sacramental dimensions in Flannery O'Connor's fiction might well begin with fellow writer Walker Percy's observation about how difficult it is for people possessed of a modern consciousness to hear the "Good News" of Christian revelation. Responding to the conventional notion of the "death" of God and the increasing "irrelevance of traditional religion," Percy wrote,

> The question is not whether the Good News is no longer relevant, but rather whether it is possible that man is presently undergoing a tempestuous restructuring of his consciousness that does not presently allow him to take account of the Good News. For what has happened is not merely the technological transformation of the world but something psychologically even more portentous. It is the absorption by the layman of the magical aura of science. ...Thus in the lay culture of a scientific society nothing is easier than to fall prey to a kind of seduction which sunders one's very self from itself into an all-transcending "objective" consciousness and a consumer-self with a list of "needs" to be satisfied. It is this monstrous bifurcation of man into angelic and bestial components against which old theologies must be weighed before new theologies are erected. Such a man could not take account of God, the devil, and the angels if they were standing before him, because he has already peopled the universe with his own hierarchies. When the novelist writes of a man "coming to himself" through some catalyst as catastrophe or ordeal, he may be offering obscure testimony to a gross

disorder of consciousness and to the need of recovering oneself as neither angel nor organism but as a wayfaring creature somewhere between.[1]

Percy's description of the layman whose mind has become absorbed by the "magical aura" of science, by which he meant principally the abstract theories of modern secular philosophy and the social sciences, fits such "intellectuals" as Hulga Hopewell, Sheppard, Asbury Fox, and George Rayber in O'Connor's stories. All of these characters have implicitly or explicitly rejected the possibility of the "Good News" as well as the sacramental vision that sees creation as infused with the spirit of God. Instead, they have substituted their own "hierarchies" of belief and action, such as Hulga's pseudo-nihilism or Asbury's idolatrous worship of art. In doing so they become those bifurcated beings—tilted toward "angelism" or "bestialism"—that Percy identified as characteristic modern personalities. Each of these characters tries to live as an abstract "objective" being separated from the vicissitudes of flesh. Such a bifurcation of the self stands in stark opposition to the Christian doctrine of the Incarnation and its affirmation of the self as a whole and unique incarnated person, and to the Catholic sacramental vision of the divine spirit indwelling in matter. Percy's notion of the writer who depicts a character's "coming to himself" through catastrophe or ordeal is apposite O'Connor's use of shock and violence to unmask the "hierarchies" that govern her "intellectual" characters and thereby return them to their truly incarnate selves. In this process of "recovery," O'Connor exposes these heretical hierarchies, as we shall see in Rayber's case in *The Violent Bear It Away*, to be perverse imitations or parodies of the Christian sacramental vision, especially the central doctrine of the Eucharist. O'Connor shatters these heretical hierarchies through her characters' encounter with mystery, especially the mystery of grace, which they are free either to accept or reject.

To understand how the Catholic sacramental vision is a shaping power in O'Connor's fiction, even in the case of the heretical

---

[1] Walker Percy, "Notes for a Novel about the End of the World," *The Message in the Bottle* (New York: Farrar, Straus and Giroux, 1975) 112–13.

"intellectuals," it is well to recall some primary truths about that vision. All of the sacraments devolve from the sacrament of the Eucharist in the Mass, the mystery of Christ's sacrifice, death, and glorious resurrection in body achieved through the power of the Holy Spirit. The Eucharist is the only sacrament that involves transubstantiation, the changing of bread and wine into the body and blood of Christ, who is real and present in the sacrament.[2] George Steiner has indicated the decisive importance of the doctrine of transubstantiation in Western culture since the medieval age: "[T]he [I]ncarnation of the Father in the Son and the transubstantiation of the Son in the self-donation of the rites of *Corpus Christi* constitute a *mysterium*, an articulated, subtly innervated attempt to reason the irrational at the very highest levels of intellectual pressure."[3] Steiner then emphasizes the significance of this doctrine for rhetoric and art, as well as for theology and philosophy:

> When we speak of analogy, of allegory, of symbolism, for formal and substantive Transformations…we adduce, consciously or not, the evolution of these key terms from within the patristic, early medieval and scholastic labours to define, to explain, the perpetually repeated miracle of Holy Communion. *…At every significant point, Western philosophies of art and Western poetics draw their secular idiom from the substratum of Christological debate.* Like no other event in our mental history, the postulate of God's *kenosis* through Jesus and of the never-ending availability of the Savior in the wafer and wine of the [E]ucharist, conditions not only the development of Western art and rhetoric itself, but at a much deeper level, that of our understanding and reception of the truth of art[.][4]

---

[2] Joseph M. Powers, S.J., *Eucharistic Theology* (New York: Herder and Herder, 1967) 131.

[3] George Steiner, *Grammars of Creation* (New Haven and London: Yale University Press, 2001) 66.

[4] Ibid., 67; my emphasis.

Moreover, and apropos O'Connor's intellectual characters, Steiner argues for the ineradicable influence of the mystery of transubstantiation on those "thinkers and artists [who] have sought to break from this matrix." Modern strategies of revolt, rejection, and denial are "one more attempt to liberate our experience of sense and of form from the grips of the theophanic," to "flee from [I]ncarnation" and the mystery of spirit in flesh.[5] This "flight" from Incarnation aptly describes the attempted escape from the *mysterium* of flesh/spirit of Percy's modern secularists and O'Connor's self-appointed intellectuals.

As Steiner has argued, transubstantiation in the Eucharist is *the* central sign action in history, transforming human actions by elevating their meaning and "re-signifying" them in relation to the Christian Incarnation. Theologian Joseph M. Powers points out that the meaning of the Eucharist (and therefore all other sacraments) is not in the explicit ritual per se, but in Christ's transformation of the inner meaning and value of those ritualistic actions through his creative word.[6] Therefore, transubstantiation is not a physical or chemical reality; it is the spiritual reality of Christ coming as Real Presence into the concrete world of ordinary things—bread and wine.[7] Christ is the principal agent in the sacrament. His coming is an action or movement of love, a free gift of the divine self to humankind. Using a phenomenological approach, theologian Edward Schillebeeckx characterizes the sacraments as a radical encounter with Christ, a call to a personal relationship and dialogue. Yet this mysterious encounter, the action of grace, "never comes just interiorally; it confronts us in visible shape as well."[8] Thus the physical world becomes the matrix of this encounter with Christ in word, in deed, and in things. As O'Connor expressed in her essay "Catholic Novelists and their Readers," quoting Baron von Hügel, "'the Supernatural experience always appears as the transfiguration of Natural conditions, acts, states...,' that 'the Spiritual generally is always

---

[5] Ibid., 67–68.

[6] Powers, *Eucharistic Theology*, 50.

[7] Ibid., 120, 313–33; 151 passim.

[8] E. Schillebeeckx, O.P., *Christ the Sacrament of Encounter with God* (New York: Sheed and Ward, 1963) 7–10, passim.

preceded, or occasioned, by the Sensible.... The highest realities and deepest responses are experienced by us within, or in contact with, the lower and the lowest'" (*MM*, 176).

While many characters in O'Connor's stories and novels attempt, in Steiner's phrase, to "break free" of the matrix of eucharistic transubstantiation and "flee from [I]ncarnation," the principal example of such a fugitive is George Rayber in *The Violent Bear It Away*, a novel O'Connor called "a minor hymn to the Eucharist" (*HB*, 387). The Eucharist, as we have seen, commemorates in the mystery of transubstantiation the sacrificial suffering, death, and bodily resurrection of Christ. Thus it instantiates a new order of meaning for the human body. Speaking of the doctrine of bodily resurrection in a letter to Cecil Dawkins, O'Connor argued that the "Church doesn't say what this body will look like, but the doctrine proclaims the value of what is least about us, our flesh. We are told that it will be transfigured in Christ, that what is human will flower when it is united with the Spirit" (*HB*, 366). Implicitly the doctrine offers a new spiritual conception of what it means to be human, a point that George Rayber emphatically denies. In addition, the doctrine of the Eucharist affirms a new spiritual freedom for humankind, a power to act in terms of one's eternal destiny, a point crucial for understanding the struggle between Rayber and young Tarwater in *The Violent Bear It Away*. Finally, the doctrine of the Eucharist also affirms the ultimate meaning of suffering and sacrifice, seen in Jesus' gift of himself in the sacrificial act of redemptive *kenosis* or self-emptying.

George Rayber's adult life is a parody of the meaning of the mystery of the Eucharist and the action of transubstantiation. Once baptized and schooled by Mason Tarwater in the "Good News" of redemption, Rayber has tried desperately to deny the "seed" of belief implanted in him as a child. As a grown man, he renounces his spiritual birthright in favor of the "hierarchy" of secular psychological theory. In so doing, Rayber becomes a caricature of the suffering savior; he would displace Christ and appropriate the role of victim-savior for himself. Thus his relation to the genuine sacrament is necessarily mimetic, as Steiner argues. In his important study of ritual sacrifice in relation to

Christianity, *I See Satan Fall Like Lightning*, Rene Girard has argued that human behavior is fundamentally imitative, and that the conscious rejection of a particular ritual does not eradicate the human need for ritualistic imitation.[9] He also argues that one of the cleverest guises of Satan is to imitate, paradoxically, the role of Christ as suffering servant and savior. His view, it seems to me, points to the inner core of Rayber's thoughts and actions as a pseudo-Christ. As a rationalist, Rayber rejects any notion of mystery, though he is himself caught in the grip of his own mysterious (what he calls "irrational") impulse to love creation. Rayber is Percy's "objective" man, dissociated from his body, his mind filled with the "hierarchy" of abstract theory. The novel's narrator says, "All his professional decisions were prefabricated and did not involve his participation" (*CW*, 399). As an "expert" in psychological testing, Rayber labels old Mason Tarwater as a "type" almost extinct and would abstractly pigeonhole Frank Tarwater in similar fashion if he could.

Critics sometimes see Rayber as a personification of the modern secular humanist. But judged in the light of the Eucharist's transformation of the meaning of "human," in the light of the resurrection of the body, Rayber's claimed humanism is truly anti-human. He would scale the meaning of humanity down to include only natural man. As he tells Tarwater, "The great dignity of man...is his ability to say I am born once and no more" (*CW*, 437). In a similar vein, he denies the possibility of bodily resurrection: "No...they won't rise again" (*CW*, 391). Ridden with abstract theory, Rayber attempts unsuccessfully to limit the "Real" only to what can be grasped by the senses and apprehended and understood by reason. For example, when faced with the mystery of the woods at Powderhead, he quickly abstracts it into the amount of board feet and profit it might produce as lumber. Corollary to his thinking is the rational *control* of experience through the exercise of rigid human will, thus denying the divine power of grace incarnated in the action of the Eucharist. The freedom from religious "superstition" he thinks he has achieved is a parody of genuine spiritual freedom, as his obsessive actions gradually reveal. In sum, Rayber's

---

[9] Rene Girard, *I See Satan Fall Like Lightning* (Maryknoll NY: Orbis Books, 2001) 178–81.

mental posture and creed involves a gnostic displacement of the reality of the sacrament, an "anti-transubstantiation" that tries to reverse the real condition of enfleshed humanity.

As Powers has noted, the center of the Eucharist sacrament is action, the redemptive action of Christ's *kenosis*. Rayber's "ascetic" life, as Richard Giannone has suggested, is a parody of a loving asceticism rooted in Christ's self-sacrifice.[10] In her book review of Teilhard de Chardin's *The Phenomenon of Man*, O'Connor cites with approval theologian Claude Tresmontant's view that for Teilhard asceticism "no longer consists so much in liberty and purifying oneself from 'matter'—but in further spiritualizing matter."[11] Genuine asceticism has as its object not the denial of the body but the disciplining of the flesh toward union with the will of God. Thus it imitates the transubstantiative action of the Eucharist and in so doing prefigures the final resurrection of the body. The genuine ascetic's self-denial is bound to the mystery of the body and of divine love. Rayber's "rigid ascetic discipline," in contrast, is an attempt to disincarnate himself, to control rigidly what he regards as the "irrational" side of his nature, the mysterious "seed" implanted in him at baptism that opens him to the demands of love.

Thus his self-denial is an attempted exaltation of his own willpower, not a disciplined attempt to ground his life in the will of the divine Father. His object is to "recreate" himself, he says, as a fully "human" (i.e., rational) being. Seeing young Tarwater as suffering from an "emotional disease," a "compulsion" to baptize Bishop, Rayber tells the youth that he must be "born again the natural way—through your own efforts. Your intelligence" (*CW*, 457). But the way of Christ, as Schillebeeckx and von Hügel suggest, is the "downward," incarnating movement into full humanity, which inevitably involves suffering as a whole person. O'Connor reveals this in the fact that Tarwater's destiny as prophet is not grandiose but modest—to baptize an ordinary idiot

---

[10] Richard Giannone, *Flannery O'Connor: Hermit Novelist* (Chicago and Urbana: University of Illinois Press, 2000) 158–160, passim.

[11] Flannery O'Connor, *The Presence of Grace, and Other Book Reviews*, comp. Leo J. Zuber, ed. Carter Martin (Athens: University of Georgia Press, 1983) 87.

child. But Tarwater only fully experiences the suffering that confirms his broken humanity in his violation by rape at the hands of a stranger. What Rayber offers, in contrast, is a mock transformation, involving only the mind.

As Rayber's asceticism parodies Christ's self-giving in the Eucharist, so also do his overt actions in relation to Bishop and young Tarwater mimic Christ's saving sacrifice. Rayber sees himself as both sacrificial victim and savior. He imagines himself to be a victim of fate in his fathering of Bishop. "His normal way of looking at Bishop was as an X signifying the general hideousness of fate" (*CW*, 401), a fate to which he has been doomed. Thus his role as detached parent mimics that of the suffering servant who offers his life for others. Bishop is a living reproach to Rayber's abstract theory of man, a "mistake of nature" (*CW*, 403). Rayber sustains the child mainly as a device by which to control his own impulse to love. Thus the real object of his sacrifice and asceticism is power and control by human intellect and will, contrary to Christ's free acceptance of the role of suffering servant. Rayber's "sacrifice" perversely mocks the salvific victimization of Christ memorialized in the Eucharist. Yet Rayber fears that his deep impulse to love unconditionally might overwhelm him, undermining his self-constructed identity:

> It was love without reason, love for something futureless, love that appeared to exist only to be itself, imperious and all-demanding, the kind that would cause him to make a fool of himself in an instant. And it only began with Bishop. It began with Bishop and then like an avalanche covered everything his reason hated. He always felt with it a rush of longing to have the old man's eyes—insane, fish-colored, violent with their impossible vision of a world transfigured—turned on him once again. The longing was like an undertow in his blood dragging him backwards to what he knew to be madness. (*CW*, 401)

The "undertow" strikes Rayber when he stops in the park with Bishop and Tarwater and recalls his aborted attempt to drown his son. In a parodic crucifixion, he sits as if "nailed to the bench" as he recalls the scene at the beach. On that day, Rayber was stricken with an epiphany of what life would be like without his son, how the impulse to love that he can "contain and limit" in Bishop would threaten to overwhelm him. Frantic, Rayber cried for help, and a stranger in "red and blue Roman striped shorts" resuscitated Bishop while "three wailing women" looked on.

Rayber's actions toward Tarwater are also an attempt to usurp Christ's role as savior and the saving act of the Eucharist. As mock-redeemer Rayber imputes to himself the power to "save" and liberate young Tarwater from his "obsession" to baptize Bishop. He sees the youth as a victim of Mason Tarwater's "madness." In another perversion of the eucharistic action, Rayber would transform his nephew into a "new man," fashioned according to Rayber's psychological theories. As with Bishop, his real motive is to deny Tarwater's spiritual nature, hence the boy's full humanity, so as to control him. He would recreate his nephew as a new "son" made in his image. In his relations with Tarwater, Rayber acts out what Girard sees as the role of those pagan self-appointed saviors who wear the mask of concern for victims, but whose real goal in their "humanitarianism" is personal power and self-aggrandizement. As Girard says, we "are living through a caricatural 'ultra-Christianity' that tries to escape from the Judeo-Christian orbit by 'radicalizing' the concern for victimization in an anti-Christian manner."[12] Rayber is such a caricature, seen especially when he thinks of himself during an encounter with the Carmody revivalist as a saving "angel" who would protect the "innocence" of all children from worldly contamination. Yet as Steiner and Girard suggest, the role of humanitarian savior is inextricably, and perversely, dependent for its meaning upon the transubstantiation represented in the sacrament of Eucharist in the Mass. Such actions appropriate the *form* of salvific agency without the substance, i.e., the power of the Holy Spirit, to effect real spiritual change. Girard sees this pagan humanitarianism as a satanic imitation of Christ. O'Connor dramatizes this in the novel by linking the

---

[12] Girard, *I See Satan Fall*, 178–79.

"wise counsel" of Rayber to the voices of the demonic strangers both within and outside Tarwater, all attempting to control his life.

While Rayber rejects the validity of baptism and blasphemes against it by "baptizing" Tarwater's bottom, and while he rejects the resurrection of the body, he cannot escape the encounter with Christ signified in the sacraments. O'Connor dramatizes Schillebeeckx's notion of the Eucharist as encounter with the incarnate Word in Rayber's meeting with the Carmody child preacher on the night he follows Tarwater through the city. As he angrily listens to her sermon, Rayber feels—in a parodic communion—"the taste of his own childhood pain laid on his tongue like a bitter wafer" (*CW*, 412). To Rayber the girl is only an exploited child, yet worthy of his "pity." He mentally casts himself in the role of a divine agent "moving like an avenging angel through the world" to gather all the children and save them from baptism and membership in the kingdom of God. Rayber would bring the children to a "new life" in an imagined Edenic world of innocence, thereby displacing Christ in his role as Lord and savior. "Rayber saw himself fleeing with the child to some enclosed garden where he would teach her the truth, where he would gather all the exploited children of the world and let the sunshine flood their minds" (*CW*, 414). But Rayber's sentimental fantasy is shattered by a real encounter with the living Word in the voice of the Carmody child. Just when he thinks there is "some miraculous communication between them" and that the "child alone in the whole world was meant to understand him," the young preacher rains judgment down on Rayber's head: "I see a damned soul before my eyes! I see a dead man Jesus hasn't raised. His head is in the window but his ear is deaf to the Holy Word!" (*CW*, 414–15). Scalded by her piercing truth, Rayber scrambles to turn off his hearing aid and silence the Word coming into his world.

Having explicitly rejected the "Good News" announced in the Carmody child's fiery judgment, Rayber is revealed as one who suffers the bifurcation of self that Percy described as the prototypically modern experience. Rayber now sees himself "divided in two—a violent and a rational self" (*CW*, 417). He is unable to conquer the pain of longing—of love—at the center of his being, and he fears that it will erupt beyond his affection for Bishop into an "irrational" love of all creation. In a perversion of genuine charity, Rayber mentally reduces Bishop to an object, now a pawn in his battle to control and reshape Tarwater. For Rayber to act freely upon his own impulse toward unconditional love would be to admit a need that to him is beneath "human" dignity. Since Bishop embodies this need and call to unconditional love, Rayber hates the pain caused by his tie to his son. His profound ambivalence toward his son, his sense of guilt over having fathered a retarded child, and his desire to "replace" Bishop with a son (i.e., Tarwater) remade in his own image all make Rayber deeply complicit in Bishop's sacrifice.

In his determination to take Tarwater to the Cherokee Lodge and then to Powderhead so the boy can confront his "compulsion," Rayber also parodies the sacramental rite of reconciliation. Unable to restrain his own urge "to confess," he tells Tarwater of his failed attempt to drown Bishop. Tarwater scoffs at the confession as proof of Rayber's inability "to act." But Rayber persists, determined to "save" his nephew from becoming "a freak." He rightly recognizes in Tarwater's eyes a need for repentance (*CW*, 392), but he would expunge the guilt Tarwater feels by means of a secular rite of therapeutic "confession," convinced that it is sufficient to relieve what he sees as Tarwater's "guilt." After Tarwater vomits in the lake, Rayber sermonizes, "It's just as much relief...to get something off your mind as off your stomach. When you tell somebody else your troubles, they don't bother you so much, they don't get in your blood and make you sick. Somebody else shares the weight. God boy...you need help. You need to be saved right here and now from the old man and everything he stands for. And I'm the one who can save you" (*CW*, 438).

But such an offer of absolution and "salvation" is powerless. Rayber's offer is a satanic temptation that his nephew intuitively recognizes as hollow. Tarwater's response is to jump in the lake and escape. When they return to the lodge, Rayber's pathetic "gift" to his nephew if he will be reborn as his "son" is a new suit of clothes and a "combination corkscrew-bottle-opener," trappings of the desacralized world he inhabits.

Sensing the failure of his attempted confession-purgation ritual of taking Tarwater to Powderhead to eradicate the boy's "compulsion," Rayber now realizes the danger of losing control of Bishop to his nephew. He knows that "his own stability depended upon the little boy's presence" and that "he could control his terrifying love as long as it had a focus in Bishop, but if anything happened to the child, he would have to face it in itself. Then the whole world would become his idiot child" (*CW*, 442). Without Bishop, Rayber concludes, he would have to "sacrifice" his need to love, "resist feeling anything at all, thinking anything at all. He would have to anesthetize his life" (*CW*, 443). Such is the logic of the abstract man, who now imagines his fate as an obliteration of the self, an ultimate ascesis, an end to consciousness. Rayber conceives of his fate as an abstraction, a mental move of separating himself from both Bishop—whom he knows will be killed—and the irksome Tarwater, whom he now wants only to "get rid of." His self-pitying image of his future destiny is one of an achieved state of "indifference" in which to "feel nothing was peace." In this destiny O'Connor projects the imagined end of the disincarnate man. When Bishop's dying howl comes to Rayber across the water, "the sound seemed to come from inside him as if something inside him was tearing itself free." Rayber determines that no cry will escape him, so that "he continued to feel nothing...and it was not until he realized that there would be no pain that he collapsed" (*CW*, 456).

In Rayber's painless collapse O'Connor seems to dramatize the fate of the abstract man *in extremis*, a kind of spiritual suicide committed by one who renounces the body and the created world that she found validated and spiritualized through the sacrament of the Eucharist. Rayber's "end" seems a fitting judgment on his refusal to love. But it is well to remember that Rayber still lives. Might not his defeat at the hands of Tarwater and the devastating loss of Bishop be the "catastrophe," to use Percy's term, that could possibly open him to a new, more human existence in the world? Might not the "seed" of a love beyond reason that was implanted in him at baptism begin to blossom? O'Connor does not say, of course, but the possibility remains as long as he lives. She leaves him "light-headed" and unfeeling, but the "self" annihilated here may be the false idol Rayber made of himself. His "dying," at least potentially, opens the door to the chance of rising again as a broken, yet human, being. The grace of a new beginning may yet be offered and accepted. Rayber has attempted to "break free" of the "matrix" of the Eucharist, as Steiner phrased it, as indeed have all the secular theorists of the age. But the definitive action of the transubstantiation of the physical world into the body and blood of Christ lives on as the shadowing light that measures ordinary humanity against the fullness of being encompassed in the transformed bread and wine.

II.

The Congregation:
Cultural and Artistic Influences on O'Connor's Fiction

Beholding the Handmaids: Catholic Womanhood and "The Comforts of Home"

Robert Donahoo

> This practice of making the saint appear edifying according to the popular convention of what is edifying is of long standing in hagiography and is based on a different conception of truth from the one we hold now. It is a conception that does not scruple to permit the rearranging of nature in order to make it fit the ideal type; as such, it is more closely related to fiction than to history.
>
> —Flannery O'Connor's review of
> *Two Portraits of St. Thérèse of Lisieux*

I.

Though few literary critics have probably ever thought of themselves as writing hagiography, it is difficult to read Flannery O'Connor's words and not be struck by the similarity between what we often do and what she describes as "rearranging nature in order to fit the ideal type." We have our theoretical commitments, and if we stare at a text long enough, we can generally uncover a way of reading it that not only validates those commitments but often enables us to embrace or reject the author/text as we wish. By embracing an antifoundationalist credo, we can even be quite comfortable with, say, a high modernist Faulkner, a Marxist Faulkner, a feminist Faulkner, an environmentalist Faulkner, a Christian Faulkner, and even a post-colonial Faulkner all residing together within the same book covers. Though on its face such a situation may strike the non-academic as schizophrenic if not plainly ridiculous, it is the air we breathe, academic *terra firma*. Such an observation, however, does not constitute an attack upon contemporary theoretical approaches to literature; rather, it serves as a cautionary reminder of the precipice upon which all interpretation dances and as an endorsement of the value of history in seeking to avoid a fall into the kind of fictive criticism that O'Connor's review rejects.

It is especially appropriate to give some heed to O'Connor on this issue since her writing and reputation have often been the subject of criticism taking either a hagiographic or debunking approach. It is only a slight exaggeration to say that the first twenty years of O'Connor criticism seemed frequently aimed at declaring O'Connor, if not St. Flannery, at least a bold bearer of light into the literary darkness. Encouraged by O'Connor's own nonfiction writing, generally conservative and/or Christian critics taught a generation to read her work as artistic demonstrations of divine grace as understood through an unswerving Roman Catholic orthodoxy. Richard Giannone, one of O'Connor's most convincing religious commentators, sums up the experience of her characters by stating, "[T]hey learn that all of their previous yearning has been a preparation for a desire for God. The will to live by this yearning and the communication of grace to fulfill the decision constitute the sacrament, which in turn signifies the particular realization of Christian life in the character—a rebirth in spirit or an anointing for imminent death."[1] Giannone's reading is indicative of the prevailing point of view of many decades. In contrast, by the start of the 1990s, Frederick Crews was pointing out that "[a]cademic second thoughts about O'Connor" had begun to appear as the "iconoclastic mood of academic trendsetters" became "restless with O'Connor's latent premise of a fixed theological backdrop to human action, with God and Satan vying for possession of the individual soul."[2] However, where Crews predicted that O'Connor's depiction of and ideas about race

---

[1] Richard Giannone, *Flannery O'Connor and the Mystery of Love* (Urbana: University of Illinois Press, 1989) 251–52.

[2] Frederick Crews, *The Critics Bear It Away: American Fiction and the Academy* (New York: Random House, 1992) 146.

would serve as the major battleground for the reassessment, critics concerned with gender issues have instead frequently led the charge.

Beginning most forcibly with Louise Westling's *Sacred Groves and Ravaged Gardens*, O'Connor is sketched as an author limited by her conception of women—a writer who depicts women as deserving or needing to remain subservient to a stifling patriarchy. Westling states that O'Connor's "world was ruled by a patriarchal authority which guarded His pastoral landscape as the Yahweh of the ancient Hebrews watched over Eden and the pastures of the Old Testament" and that O'Connor "inadvertently presented" "doubles of herself" that reveal "female self-loathing, powerlessness, and justified fear of masculine attack."[3] More than a decade later, Cindy Beringer, in a contribution to the essay collection *Southern Mothers: Fact and Fictions in Southern Women's Writing*, offered a similar judgment: "All of [O'Connor's] frantic and class-conscious female farm managers must operate in a system that devalues them while highly valuing men and fathers." She further argues that O'Connor's vision required any woman who "displaced a man as the head of the patriarchy" to be "brought down and forced to face her weakness before men as well as before God."[4] Both these scholars imply that the cause or source of O'Connor's problems is her religious commitment and, given O'Connor's undisguised Catholicism, the teachings of the faith that she embraced.

Other critics, writing in the same period, sought to mitigate O'Connor's depiction of women. Claire Kahane analyzes "A Temple of the Holy Ghost" to find in the hermaphrodite "a symbolic resolution to the problem of gender limitation."[5] For Kahane, the hermaphrodite, and

---

[3] Louise Westling, *Sacred Groves and Ravaged Gardens: The Fiction of Eudora Welty, Carson McCullers, and Flannery O'Connor* (Athens: University of Georgia Press, 1985) 180, 174.

[4] Cindy Beringer, "'I Have Not Wallowed': Flannery O'Connor's Working Mothers," in *Southern Mothers: Fact and Fictions in Southern Women's Writing*, ed. Nagueyalti Warren and Sally Wolff (Baton Rouge: Louisiana State University Press, 1999) 140.

[5] Claire Kahane, "The Gothic Mirror," in *The (M)other Tongue: Essays in Feminist Psychoanalytic Interpretation*, ed. Shirley Nelson Garner, Claire Kahane, and Madelon Sprengnether (Ithaca: Cornell University Press, 1985) 350.

its double, the nun, "restore to women at least conceptually the breadth of human potential."[6] Three essays in *Flannery O'Connor: New Perspectives* (1996) try similar absolutions. Jeanne Campbell Reesman and Bruce Marshall Gentry both draw on Bakhtinian theory to deal with complaints about O'Connor's depiction of women. Reesman argues that O'Connor's women are less attempts to mirror her reality than Bakhtinian grotesques whose negative example "reasserts an outraged individual or social norm."[7] Bruce Marshall Gentry examines her work in terms of a Bakhtinian dialogue between "the typical O'Connor narrator," described as "a rigidly patriarchal female who promoted gender separation," and other voices of the feminine that "compete with the narrator's voice for authority"—a dialogue that results in "O'Connor characters frequently find[ing] redemption as they move toward androgyny."[8] More surprisingly and persuasively, Richard Giannone argues that O'Connor may turn out to be "a feminist despite herself."[9] Through an analysis of "A View of the Woods," Giannone asserts that O'Connor sought to eradicate "gender as a basis for human identity" through that story's clear depiction of the "[s]ubordination of Mary Fortune" as "an unjust violation of a female's original equality in creation."[10] Nevertheless, despite their different approaches and varying degrees of success, the very existence of these articles demonstrates the perceived need to account somehow for O'Connor's women, to explain away their obviously unpalatable qualities—qualities that Kahane, Gentry, and Giannone, directly or by implication, link to her Catholicism.

More recently, the new millennium has seen two major feminist examinations of O'Connor, and in both the issue of O'Connor's

---

[6] Ibid.

[7] Jeanne Campbell Reesman, "Women, Language, and the Grotesque in Flannery O'Connor and Eudora Welty," in *Flannery O'Connor: New Perspectives*, ed. Sura P. Rath and Mary Neff Shaw (Athens: University of Georgia Press, 1996) 40.

[8] Bruce Marshall Gentry, "Gender Dialogue in O'Connor," in *Flannery O'Connor: New Perspectives*, 57.

[9] Richard Giannone, "Displacing Gender: Flannery O'Connor's View from the Woods," in *Flannery O'Connor: New Perspectives*, 73.

[10] Ibid., 79, 93.

commitment to Catholic views of women is emphasized. Sarah Gordon's *Flannery O'Connor: The Obedient Imagination* approvingly cites Westling's book, refers to O'Connor's "attacks on female culture," and claims "*Obviously* O'Connor did not embrace the matrilineal tradition, either in literature or in life; instead, she appears to have followed the route that Freud…describes as normative: that of embracing the male tradition."[11] For Gordon, the drive for this embrace is twofold: O'Connor's desire to be an heir of the male literary masters who dominated critical opinion of her time and "the strongly misogynistic tradition of the Roman Catholic Church."[12] Gordon writes, "[T]he conflict between O'Connor's own situation as a southern white woman who—though she wanted to leave home to write and thereby create her own territory apart from conventional social expectations and in so doing to reject the matrilineal in favor of the power and authority of the patrilineal—could not leave home, and her strong belief that her art must be used in the service of her faith is, I believe, largely responsible for the shape and content as well as the tension of her fiction."[13] Though Gordon clearly wants to praise O'Connor, one cannot read her book without getting the sense that O'Connor was unfortunate in her literary and spiritual alliances. Similarly, Katherine Hemple Prown's *Revising Flannery O'Connor* examines O'Connor manuscripts and concludes O'Connor "reshaped her work to appeal to a literary and critical community built on the gender-based and racial hierarchies that had traditionally characterized southern culture," with the result that her novels have an "androcentric orientation" in their published versions and that "misogyny…imbues her short stories."[14] For Prown, Catholicism is one of the forces that led O'Connor to revise her manuscripts, suppressing their initial feminist tendencies. She finds, for instance, that the manuscript fragment of *Wise*

---

[11] Sarah Gordon, *Flannery O'Connor: The Obedient Imagination* (Athens: University of Georgia Press, 2000) 26, 29; my emphasis.

[12] Ibid., 30.

[13] Ibid.

[14] Katherine Hemple Prown, *Revising Flannery O'Connor: Southern Literary Culture and the Problem of Female Authorship* (Charlottesville: University Press of Virginia, 2001) 3, 12.

Blood that was ultimately published as "A Stroke of Good Fortune" includes a more positive attitude toward abortion and that "the manuscripts revise Catholicism itself to include female subjectivity." Prown quickly adds, "It thus remains little wonder that O'Connor always hated the published version of Ruby's story, which originated as a radical revision of the Catholic stance on abortion and functions as yet another example of the female-sexed voice she strove so hard to eliminate."[15] As with Gordon and indeed almost all of the critics who link O'Connor's view of women with her religion, the portrait Prown paints is of a writer led astray by the Church.

But is it so? Undoubtedly, these portraits, like those of St. Thérèse of Lisieux that O'Connor criticizes,[16] do justice to our current sensibilities and are fascinating to consider, but even as these critics so clearly desire to present a complex, multidimensional image of O'Connor, they present a largely one-dimensional image of Roman Catholicism as O'Connor would have known it. In other words, these critics assume that the Catholicism O'Connor knew and practiced at Sacred Heart Catholic Church in Milledgeville, Georgia, is the Catholicism pronounced from the papal throne in Rome. Such a complete, direct, and unmitigated chain must strike anyone who has ever been involved at a local level with a national or international organization as difficult to accept. For even if the Roman Catholic Church speaks in a unified voice in its dogma, at the local level where individuals such as O'Connor had to live and work, that voice is likely to become fragmented and multi-vocal—particularly in a nation as diverse as the United States.

In fact, evidence of these multiple voices is found in the historical documents of the period—not the official pronouncements of the Catholic Church, but the publications of the wider Catholic press in America. Even a brief scan of the items under the heading "Women" in *The Catholic Periodicals and Literature Index* for the active years of O'Connor's career suggests this diversity. The entries for the period 1948–1964 number literally in the thousands, and the titles of the

---

[15] Ibid., 125.

[16] See my opening epigraph.

periodicals—*The Catholic Digest, Ave Maria, The Sign*, and *The Homiletic and Pastoral Review*, not to mention better known magazines such as *America* and *Commonweal*—hint at their diversity. Even an examination of only a fraction of the journals reveals that, though undoubtedly more conservative than today's academic feminists, post-World War II Catholic commentators on the nature of women and their roles show limited homogeneity.

Consider some highly conservative articles. Writing in a 1949 issue of *America*, Virginia Rowland, described by the author's note as "a self-confessed refugee from the teaching profession" and the mother of a fifteen-month-old son, complains that modern parents are failing to fulfill "their God-given responsibilities" and are producing children who are "disrespectful, uncooperative, lacking in self-restraint."[17] Writing that she gave up her own job when she married, Rowland, not surprisingly, places much of the blame for this parental failure on women who have "the main responsibility of training children" because they are "with them all day while the father works."[18] Complaining that modern women fail to see motherhood as "a glorious career," she argues that "our schools must prepare young women for motherhood. ...They can be shown that motherhood is not only a sacred obligation, but an exciting, challenging career."[19] The same journal sounds similar notes in two pieces from 1950 and 1954. In its "Current Comment" section, the editors interpret a Soviet boast of having attained equal rights for women as meaning "[e]quality to engage in back-breaking physical toil," and they conclude, "May is a good month for the women of the free world to ask Our Lady to liberate the women of the slave world from the burden of such 'equality.'"[20] A 1954 editorial in the journal denounces mothers who work without true economic need. "Such women," the editorial declares, "are contributing to juvenile delinquency and actually

---

[17] Virginia Rowland, "Modern Parenthood," *America* 82/7 19 November 1949): 182.

[18] Ibid.

[19] Ibid., 182, 183.

[20] "Women Workers Behind the Iron Curtain," *America* 83/5 (6 May 1950): 132.

helping to undermine the very homes they are working (they say) to support."[21]

An editorial in *The Homiletic and Pastoral Review* from 1958 also addresses the working mothers issue, though less directly. Responding to a statement by the U.S. undersecretary of health, education, and welfare that 22,000,000 married American women were working, the editorial raises a series of rhetorical questions: "What are the consequences upon the emotional and spiritual growth of children brought up in a home with a part-time mother? Is our society so disoriented economically, so geared to a 'high consumption' production line that only those families can live 'decently' in which both parents work? Doesn't this foster materialism? What is the effect on American women of a culture that relegates, to a place of subsidiary dignity and respect, the role of housewife-at-home?"[22] Not surprisingly, the same journal in a 1952 article titled "The Christian Ideal of Womanhood" finds that ideal in motherhood, exemplified by the Virgin Mary—the true subject of the article.[23]

Two very different magazines, *The Sign*, a general-interest magazine for Catholics resembling the *Look* or *Life Magazine* of its day, and *Ave Maria*, a weekly magazine aimed at Catholic families and published in Notre Dame, offer male perspectives on the modern woman. Joe Breig used his 1957 monthly column in *Ave Maria* to try to mine humor from what he described as the bewildering way women talk: "[T]hey never bother to tell you what they are talking about. Their sentences have predicates but no subjects—no subject, at least, that you can make head or tail of."[24] The smug leadenness of this humor is also found in a 1953 article in *The Sign* titled "What Every Man Knows." According to its author, Ray Neville, what every man knows is that

[21] "Working Mothers," *America* 91/2 (10 April 1954): 35.

[22] Aidan M. Carr, "Where Women Work," editorial in *The Homiletic and Pastoral Review* 59/2 (November 1958): 208.

[23] A. Durand, "The Christian Ideal of Womanhood," *The Homiletic and Pastoral Review* 52/8(May 1952): 700–705.

[24] Joe Breig, "The Way That Women Talk," *The Ave Maria* 85/1 (5 January 1957): 7.

women are taking over: "[A] great many American men have quietly relinquished their traditional authority as 'head of the family' and settled for the secondary role of mere breadwinner."[25] This relinquishing is linked directly to the rise of "a whirlwind movement which our grandparents called feminism" that has misled "softheaded" men to become the "truly effective feminists." Neville concludes, "and where it will end nobody knows. *A woman's world!* If it came to pass, who would have the best of it? The answer to that is 'what every man knows.'"[26]

Three particularly anti-feminist pieces appear in *The Catholic Educator*, *The Catholic World*, and *The Catholic Digest*. Sister Mary St. Beatrice Brennan's article in *The Catholic Educator*, "Marriage *Is* a Career," refers directly to the "evil effects of 'working wives'" and sees it leading to "the same shapeless leveled-off society that Marxist communism holds up to the world as an ideal."[27] For Brennan, only participation "in the life of the Church through her piety and the assistance she gives to every needy brother" can move a woman "from the seclusion of her home without corrupting her."[28] For Brennan this is not a matter of inequality: "Woman enters Christian society endowed with equal rights with men because she enters it also with a soul, and among souls there is no distinction of sex or class. But she enters it with the distinctive nature of woman and duties are imposed on her which are most suited to that nature."[29]

A far more detailed argument of similar ideas is found in Fordham University professor William J. Grace's 1956 article, "The Dilemma of Modern Woman: Can She Solve It?" published in *The Catholic World*. Pressed by the feminist movement, the modern woman finds herself "expected to be prepared for two roles, either simultaneously or consecutively, of a business or professional career and of a wife and

---

[25] Ray Neville, "What Every Man Knows," *The Sign* 33/4 (November 1953): 51.

[26] Ibid., 52; emphasis in original.

[27] Sister Mary St. Beatrice Brennan, "Marriage *Is* a Career," *The Catholic Educator* 29/9 (May 1959): 665, 666.

[28] Ibid., 666.

[29] Ibid.

mother."[30] Consequently, modern woman loses "contact with that cultural wisdom from the past that is transmitted through family life. The many things she would instinctively know or subconsciously learn through family tradition she has to reacquire through manuals, pamphlets, and the technical advice of counselors, doctors and psychiatrists. Have you ever seen a professional woman handle a baby? She is frequently far less at home with it than an old male bachelor."[31] Like Brennan, Grace believes the solution is for women to return to the home to "be released from jobs of a non-creative mechanical kind in order that they may be free to do things far more rewarding and fundamental."[32]

Only the last of these three offers much of a surprise. In "The Woman in the Gray Flannel Suit," Sloan Wilson seeks to combine the humor approach of Brieg and Neville with Grace's detailed reasoning. However, his conclusions are much the same: "Maybe even in 1956 the place for women is in the home," and "Obviously, the women are trying to play the game under the men's rules. Schools and universities are doing all they can to help them."[33] Instead of women pursuing their own careers, Wilson encourages the idea of "the executive wife," alternately known as "an old-fashioned woman around the house."[34] The surprise in all this is not the content but that its Catholic publication, *The Catholic Digest*, like its role model, *Reader's Digest*, reprints articles from other sources, and the source for this conservative piece is *The New York Times Magazine*. In other words, what initially looks like merely *Catholic* conservatism is, at least potentially, American sectarian conservatism—a possibility that suggests most of these pieces had their ideological genesis to some extent in the American culture of *Leave It To Beaver* and *I Love Lucy*, not religious doctrine only. If that's the case, then it seems

---

[30] William J. Grace, "The Dilemma of Modern Woman: Can She Solve It?" *The Catholic World* 183/1093 (April 1956):16.

[31] Ibid., 20.

[32] Ibid., 21.

[33] Sloan Wilson, "The Woman in the Gray Flannel Suit," *The Catholic Digest* 20/9 (July 1956): 35, 36.

[34] Ibid., 37.

questionable to attribute perceived anti-feminist ideas in O'Connor to her religion only.

However, an examination of more moderate and liberal Catholic articles raises even further questions about the relation of Catholicism and O'Connor's views of women. Some of the more moderate commentary comes from women rejecting what they perceive as Madison Avenue propaganda defining equality of the sexes in terms of women who manage to do everything well. Writing in a 1949 issue of *The Ave Maria*, Clarice Cox complains about women's magazine fiction in which "the heroine, who looks a mere seventeen, runs a successful business, keeps up an elaborate ménage, and is the perfect mother to at least two children. This paragon stands out in my mind as the Woman's Magazine Femme since she exists largely in the editor's mind and has little counterpart in fact."[35] Cox dismisses the pop psychology of her day that claimed the modern woman was frustrated because "'she feels she is not making an adequate contribution to modern life.' Nonsense! She is just atwitter from trying to vie with the ideal W.M. [Women's Magazine] Femme with her hyperthyroid housekeeping and her combination of careers."[36] Despite her rejection of this image, Cox includes neither a call for women to return to the kitchen nor a pining for better times in the past. Rather, her article presents a clear-headed, commonsense perspective that sees women not as a collective situation or problem but as individuals struggling with both success and failure in their daily lives. In a 1957 issue of the same periodical, Dorothy Dohen offers a similar view of women as she, too, attacks propaganda-like role descriptions for single women. However, for her the source of these unrealistic guides is not Madison Avenue but "Victorian novels," "pious books," articles in Catholic magazines, and even the Pope. After humorously considering each of these "solutions" and finding them wanting, she advocates self-acceptance, using "my head to find out what I should do," and practical piety, concluding, "all I can ask is that God

---

[35] Clarice Cox, "Make-Believe Perfection," *The Ave Maria* 70/5,19 (5 November 1949): 597.

[36] Ibid., 599.

will help me to understand [my role]."[37] While hardly models of feminist empowerment, both of these articles take an existential view of women's roles, never demanding or hoping that they conform to any secular or religious model.

Moreover, these less rigid views of women's roles crop up even in generally conservative periodicals such as *America*. An editorial titled "Women: Equal but Different" in a 1950 issue notes positively the passage of an Equal Rights for Women Amendment in the United States Senate. The thrust of the editorial favors the amendment, which reads, "The provisions of this article shall not be construed to impair any rights, benefits or exemptions now or hereafter conferred by law upon any persons of the female sex."[38] In supporting the amendment, the writer reasons that "[w]omen can and do perform much of the work of today's world as well as men. But in bearing and rearing the youth on whom the whole future of society rests they have a responsibility in which no man can compete. Social legislation protecting women is society's acknowledgement that women, though entirely equal with men as *human persons*, have an entirely *unique role to perform in our national life*."[39] This distinction between personhood and role, while clearly a sign of paternalism toward women, marks at least some improvement over the direct calls for women to disappear into the private world, and it surfaces in a number of *America* pieces, including an endorsement of a challenge to Alfred Kinsey's *Sexual Behavior in the Human Female* as "equat[ing] human and sub-human sex activity"[40] and an attack on the film and advertisement industries for "hawking women on the movie-ad auction-block as animals."[41] It even appears in generally conservative pieces such as the article "American Feminism a Century After" by Jesuit priest W. B. Faherty. While acknowledging the economic benefits

---

[37] Dorothy Dohen, "Answers for Single Women!" *The Ave Maria* 86/24 (14 December 1957): 15.

[38] "Women: Equal but Different," editorial in *America* 82/19 (11 February 1950): 543.

[39] Ibid.; emphasis in original.

[40] "Challenge to Dr. Kinsey," *America* 90/18 (30 January 1954): 432.

[41] "Hucksters Hawking American Womanhood," *America* 92/2 (9 October 1954): 31.

achieved by American feminists since the 1848 Woman's Rights Convention at Seneca Falls, he deplores U.S. Department of Labor statistics that show most working women "doing outside the home the very work which was termed 'drudgery' when done by the wife in the home."[42] For Faherty the major failing of feminism in America is the failure to value the home and the work that women have done in it. Still, he concludes,

> Should one hundred years of American feminism be written off, then, as a loss for the nation? No, that conclusion would be hasty and unjust. Some results have been fine, others bad. The possibilities of an alert, educated American womanhood for lasting good are tremendous, but so far largely unrealized. There must be a re-evaluation of the past, honest analysis of the present, and above all some thoughtful planning for the future. This planning must be based on an accurate knowledge of woman's nature and her relations to man, and must give proper attention to the American home. That feminists did not do this a century ago has made much of their work vain.[43]

The picture of American Catholics propounding a moderate, individualistic view of women as well as a protective, paternalistic one is rounded out by two other articles from this period. The earliest, "The Characteristics and the Social Role of Women," appears in a 1948 issue of the academic journal *The American Catholic Sociological Review*. Written by Louis A. Ryan of the Dominican Institute of Sociology in Washington, D.C., the article claims to grow out of "the current dissatisfactions with the social relationships of man and woman in and out of marriage"[44] and attempts to draw conclusions based on a survey of sociological writing about women. Ryan begins with the work of

---

[42] W. B. Faherty, "American Feminism a Century After," *America* 80/9 (4 December 1948): 235.

[43] Ibid., 236.

[44] Louis A. Ryan, "The Characteristics and the Social Role of Woman," *The American Catholic Sociological Review* 9 (1948): 230.

Auguste Comte and includes texts by both Catholic and secular thinkers such as Havelock Ellis, Gina Lombroso, Helene Deutsch, G. K. Chesterton, Jacques Maritain, Ferdinand Lundberg, and Marjorie F. Farnham. Ryan's conclusion is this: "At the present stage of the research, the general psychological tendencies or traits which seem best to describe the feminine nature are the following three: *to be reserved, to conserve, to serve*."[45] As Ryan explains these terms, they are a mixture of positive and negative traits. "To be reserved," for instance, includes both "psychological passivity" and "reflective intelligence."[46] "To conserve" includes both the predictable "motherly" and the surprising "more retentive memory" and "patience."[47] "To serve" includes both "intuitive superiority" and "adaptability."[48] While any one of the terms can be criticized from a feminist perspective, as can Ryan's choice of sociological sources, perhaps the most valuable insight is the very complexity he acknowledges in women—something best illustrated by a detailed chart of qualities inserted at the end of his article. Clearly he rejects the simplistic designation of woman as merely a child bearer and nurturer; indeed, his final statements convey his work in terms of a cultural test as he asks that cultures be measured by the degree to which they allow and encourage women to fulfill all their aspects.

Jesuit John L. Thomas presented a similar but more complex view of women in an article for *The Commonweal* in 1956. Setting his topic in the context of the centuries-long "Battle of the Sexes," Thomas quickly rejects simplistic solutions: "We are sometimes assured that all would be well if we returned to the good old days when 'men were manly and women were womanly.' But what does it mean to be 'manly' or 'womanly' today? Each age tends to develop its own definition, and in a pluralistic culture like our own, there will be several."[49] Rejecting both novelistic and scriptural "pat phrases," Thomas sees women struggling

---

[45] Ibid., 251; emphasis in original.
[46] Ibid.
[47] Ibid., 252.
[48] Ibid.
[49] John L. Thomas, "The Role of Woman," *The Commonweal* 64/7 (18 May 1956): 171.

to cope with role choices in the midst of a society that has devalued their traditional work in the home. For Thomas, the modern woman's dilemma is wrapped up in larger changes, particularly in the status and image of the family. In other words, the difficulty women have in finding a fulfilling role is part of a conceptual, philosophic situation that requires conceptual, philosophic solutions. He writes, "it is necessary to think in terms of essential human values and integral personal fulfillment. This is not a plea that women return submissively to the home. Rather it is a statement that the two aspects of a woman's vocation—as a person and as a feminine person—achieve normal integration in the family. In a very real sense, this statement holds for the man."[50] While this solution, like most of the moderate ideas floated in the Catholic press, lacks practical application for improving women's status or position, it is difficult to label it as being purely misogynistic; yet it has just as valid a claim to being Catholic practice as do the more repressive ideas considered earlier.

In addition to the view of Thomas and other moderate voices, even more progressive thinking, admittedly rare, also surfaces in the Catholic press of this period. Writing in *The Catholic World*, Priscilla O'Brien Mahoney opens her defense of women's intellectual capacity, "The Lady Has a Brain!" by an analogy to Scriptures: "The Lord scolded the apostles when they disputed about who among them would be given the highest place in heaven. It would not be surprising if He looked with equal disfavor on the so-called 'battle of the sexes' which, without a doubt, is the longest unarmed conflict in the annals of the world."[51] She continues her argument by connecting the intellect to the soul and by citing the examples and statements of Catholic saints while scoffing at a male cleric's claim "that while women might be forging ahead in their claim to holiness, nevertheless, men assuredly took first place in the *quality* of their sanctity."[52] Mahoney directly encourages her readers to give women "respect as a rational being," and she claims that doing so

---

[50] Ibid., 173–74.

[51] Priscilla O'Brien Mahoney, "The Lady Has a Brain!" *The Catholic World* 178/1068 (March 1954): 451.

[52] Ibid.; emphasis in original.

may produce in women the "self-confidence" they need "to produce works comparable to those of the male," though she admits sarcastically that it may lead to "fewer pink teas and bridge sessions."[53] That Mahoney feels the need to make what most modern readers would take as self-evident claims for women's intellect may speak to her perception of Catholics holding women's intellect in low esteem, but the fact that she gained a hearing in a journal published by the Missionary Society of St. Paul the Apostle demonstrates an openness in the American Catholic world to such views.

Moreover, in 1959, *The Sign* published an article specifically addressing the problem of discrimination against women. Alba Zizzamia's provocative article opens with a story of a woman in French West Africa who is denied property, ill-treated, and forced to marry without her consent due to her status as a woman.[54] After discussing efforts by the United Nations to address such conditions, Zizzamia affirms the contributions of Catholic women's organizations to several UN Commission studies. After a reminder that "the facts of [women's] social and legal inferiority in many areas of the world are very real and often cruel," she ends on this pious note: "The role of Catholic women, said Pius XII, 'is in general to work toward making woman always more conscious of her sacred rights, of her duties, and of her power to help mold public opinion through her daily contacts, and to influence legislation and the administration by the proper use of her prerogatives as a citizen.'"[55] While Zizzamia may be distorting the intent of the Pope's words, she shows them to be highly flexible and is willing to use them to women's advantage.

Such an article plainly suggests that at least part of American Catholicism was working—and trying to motivate others to work—on behalf of women's justice and equality. It does not, of course, refute or reconfigure the Catholic Church's patriarchal structure or its history of understanding the Supreme Being in male terms. However, even if it

---

[53] Ibid., 453, 454.

[54] Alba Zizzamia, "Talk to the Women...and See," *The Sign* 38/9 (April 1959): 24.

[55] Ibid.

reflects only a small segment of American Catholic thought and belief, it counterbalances the view that for an American Catholic of this period faith was inevitably a misogynistic force. Moreover, for Flannery O'Connor studies, it serves to refute the easy assumptions of critics who, acknowledging O'Connor's commitment to Catholicism, assume that her Catholicism necessarily made her antifeminist. At the same time, it enables us to avoid going to the other extreme—a position that can probably best be defined as that staked out by John Hawkes when he declared O'Connor an unknowing member of the devil's party—when one discovers any material not in line with the monolithic conception of Catholic beliefs. Put another way, it challenges the preconceptions, derived from awareness of O'Connor's Catholicism, of what O'Connor's fiction *must* say or mean in terms of gender. The importance of such a challenge appears when, specifically rejecting preconceived views of how O'Connor must have viewed women, we examine one of her stories that has drawn relatively slim scholarly commentary despite the key role that gender and sexuality play in it: "The Comforts of Home."

II.

O'Connor's "The Comforts of Home" is one of the few stories for which her own interpretation has not dominated critical response. Writing to John Hawkes in 1961, O'Connor explicates the story, beginning with a complaint about reader expectations of Catholic writers:

> The sheriff's vision is not meant to be taken literally, but to be the Devil's eye view. And nobody is "redeemed." I am afraid that one of the great disadvantages of being known as a Catholic writer is that no one thinks you can lift the pen without trying to show somebody redeemed. To me, the old lady is the character whose position is right and the one who is right is usually the victim. If there is any question of a symbolic redemption, it would be through the old lady who brings Thomas face to face with his own evil—which is that of putting his own comfort

before charity (however foolish). His doing that destroys the one
person his comfort depended on, his mother. The sheriff's view
is as the world will see it, not as it is. Sarah Ham is like Enoch
and Bishop—the innocent character, always unpredictable and
for whom the intelligent characters are in some measure
responsible (responsible in the sense of looking after them). I am
much interested in this sort of innocent person who sets the
havoc in motion[.] (*HB*, 434)

Four ideas in this comment are relevant to the issues I have been
discussing: (1) "the old lady is the character whose position is right"; (2)
Sarah Ham is an "innocent character"; (3) "nobody is 'redeemed,'" but
Thomas is brought "face to face with his own evil"; and (4) "the sheriff's
view is as the world will see it, not as it is."

A feminist reading of the story that sees American Catholicism as
monolithic could well respond to the first idea by saying, "Of course, the
old lady's right from O'Connor's view. She behaves like a good Catholic
mother, keeping house for her child and even sacrificing her life in the
pursuit of her nurturing, motherly duties." However, such a view overly
simplifies the actual text. As Anthony Di Renzo has observed, the
behavior of Thomas's mother consists of "maddening paradoxes,"[56] and
he suggests that the story encourages a reading of her that changes and
develops until she is seen as "ridiculous *and* heroic."[57] Moreover,
recognizing that American Catholicism contained, in O'Connor's era,
varying expectations for women and their roles, as my survey of
periodicals suggests, allows us to see as well that this progression is
paralleled by her movement beyond the caricature of the good Catholic
mother. When the story begins, she is that caricature, appearing to be as
Sarah Ham tells Thomas, "about seventy-five years behind the times"
(*CS*, 391). She appears to devote herself almost purely to homemaking,
interrupted only by giving boxes of candy to mark every occasion from
birth to illness. Thomas makes clear the subservient nature of the role

---

[56] Anthony Di Renzo, *American Gargoyles: Flannery O'Connor and the Medieval
Grotesque* (Carbondale: Southern Illinois University Press, 1993) 101.

[57] Ibid., 108; emphasis in original.

she has assumed when, as she moves beyond that role, he accuses his mother of caring "nothing about me, about my peace or comfort or working conditions" (CS, 398). Moreover, her movement beyond caricature is linked to her involvement in the social problem Sarah Ham represents, and it intensifies as her involvement with Sarah grows. Though she still is willing to serve Thomas meals in his room (CS, 396), she will not bow to his male authority by abandoning Sarah. Additionally, at the story's climax, when Sarah "lunge[s] at Thomas's throat," Thomas's mother "throw[s] herself forward to protect *her*" (CS, 403; my emphasis)—to protect Sarah, not her son. If this is still motherly behavior, it is not the behavior of the traditional homemaker but of someone who sees motherhood as requiring action beyond her home and family.

In addition to this progression, it is also important to see, as Miles Orvell has pointed out, that the story self-consciously depicts Thomas's mother as a victim long before she is shot. By denying her a name and control of any narrative point of view, the story makes clear that her position is a diminished one—a diminishment only emphasized by the failure of any of the characters to take her seriously. She is lectured to by Thomas, is lied to by Sarah Ham, is the subject of wrath by her husband, and is dismissed as an "old lady" by the sheriff. With her "heavy body on which sat a thin, mysteriously gaunt and incongruous head," her "greasy" face "framed in pink rubber curlers," and her "small swollen feet," she is constantly reduced to a grotesque figure (CS, 384, 387). However, as Patricia Yaeger has argued, such bodies are part of the work of "constructing a female tradition that refuses the genteel obsession with writing (or inhabiting) the beautiful body, in exchange for something more politically active and vehement."[58] In other words, despite expectations, Thomas's mother exemplifies the "gargantuan body [that] both maps its own limits and refuses to stay within bounds, to serve asked-for ends."[59] Moreover, in linking her view to that of the mother, O'Connor signals not the "rightness" of the mother's

---

[58] Patricia Yaeger, *Dirt and Desire: Reconstructing Southern Women's Writing, 1930–1990* (Chicago: University of Chicago Press, 2000) 139.

[59] Ibid., 126.

oppression/suppression but rather an identification with her course of development, even when the cost of that development in 1950s American society is life itself.

In a similar way, recognizing the diverse views of women in American Catholicism allows us to consider new possibilities for Sarah Ham and to take seriously O'Connor's description of her as innocent—something few critics have done. Indeed, critics as diverse as Jill Peláez Baumgaertner, D. G. Kehl, and George G. Murphy and Caroline L. Cherry have defined her in negative terms, with Bryan N. Wyatt going so far as to label her "an utterly repulsive character."[60] Two critics who do view her positively focus, perhaps surprisingly, on her sexuality. Anthony S. Magistrale, in a brief Freudian reading of the story, refers to Sarah Ham as "an independent and passionate woman" with "energy and enthusiasm" who is "unafraid of her sexuality."[61] Giannone links her to "ancient monastic sources" who, like Sarah Ham, admit and accept their sexuality and seek "to integrate its power into their search for God."[62] Such comments are useful in reconfiguring her character, but Miles Orvell comes perhaps closer to O'Connor's own sense when he parenthetically questions Thomas's moral superiority to Sarah by contrasting the family dog's favorable response to her versus the dog's ignoring Thomas.[63] Such an image, buried in O'Connor's text and in Orvell's parenthesis, does serve to link Sarah more closely to nature as does her nudity—described in terms of nature: "wide apple cheeks,"

---

[60] Bryan N. Wyatt, "The Domestic Dynamics of Flannery O'Connor: *Everything That Rises Must Converge*," *Twentieth Century Literature* 38 (1992): 79. See also Jill Peláez Baumgaertner, *Flannery O'Connor: A Proper Scaring* (Wheaton: Harold Shaw, 1988); D. G. Kehl, "Flannery O'Connor's 'Fourth Dimension': The Role of Sexuality in Her Fiction," *Mississippi Quarterly* 48 (1995): 255–76; George D. Murphy and Caroline L. Cherry, "Flannery O'Connor and the Integration of Personality," *The Flannery O'Connor Bulletin* 7 (1978): 85–100.

[61] Anthony S. Magistrale, "O'Connor's 'The Comforts of Home,'" *The Explicator* 42/4 (1984): 52.

[62] Robert Giannone, *Flannery O'Connor, Hermit Novelist* (Urbana: University of Illinois Press, 2000) 189.

[63] Miles Orvell, *Invisible Parade: The Fiction of Flannery O'Connor* (Philadelphia: Temple University Press, 1972) 163.

"feline empty eyes," and "a dangerous cat"—that so alarms Thomas (*CS*, 384). This, then, is Sarah Ham's innocence: she is an embodiment of natural impulses and desire. While a monolithic Catholicism would want Sarah buried safely in a marriage, home, and children, O'Connor did not. Rather, her letter to Hawkes implies that she found value in setting such characters as Sarah loose—found value in "the havoc" they set in motion. With this positive assessment, Sarah becomes a twin body, not just to Thomas as many critics have noted,[64] but to Thomas's mother, suggesting the value of women who do not conform to Southern or conservative Catholic expectations for women. If O'Connor is suggesting women's work be limited to the home, her delineation of Sarah Ham does so ironically and defines "women's work" in unexpected and devastating terms.

The remaining two points from O'Connor's letter to Hawkes take her ideas about women even further because they challenge the idea of patriarchal authority itself. For in one sense, all that I have argued about Thomas's mother and Sarah Ham could be countered if it can be shown that both women work ultimately to maintain the traditional authority of men over women. If the story supports masculine authority, such support suggests that O'Connor saw Catholicism as requiring her voice to sing in unison with its patriarchal tradition. However, her letter to Hawkes, with its plain assertion that "nobody is 'redeemed,'" does not encourage such a view. In O'Connor's gloss of the story, neither Thomas's mother nor Sarah Ham have worked to redeem him. Rather, their actions have brought him, so the letter asserts, to judgment, forcing him to come "face to face with his own evil" (*HB*, 434).

The story itself tends to support O'Connor's reading, as Frederick Asals unconsciously suggests in his complaint that the plot "is surely one of the least convincing O'Connor ever devised."[65] Central to Asals's criticism is what he calls the "awkward business of the disappearance and reappearance of the gun," which he claims is "crucial to the action as a

---

[64] See especially Bruce Marshall Gentry, "The Hand of the Writer in 'The Comforts of Home,'" *The Flannery O'Connor Bulletin* 29 (1991): 67.

[65] Frederick Asals, *Flannery O'Connor: The Imagination of Extremity* (Athens: University of Georgia Press, 1982) 108.

means of involving the sheriff and setting up the violent denouement."[66] In a literal sense, Asals is incorrect. The text mentions several ways the sheriff could have been involved when it raises the possibility that Thomas's father could "have pulled the necessary strings with his crony, the sheriff, and the girl would have been packed off to the state penitentiary to serve her time" (*CS*, 387). Moreover, O'Connor could have dispatched Thomas's mother by other means, the most easily conceived being a stroke, given her large body and swollen feet, similar to the one Julian's mother suffers in "Everything That Rises Must Converge." That O'Connor elected to use the gun, an object that, in view of the Freudian sexual imagery Asals and others have observed,[67] works as an obvious phallic symbol, suggests an intent to place the issue of the phallus at the core of the tale. The gun, then, is crucial to the story not because of its role in the plot but because it allows the reader to see that control of the phallus is, to phrase it comically, up for grabs. Thomas is driven to act only when his physical control of the phallus is challenged as Sarah becomes the controlling force in his house, isolating him to his room and directing his mother's activity. However, Sarah has no such focus on the gun/phallus, and she quietly returns it to Thomas's "center drawer" (*CS*, 402). Yet physical possession of the gun/phallus fails to give Thomas the control/authority he desires. He is caught trying to slip it into Sarah's purse (*CS*, 402), and when he fires it, the wrong target is hit (*CS*, 404). In short, for Thomas, having and controlling the phallus may "shatter the laughter of sluts" and bring the "peace of perfect order" (*CS*, 403–404), but it also robs him of the one natural love in his life and propels him toward an almost certain punishment. Such a plot is unconvincing only if one has the expectation that questioning male domination, the rule of the phallus, is out of place in O'Connor's religious world. However, it is convincing from a female Catholic writer chaffing, as the letter to Hawkes suggests, against limited views of her religion.

---

[66] Ibid., 109.

[67] See Asals, *Imagination of Extremity*, 112–13; Gentry, "The Hand," 62 and Magistrale, "O'Connor's 'The Comforts of Home,'" 52–54.

Such an idea is encouraged by O'Connor's last point in the Hawkes letter: that "the sheriff's view is as the world will see it, not as it is" (*HB*, 434). Though both Orvell and Gentry deem puzzling the final paragraphs giving the sheriff's view that the shooting of Thomas's mother is a planned murder by two sordid lovers,[68] Di Renzo is closer to the mark when he labels it "a piece of pulp fiction"[69]—the literature of the masses. As such, it serves to emphasize the tendency to read to a pre-set formula: we see what we want and expect to see. If Miles Orvell is right—and I think he is—in seeing this tale as a satire,[70] perhaps we would do well to recognize that the closing paragraph turns the satire upon readers who find the meanings that meet their expectations. As I have tried to suggest, I don't think O'Connor would be surprised that much of those expectations derive from readers knowing of her Catholicism. The danger, of course, is that we will ignore history and fail to see the Catholicism of her time as more complex in its view of the world and especially of women than knowledge of Catholicism's official doctrines would lead us to expect. If we fail to see that danger, we are likely also to fail to see the women O'Connor imagined and wrote about, beholding instead the old ladies, sluts, and handmaids of our own ideologies.

---

[68] Orvell, *Invisible Parade*, 164; Gentry, "The Hand," 69.

[69] Di Renzo, *American Gargoyles*, 109.

[70] Orvell, *Invisible Parade*, 166.

Flannery O'Connor and the
Cartoon Catechism

Jill Peláez Baumgaertner

Before catechisms were books of instruction, they were parts of an oral tradition, appearing as portions of sermons. Doctrinal teachings were presented in a standard order that included the creed, the Ten Commandments, the teaching of the love of God and neighbor, the seven deadly sins, the seven virtues, and the seven sacraments. Not until 1357 was the first vernacular book of instruction produced by Archbishop John Thoresby of York and named *The Lay Folks' Catechism*. More than three hundred years later, priest and church historian Claude Fleury, who felt that contemporary catechisms were spiritually dry because they were so heavily rational, argued for more use of narration and illustrations. When he published his *Catechisme historique* in 1683, he included his own illustrations.[1] Not until the twentieth century, however, did other illustrated catechisms appear.

In one form or another the version of the catechism with which Flannery O'Connor and most American Catholics in the first half of the twentieth century grew up was the *Baltimore Catechism*, published in 1885 to immediate complaints about its dull and ponderous style. One anonymous author of nine articles published in 1885–1886 complained that "the work was pedagogically unsuitable for children...because of its incomprehensible language, its small size (children are more comfortable with a larger volume), the disproportionate number of yes-no questions (91 of 421), the stunting of thought processes involved in questions that

---

[1] Berard L. Marthaler, *The Catechism Yesterday & Today: The Evolution of a Genre* (Collegeville MN: The Liturgical Press, 1995) 9, 68.

contain complete answers, and finally, the monotony of the entire text."[2] In 1896 a committee was appointed to revise the *Baltimore Catechism*, but a revised edition did not appear until 1941, with a First Communion edition following in 1943.

Catechetical scholar Monsignor Michael J. Wrenn speaks of the *Baltimore Catechism* as a "symbol of everything some people thought was bad in preconciliar Catholicism in America; included in that, apparently, were propositional formulations of the belief of the Church of any description."[3] In spite of the prevalence of this attitude toward the *Baltimore Catechism* and the general dissatisfaction with it, it gained a particular kind of authority as its use increased, and with this occurrence arose another phenomenon: teachers and pastors began to write their own manuals and supplements, often in workbook style and with illustrations that would appeal to children. Some of the titles of these works are self-explanatory: Joseph Baierl's *The sacraments explained according to the Munich or psychological method: for children of the intermediate and higher grades: based on the Baltimore catechism an aid to catechists* (1921; 1929); Thomas Kinkead's *An Explanation of the Baltimore Catechism of Christian doctrine: for the use of Sunday-school teachers and advanced classes* (1921); and Magnus Schumacher's *How to teach the catechism: a teacher's manual containing a systematized presentation of lessons in the Baltimore catechism, in correlation with Bible and church history, the ecclesiastical year, liturgy, and the lives of the saints. Also a definite schedule of lesson plans for the religion curriculum of every grade* (1933, 1934).

Notice how the dates of publication of some of these books coincide with the dates of O'Connor's own catechetical instruction and suggest that those who catechized O'Connor could have been in some way influenced by the verbal examples these manuals provided and the illustrations they contained. O'Connor entered St. Vincent's Grammar School at the Cathedral of St. John the Baptist in Savannah, Georgia, in

---

[2] Mary Charles Bryce, "The *Baltimore Catechism*—Origin and Reception," *Sourcebook for Modern Catechetics*, ed. Michael Warren (Winona MN: St. Mary's Press, 1983) 141.

[3] Michael J. Wrenn, *Catechisms and Controversies: Religious Education in the Postconciliar Years* (San Francisco: Ignatius Press, 1991) 33.

1931, made her First Communion at the Cathedral in 1932, transferred to Sacred Heart School in 1936 where she was taught by the Sisters of St. Joseph of Corondolet, furthered her primary education at St. Joseph's Church in Atlanta, and moved with her mother to Milledgeville later that year, where because there were no parochial schools, she entered her first public school, Peabody High School (*CW*, 1238–39).

That O'Connor used the catechism as a child is a given.[4] How it entered her developing intellect with all of its sensitivities for spiritual realities, how it combined with her Christian aesthetic, is, of course, a mystery. When we look at her work for evidence of the influence of the catechism, we find that at least a few of her stories contain catechetical moments—some indirect, some very direct. "The Enduring Chill" is probably the only story in which a character quotes directly from the *Baltimore Catechism*. "Do you know your catechism?" Father Finn asks Asbury, who thinks he is dying and has, to the dismay of his mother, called for a priest. "Certainly not," Asbury replies. The priest then fires the first and second questions of the Catechism at him:

> "Who made you?" the priest asked in a martial tone.
> "Different people believe different things about that," Asbury said.
> "God made you," the priest said shortly. "Who is God?"
> "God is an idea created by man," Asbury said, feeling that he was getting into stride, that two could play at this.
> "God is a spirit infinitely perfect," the priest said. "You are a very ignorant boy." (*CS*, 376)

---

[4] In a phone interview on 8 February 2006, O'Connor friend and scholar W. A. Sessions confirmed that the published inventory of O'Connor's library is correct and that it did not include a catechism. "There wasn't a book source in her library," Sessions stated. "But the religious teaching and images from her youth remained firmly in her mind. The catechism was just understood. It was like a law text—you didn't keep it around, but you knew the law." In addition, Jean W. Cash's biography, *Flannery O'Connor: A Life*, quotes O'Connor classmates as affirming that the *Baltimore Catechism* was used for instruction in their grammar school. (Knoxville: University of Tennessee Press, 2002), 14.

The actual answer in the St. Joseph edition of the *Baltimore Catechism* is "God is the Supreme Being, infinitely perfect, who made all things and keeps them in existence."[5] The priest continues with the third question in the catechism and then follows with a conflation of the answers to questions three through five in the catechism:

> "Why did God make you?"
>
> "God didn't...."
>
> "God made you to know Him, to love Him, to serve Him in this world and to be happy with Him in the next!" the old priest said in a battering voice. "If you don't apply yourself to the catechism how do you expect to know how to save your immortal soul?" (*CS*, 376)

In another story, "The Displaced Person," Father Flynn regularly visits Mrs. McIntyre to give her instruction and to check on the Guizacs, the Polish displaced people she has hired. O'Connor writes, "She had not asked to be instructed but he instructed anyway, forcing a little definition of one of the sacraments or of some dogma into each conversation he had, no matter with whom. He sat on her porch, taking no notice of her partly mocking, partly outraged expression as she sat shaking her foot, waiting for an opportunity to drive a wedge into this talk" (*CS*, 229). At the end of the story Father Flynn's catechetical instruction continues at Mrs. McIntyre's bedside, as she lies there devoid of mobility and eyesight and voice.

In both of these stories the protagonists—Mrs. McIntyre and Asbury—are spiritually blind, and in both of these stories, while the priests have some physical infirmities (both Father Flynn and Father Finn are elderly, and Father Finn is "blind in one eye and deaf in one ear"[*CS*, 375]), they recognize a truth they have difficulty communicating in a winning, pastoral manner. Notice that their communication almost entirely adopts the impersonal tone of the catechism. But these priests do have a gargantuan task—the same one

---

[5] *The New Saint Joseph Baltimore Catechism* (New York: Catholic Book, 1962) 9.

O'Connor faced in every story she wrote: how to communicate the truths of the Church to a deaf and blind generation. That O'Connor chose narrative to communicate truth is a sign of where she stood. In "The Enduring Chill" the priest *is* partially deaf and partially blind—he is a country priest of no sophistication—certainly not what Asbury expects to find after his New York encounter with Ignatius Vogle, S.J. But Father Finn recognizes spiritual ignorance when he sees it (after all, his good eye is "blue and clear" and "focuse[s] sharply" [*CS*, 375])—and Asbury's inevitable capture by the Holy Spirit, as it appears in the last paragraph, seems to have everything to do with the priest's words, which leave him "pale and drawn and ravaged, sitting up in his bed, staring in front of him with large childish shocked eyes" (*CS*, 377).

Similarly, in "The Life You Save May Be Your Own," Mr. Shiftlet asks Mrs. Crater some pointed catechetical questions reminiscent of the priest's conversation with Asbury:

> He leaned back against the two-by-four that helped support the porch roof. "Lady," he said slowly, "there's some men that some things mean more to them than money." The old woman rocked without comment and the daughter watched the trigger that moved up and down in his neck. He told the old woman then that all most people were interested in was money, but he asked what a man was made for. He asked her if a man was made for money, or what. He asked her what she thought she was made for but she didn't answer, she only sat rocking and wondered if a one-armed man could put a new roof on her garden house. He asked a lot of questions that she didn't answer. (*CS*, 148)

By the end of the story Shiftlet seems almost ready to come up with the right answers to the questions Mrs. Crater ignores.

A different kind of catechism—a perversion of it—appears in "The Artificial Nigger," where the unwitting Nelson, having never seen an African American in his life, even though he had been exposed since birth to his grandfather's racist pronouncements, is, on their train ride to Atlanta, catechized in the basic doctrines of racism:

> A huge coffee-colored man was coming slowly forward.... Mr. Head's grip was tightening insistently on Nelson's arm. As the procession passed them, the light from a sapphire ring on the brown hand that picked up the cane reflected in Mr. Head's eye, but he did not look up nor did the tremendous man look at him. The group proceeded up the rest of the aisle and out of the car. Mr. Head's grip on Nelson's arm loosened. "What was that?" he asked.
>
> "A man," the boy said and gave him an indignant look as if he were tired of having his intelligence insulted. (CS, 254–55)

When Mr. Head asks him "what kind of man," Nelson replies "fat" and then adds "old."

> "That was a nigger," Mr. Head said and sat back.
>
> Nelson jumped up on the seat and stood looking backward to the end of the car but the Negro had gone.
>
> "I'd of thought you'd know a nigger since you seen so many when you was in the city on your first visit," Mr. Head continued. "That's his first nigger," he said to the man across the aisle.
>
> The boy slid down into the seat. "You said they were black," he said in an angry voice. "You never said they were tan. How do you expect me to know anything when you don't tell me right?"
>
> "You're just ignorant is all," Mr. Head said and he got up and moved over in the vacant seat by the man across the aisle. (CS, 255)

Notice how Mr. Head's conclusion here about Nelson's ignorance is the same as Father Finn's about Asbury, and this conclusion follows a series of questions that Nelson, like Asbury, answers incorrectly—at least in Mr. Head's estimation. As in "The Enduring Chill," the character being catechized is profoundly altered by the experience. In "The Artificial Nigger," "Nelson turned backward again and looked where the Negro had disappeared. He felt that the Negro had deliberately walked down the aisle in order to make a fool of him and he hated him with a fierce raw fresh hate; and also, he understood now why his grandfather disliked them" (CS, 255–56). We see here that both the catechisms of the Church and the catechisms of social inculturation can have life-changing effects. But then there is also the balancing example of Father Flynn in "The Displaced Person." He drones on about the doctrines of the Church to Mrs. McIntyre, who cannot respond and who may not even hear him.

In addition to these catechetical references in O'Connor's stories—references that are verbal and structural—her work may contain other, submerged references that are primarily visual. What I am not suggesting here is that O'Connor was intentionally quoting these visual images. She well may have been, but I have no proof of that. What I am prepared to suggest is that the catechetical books of her youth, the supplements, workbooks, and manuals she may have used or her teachers may have used in presenting doctrine to children, and even some of the catechetical materials published in the 1950s and early 1960s may have provided her with images that were subject to her relentless irony and that infused and informed her imagination as she wrote.

Recall, for example, that Asbury's illness in "The Enduring Chill" is finally diagnosed as undulant fever, which he has contracted from drinking unpasteurized milk. He also had defied the orders of his mother and smoked in the dairy barn, defiling two cans of milk that were returned the next day, making impure milk an informing metaphor of the story. In *Father McGuire's The New Baltimore Catechism* (1942) appears an image illustrating the difference between original sin and actual sin (figure 1).[6] Original sin is imaged as an empty milk bottle—as empty as the soul without grace that is inherited through original sin. Next to this image is another box with illustrations of the two types of

---

[6] *Father McGuire's The New Baltimore Catechism* (New York: Benziger Bros., 1942) 25.

actual sin. The first is a figuration of mortal sin, which is, like original sin, represented by an empty milk bottle. The second is an illustration of venial sin, which is a bottle filled with impure milk; the soul guilty of venial sin has not separated itself from grace, but it still contains impurities that need to be cleansed. Anecdotal evidence suggests that the image of the sin-stained soul as a bottle of impure milk entered the popular Catholic imagination at the time O'Connor was being catechized. Later she certainly could have picked up on images and developed references to material she had either seen herself or heard in various contexts in her parochial education.

Another image reminiscent of the bedridden Asbury appears and reappears in various contexts in *The New Saint Joseph Baltimore Catechism*. A sick child provides an illustration of venial sin (figure 2). In the discussion of purgatory is an illustration of a young man burning in fever in a bed in purgatory, here presented as God's hospital (figure 3). Again, in an illustration of penance is a child sick in bed who takes his medicine—penance—and rises healthy, having experienced the benefits of the blood of Christ, which has descended upon him from a crucifix on the wall (figure 4). One can't help but think of "the Holy Ghost emblazoned in ice instead of fire, continuing to descend" from the ceiling above Asbury's head (*CS*, 382).

The automobile, which figures so heavily in O'Connor's work, appears in many forms in the various editions of the catechism. In an illustration O'Connor would have enjoyed immensely, the perfection of God appears in an only-in-America comparison with an automobile (figure 5). In a cartoon analogizing the necessity of keeping God's laws, one immediately recalls Hazel Motes's car stalled in front of the sign "Jesus Saves" (figure 6). In the second frame, "Disregarding Directions," an illustration of a wrecked car that has crashed off a bridge into a body of water, one remembers the destruction of Hazel Motes's automobile by the policemen, agents of civil law, who push the car into the lake. At other places in the catechism the car becomes representative of the soul (figure 7), the lesson being that God's "actual grace" (different from sanctifying grace) allows us to avoid mishaps—getting stuck in the mud (venial sin) or running into unforeseen dangers around a dangerous

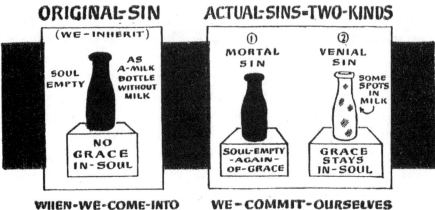

ORIGINAL-SIN

(WE-INHERIT)

SOUL EMPTY — AS A-MILK BOTTLE WITHOUT MILK

NO GRACE IN-SOUL

WHEN-WE-COME-INTO THE-WORLD

ACTUAL-SINS-TWO-KINDS

① MORTAL SIN

SOUL-EMPTY -AGAIN- OF-GRACE

② VENIAL SIN

SOME SPOTS IN MILK

GRACE STAYS IN-SOUL

WE-COMMIT-OURSELVES

Figure 1.

70. What is venial sin?

Venial sin is a less serious offense against the law of God, which does not deprive the soul of sanctifying grace, and which can be pardoned even without sacramental confession.

Venial sin is a disease in the life of grace in the soul. It is less serious than mortal sin, but much more serious than a sickness, or even the death, of the body.

71. How can a sin be venial?

A sin can be venial in two ways:

first, when the evil done is not seriously wrong;
second, when the evil done is seriously wrong, but the sinner sincerely believes it is only slightly wrong, or does not give full consent to it.

Figure 2.

PURGATORY IS GOD'S HOSPITAL

Purgatory is God's hospital for souls, where those who do not love God enough to enter heaven are cured by fire.

Only those who love God perfectly can enter heaven. But even many good people die with only a weak love of God. They had more interest in the people and the things of this earth than they did

PURGATORY

in God. They did not love Him with their whole heart and soul. They wasted many opportunities to please Him.

Love is purified, increased and perfected by suffering. This means not only bodily pain, but crosses of all kinds. (See Q. 425.) God sends everyone all the sufferings they need on earth to cleanse, strengthen, and perfect their love. But most people waste their sufferings. They do not want them, complain about them, and try to escape them in every manner possible, even by committing sin. Because of this attitude, the fires of their sufferings are unable to burn away the selfishness from their love, so that it will be perfect.

Figure 3.

PENANCE — The MEDICINE for our Soul

The sacrament of Penance is a SIGN.

Like every sacrament it is a sign of three things: past, present, and future.

1. It is a sign of the **Passion of Christ** and of His Precious Blood, which is the medicine He uses to heal our souls.

2. It is a sign of the **healing action of Christ** on the soul through the absolution of the priest.

3. It is a sign of the **spiritual health** which this sacrament gives.

Figure 4.

11. What do we mean when we say that God is infinitely perfect?

When we say that God is infinitely perfect we mean that He has all perfections without limit.

Perfections are good qualities which something has. For example, advertisements for automobiles may list the perfections of the automobiles, their size, beauty, speed, power, comfort, and so forth.

Figure 5.

Road Directions

Help us to get where we are going and to avoid danger.

Disregarding Directions

Means accidents and tragedy.

Laws of God

HONOR
THY
FATHER
AND
MOTHER

Help us to get where we are going and to avoid danger.

Breaking God's Laws

Means the tragedy of sin.

Figure 6.

Actual graces are special HELPS God gives us, like a lift to get a car out of the mud or a red light to warn of danger.

God gives us many actual graces each day. They last as long as we need them and then go. They are really actions of God to help us.

But sanctifying grace is permanent and, unless we lose it by sin, it will last until it becomes the life of glory in heaven.

114. Can we resist the grace of God?

We can resist the grace of God, for our will is free, and God does not force us to accept His grace.

If you keep the brake on in the car, it is hard to push it out of the mud. God could force us, but He will not.

Figure 7.

Extreme Unction and Holy Orders

Figure 8.

curve (mortal sin).[7] These illustrations put Hazel Motes's peculiar statement—"Nobody with a good car needs to be justified"—into a fresh context.

Another image of the automobile that finds its way into the catechism occurs in *Father McGuire's Catechism* in the section explaining the sacraments—in particular, Extreme Unction (figure 8). Notice how the image here—of a seriously injured girl being anointed by a priest—also contains the agent of the injury, another big American car, a model from the late 1930s. One recalls the scene in "The Displaced Person" after Mrs. McIntyre witnesses the tractor accident, collapses, and eventually regains consciousness, at which point she watches the priest administering last rites to Mr. Guizac under the machine of his demise.

One of O'Connor's favorite devices, which she uses frequently to illustrate the perilous closeness of the sacred and the profane, is the double-edged swearing that so many of her characters find tempting. In "A Good Man Is Hard to Find," for example, the grandmother "found herself saying, 'Jesus, Jesus,' meaning, Jesus will help you, but the way she was saying it, it sounded as if she might be cursing" (*CS*, 131). In "Parker's Back" Parker yells, "GOD ABOVE!" (*CS*, 520) as he is tossed through the air (another tractor accident). Later the tattoo artist asks him if he wants to look at images of "Father, Son, or Spirit" and Parker replies, "Just God. ...Christ. I don't care. Just so it's God" (*CS*, 522). In a remarkable image from *Father McGuire's Catechism* to which one can only imagine O'Connor's response, we find prayer described as our "spiritual telephone" to God (figure 9). Notice that the image is complete with the explosive "MY GOD!" which is certainly intended as prayer, but traverses the fine line between the sacred and the profane that either an unredeemed imagination—or one on the lookout for irony, as O'Connor's always was—would find irresistible.

---

[7] For a penetrating study of the automobile in O'Connor's work, see Brian Abel Ragan's *A Wreck on the Way to Damascus: Innocence, Guilt and Conversion in Flannery O'Connor* (Chicago: Loyola University Press, 1989).

Prayer

Figure 9.

As an undergraduate O'Connor was a cartoonist, publishing the results of her efforts in both her high school and college newspapers and her college yearbook. In fact, Sally Fitzgerald reports that O'Connor submitted several of her cartoons to trade journals and to *The New Yorker*, but they were returned to her. She was so attracted to the genre that she continued to study art while she was at the University of Iowa—in particular a course in American political cartooning (*CW*, 1240). This interest, added to her wicked sense of humor and her propensity to caricature, would most probably have made her an ironic reader of some of the illustrated versions of the catechism. As always, she would have taken the doctrines absolutely seriously, but there is no doubt that she would have found some of these cartoons worthy of at least a good chuckle, and it is even possible that some of these pictures would have played either a conscious or an unconscious part in her approach to characterization and narrative. After all, in explaining the difficulty for a religious writer in a secular age, she famously said that one must draw large and startling pictures. At any rate, even though

O'Connor undoubtedly believed that the sacraments of the Church were a means of grace, and even though she would have memorized the catechism as a child and continued wholeheartedly to believe its teachings as an adult, this would not have precluded her from imbuing characters with an ironic consideration of Church doctrine and practice. O'Connor's humor, in fact, seriously depends on the resulting tension between an absolute truth and human interpretation of it, which can be as peculiar and idiosyncratic as some of the cartoons in these catechisms.

Partaking of the Sacraments with Blake and O'Connor: A Reading

Stephen C. Behrendt

I. Innocence

In a particularly insightful 1997 essay, W. A. Sessions observes that the surest way to approach Flannery O'Connor's fiction is at the level of the text itself. It is not so much by means of a theological or ideological study of the fiction that one grasps its essence, argues Sessions, as it is from an unblinking *textual* analysis that approaches the fiction from what some might consider the "old-fashioned" approach of *explication de texte*. For Sessions, such an approach ensures—and requires—that the reader "must participate in the text on *its* own terms, not the reader's, although the reader's self is never absent."[1] As someone who regularly teaches O'Connor's short fiction, I am intrigued that Sessions's sage advice has gone so largely unheeded among scholars and teachers alike. For surely one of the greatest challenges a teacher—or a scholar—faces is the unfamiliar ways in which O'Connor's stories operate, both within their discrete individual textual entities as what Sessions further calls "a form of ritual therapy"[2] and within the consciousness of the reader who struggles with them. Indeed, Sessions himself reformulates some of O'Connor's own dicta about reading—and reading her fiction in particular—in arriving at his statement that reading her texts involves a

---

[1] W. A. Sessions, "How to Read Flannery O'Connor: Passing by the Dragon," *Flannery O'Connor and the Christian Mystery*. Ed. John J. Murphy (Provo, UT: Brigham Young University, 1977) 191–215; 194–95.

[2] Ibid., 199.

"process of entering a text" as part of a "therapeutic or baptismal resource."[3] Or, as O'Connor herself said of reading fiction, "the modern novelist merges the reader in the experience" (*MM*, 139). I want to take these observations as starting points for an examination of one aspect of the sacramental quality that characterizes the experience of reading O'Connor's fiction.

In common usage, the term "sacrament" designates both a visible sign of an inward grace and a sign, token, or pledge that is understood to possess a sacred character or a mysterious (moral and spiritual) significance. The adjectival form, "sacramental," identifies an action that enables one to receive sanctifying grace.[4] In their specifically Catholic context, sacraments are understood to be "outward signs of inward grace, instituted by Christ for our sanctification."[5] According to Cynthia L. Seel, in a sacrament "matter (the material used), form (words and actions), and grace (that is holiness and mercy) are equally present—conjoined, inseparable and instituted by Christ through his example" in order to "instruct (initiate) and to build up the Body of Christ (the community)" and facilitate acts of charity or compassion. By partaking of the sacraments and the rituals they involve, Seel writes, individuals become "more disposed to effectively interact with both the divine as it is revealed through the physical world of matter and with others in the community."[6] If by "sacrament," then, we mean a form or instrument of formal and ritualized behavior that is assumed to confer both grace and spiritual value upon the recipient/participant or "communicant," then we do well to consider the extent to which O'Connor intended her stories to perform this function upon and within the moral and spiritual consciousness of her reader. Furthermore, it is not far from the mark to suggest that O'Connor expects her readers to

---

[3] Ibid., 204.

[4] As a source for these deliberately generalist definitions, I have used that most common of resources, the *Random House College Dictionary*, rev. ed. (New York: Random House, 1980) 1159.

[5] *The Catholic Encyclopedia* online, www.newadvent.org/cathen/13295a.htm. 20 May 2002.

[6] Cynthia L. Seel, *Ritual Performance in the Fiction of Flannery O'Connor* (Rochester NY: Camden House, 2001) 30.

be seized, like John of Patmos, by the vision that befalls them and, in turn, first to "enter into" that text and then to *consume* the vehicle of that vision in the process of "digesting" it and redirecting its empowering light outward—toward the public community of the social unit—in a newly informed and empowered awareness of both "truth" and what O'Connor terms "mystery."

Many of us who read O'Connor with pleasure and satisfaction are what I would call "professional readers." Often we are professional educators for whom complicated exercises in reading are both familiar and gratifying. For the most part, we enjoy O'Connor's fiction because it challenges us with its inherent intellectual and philosophical (and spiritual) difficulty while at the same time providing a considerable measure of aesthetic pleasure. Those of us who teach, though, often find that what our students bring to—and take away from—O'Connor's fiction is different indeed from our own experience, which is in part a consequence of the very different youth culture of which they—and not we—are a part. Most typically, they do not read her fiction with pleasure but rather with a pronounced and often vocal dissatisfaction. Their responses range from shock to offense, and their complaints invariably stem from the fact that O'Connor's stories fail so visibly to conform to their expectations about how stories "work." These expectations are of course grounded in students' previous experience with the short story form, an experience that reflects their prior education, as well as with the delivery systems of television and movies, which often rely upon a visual foreshortening more striking than even the quick-hitting format of the short-short story permits. The relative brevity of the short story has, however, made the genre popular in the undergraduate curriculum. The unwillingness (or inability) of students to deal with the rigors of longer forms like the novel has prompted their teachers to substitute the ostensibly more manageable form of the short story in the assumption that students will actually *read* these works in their entirety.

Ironically, at the other end of the intellectual spectrum, O'Connor's fiction often resists, too, the efforts of professional scholars and critics to unlock its mysteries. I use the term "mystery" deliberately, both because O'Connor placed such value on the word and because it is a problematic term in professional scholarly discourse and especially among contemporary critical theorists, whose writings often suggest that they do not much care for literature (or, put another way, that they do not care for much literature) in the first place. One might expect postmodern theory to be especially receptive to O'Connor's approach, given postmodernism's fascination with the dilemma posed by the artist's struggle to represent the unrepresentable, or to give form to that which is essentially formless, as well as its insistence on the lack of viability of traditional rules and paradigms associated with fiction. The challenge of postmodern art, according to Jean-François Lyotard, is to deal with "the fact that the unpresentable exists[,]...that there is something which can be conceived and which can neither be seen nor made visible." According to Lyotard's postmodernist view of things, much of modern aesthetics lacks rigor in its applications because it is willing to be content instead with a mere nostalgia. Lyotard remarks disdainfully that this cheap nostalgia permits "the unpresentable to be put forward only as the missing contents,"[7] as if this absent "something" may be glimpsed through its empty outlines, rather as we "see" a dog or a horse that has been cut out of a picture, leaving a hole shaped in its likeness.

All of which is to say that even the most sophisticated professional reader may, paradoxically, share some of the weaknesses we tend to associate with impercipient undergraduate readers, who are neither patient nor "professional" in the sense in which I have introduced the term here. Bringing to O'Connor's work a set of preformed and experientially reinforced expectations may both limit one's flexibility and blind one to what O'Connor clearly believed would be patently obvious to a reader whose "eyes" were at all reliable. It is when one lives under the spiritually unproductive circumstances the Bible associates with "a rebellious house" that individuals have "eyes to see, and see not, [that] have ears to hear, and hear not" (Ezek 12:2). Yet seeing and hearing correctly is as difficult for O'Connor's reader as is attaining the sort of clarified "vision" that is the aim of that fiction.

---

[7] Jean-François Lyotard, "Answering the Question: What Is Postmodernism?" *The Postmodern Condition: A Report on Knowledge*, trans. Geoff Bennington and Brian Massumi (Minneapolis: University of Minnesota Press, 1984) 78, 81.

The difficulty of this is well illustrated by O'Connor's famous report to Charlotte Gafford about her exchange with some students at Vanderbilt University in 1962:

> I see that telephone call those Vanderbilt students made has got around. What they wanted was for me to write their paper for them. They asked me such things as "Miss O'Connor, why did they stop at *the Tower?*"—trying to make something of the word *tower*. They try to make everything a symbol. It kills me. At one place where I talked, one of them said, "Miss O'Connor, why was [T]he Misfit's hat *black?*" "Well," I said, "he stold it from a countryman and in Georgia they usually wear black hats." This sounded like a pretty stupid answer to him, but he wasn't through with it. In a few minutes he says, "Miss O'Connor, what is the significance of [T]he Misfit's hat?" "To cover his head," I say. When the session was over they obviously thought I didn't have sense enough to have written the story I wrote. (*HB*, 465)

O'Connor's anecdote reveals precisely the dilemma her stories pose to their readers. Even the most sophisticated professional readers learn to read by repeatedly doing so. In the process they absorb the conventions of the fiction they read: both formal features like length, arrangement, plot, character, and incident and more "internal" features like figurative language, allusion, iconography, and symbol. These conventions, which govern both reading and cognition (which I separate intentionally here), become so familiar that the readers may forget that they are learned, not inherent, and that they involve *choices* grounded in expectations that these readers have formed as part of their individual reading experiences within what Sarah Gordon has called "the myriad communities of reading that affect any one text."[8]

Students in the classroom have learned to read literary texts by bringing to them and to the reading activity a set of expectations and parameters they have gained from prior comparable experiences. Thus

---

[8] Sarah Gordon, *Flannery O'Connor: The Obedient Imagination* (Athens: University of Georgia Press, 2000) 83–84.

they typically mark up their texts in terms of a set of questions they have been conditioned to answer, usually for some sort of written or oral examination. Questioned about their annotations, they will respond that they mark what is "important," although when pressed they are often unable to say *why* something strikes them as important. So they underline or highlight names, places, dates, and the like, as well as what they have learned at least to *suspect* might be a symbol (such as The Misfit's black hat). They *almost* know how such things function in works they have read, and they *almost* know, too, what sort of questions these things elicit from instructors *and* what sort of "answers" will normally satisfy those instructors. Confronted with The Misfit's black hat, then, or with the "crooked cross" Mr. Shiftlet inscribes against the evening sky at the beginning of "The Life You Save May Be Your Own" (*GM*, 48), they immediately shift into a problem-solving mode, playing "find the symbol" much in the manner O'Connor suggests in the passage quoted above. With their readerly "eyes" fixed so intently upon what they cannot see but *expect* to see, they fail to see what is actually set before them. Readerly expectations of this sort get in the way of intellectual, imaginative, and *spiritual* cognition and are part of what O'Connor had in mind when she wrote to her unidentified correspondent, "A." (Betty Hester), "I daresay no one of us is free of these impediments to responsiveness. All education is a matter of getting rid of them. Some of them are conscious and some unconscious. The wrong kind of education can impose them" (*HB*, 465). This is certainly true of the institutionally conditioned training in reading that produces among students not the sort of "professional" readers that might reasonably be the goal of education, but rather unsophisticated and undiscriminating readers bent on "finding the symbol."

Of course, O'Connor is not entirely innocent of blame in any of this, either. She was well aware of the limitations of the readers who encountered her stories in the journals in which they first appeared, as well as in the collections that followed. Materialistic, Protestant, often pseudo-intellectual, these readers she imagined (usually correctly) as "unbelievers hostile to what she called Christian mystery"[9] were fair game for the traps she set for them in her stories. Just as she drops the seemingly innocent colloquialism "stold" in her letter to Charlotte Gafford, quoted previously, so was she also fond of others like "bidnis" that pepper her letters. But this is the private author writing to friends and acquaintances who—being trained in reading O'Connor's correspondence and being therefore also "professional" readers of that correspondence—know how to distinguish the complex spiritual writer from her colloquial witticisms.

In offering her general reader a physically deformed Mr. Shiftlet whose figure forms a "crooked cross," however, O'Connor teases the reader into assuming that both words are "loaded" and that they must therefore be "unloaded" or "unpacked" to disclose a "meaning" that has to do both with "cross" (and therefore a whole constellation of Christian signification) and with "crooked" (connoting physical shape but also a sense of dishonesty). That the name of this itinerant "tramp" is Mr. Shiftlet, moreover, prods the reader to think of "shiftless," with its own mixed connotations of dishonesty, irresponsibility, and rootlessness. Further still, having probably decided that Mr. Shiftlet's surname is designedly meaningful, the reader is then tempted to consider the surname of his victims and to conclude that "Crater" bears significant overtones not just of a large hole in the ground but also of one that has been created by an impact or an explosion, both of which readings "work" within the story's intellectual and aesthetic design. But within a few pages O'Connor subverts—or deconstructs—this pattern of apparent signification when she has Mr. Shiftlet recite a whole catalogue of names and places in support of his claim that he may be lying about the name he has given: "'Lady,' he said, 'nowadays, people'll do anything anyways. I can tell you my name is Tom T. Shiftlet and I came from Tarwater, Tennessee, but you never have seen me before: how you know I ain't lying? How you know my name ain't Aaron Sparks, lady, and I come from Singleberry, Georgia, or how you know it's not George Speeds and I come from Lucy, Alabama, or how you know I ain't

[9] Joanne Halleran McMullen, *Writing against God: Language as Message in the Literature of Flannery O'Connor* (Macon GA: Mercer University Press, 1996) 2.

Thompson Bright from Toolafalls, Mississippi?'" (*GM*, 50–51). The "how you know?" is aimed at the reader as much as it is at the elder Lucynell Crater, for the reader, too, "knows" only what the narrator reveals—or what the reader "reads." If narrative is about "telling" things, it is also about *not* telling them or, in the case of this passage, telling so *many* things that it becomes impossible to know which is "correct."

Therein lies the challenge that perplexes, annoys, and often defeats O'Connor's more impatient readers. Does it *matter*, finally, what Mr. Shiftlet's "real" name actually is? Only if we invest a fictional name of a fictional character in a work of fiction with "real" significance does it matter. I am not at all convinced that O'Connor finally intends it to matter—at least in the way such things usually "matter" to the average reader who is looking for conventional "meaning" in a story that follows the usual "rules." O'Connor's fiction everywhere requires of its reader an active *engagement* in a process of discovery that leads into the heart of mystery and into an individual and highly personal revelation that takes the form of an often still mysterious but nevertheless unmistakable in-sight (with the hyphen intended). Passive reading will not do with O'Connor; her stories are not like the pictures on the walls of an art gallery, past which a procession of viewers parade looking casually at surfaces and tracing the artists' names from the mounted labels.

Readers who attempt this sort of detached gallery gazing with O'Connor's stories find themselves no nearer the "truth" (or "meaning") than Mrs. Crater—and often further from it than when they began. This is why they emerge from the encounter disappointed or angry: their experience as readers has not prepared them to anticipate the intellectual and imaginative resilience and self-assurance that O'Connor's art demands. As she put it—significantly, to an unnamed "Professor of English" who had written her about some particularly off-the-wall interpretations of "A Good Man Is Hard to Find" he and his colleagues and students had devised and submitted to her for her comment—"The meaning of a story should go on expanding for the reader the more he thinks about it, but meaning cannot be captured in an interpretation. If teachers are in the habit of approaching a story as if it were a research problem for which the answer is believable so long as it is not obvious, then I think students will never learn to enjoy fiction. Too much interpretation is certainly worse than too little, and where feeling for a story is absent, theory will not supply it" (*HB*, 437).

A year later, at a public reading at Hollins College of "A Good Man Is Hard to Find," O'Connor said this in the remarks with which she introduced her reading:

> In most English classes the short story has become a kind of literary specimen to be dissected.... I realize that a certain amount of this what-is-the-significance has to go on, but I think something has gone wrong in the process when, for so many students, the story becomes simply a problem to be solved, something which you evaporate to get Instant Enlightenment. A story really isn't any good unless it successfully resists paraphrase, unless it hangs on and expands in the mind. Properly, you analyze to enjoy, but it's equally true that to analyze with any discrimination, you have to have enjoyed already, and I think that the best reason to hear a story read is that it should stimulate that primary enjoyment. (*MM*, 108)

For O'Connor, it is clear, the *process* of reading and cognition matters most in the reader's experience of a story, not the *product* of the "what-is-the-significance" exercise, an exercise that is more likely to lead readers *away* from the "significance" they seek than to lead them toward it.

I quoted O'Connor's anecdote about the student readers earlier not because it is particularly humorous (although it is), but because it makes so clearly the point that O'Connor was always at pains to make about her work: one needs to begin not by assessing what may not be there at all, but rather by *seeing* what in fact *is* there. The old gag about Freud ("Sometimes a cigar is just a cigar") supplies a useful analogy. The point of The Misfit's hat is that it covers his head; the hat is black because that is what color it is. To look for "meaning" here is to look in entirely the wrong place—in part because the unsophisticated reader does not know what to look for (even assuming, incorrectly, that the point of reading is to look *for* something) and in part because the search for an object of

meaning distracts that reader from the more important *process* that in fact
constitutes meaning itself. "Truth, Goodness and Beauty are abstractions
and abstractions lead to thinness and allegory whereas in good fiction
and drama *you need to go through the concrete situation* to some experience
of mystery," O'Connor wrote to Janet McKane in 1963; "you are always
bounded by what you can make live" (*HB*, 520; my emphasis). For
O'Connor, its grounding in what she called the "concrete" is
fundamental to fiction. "The beginning of human knowledge is through
the senses, and the fiction writer begins where human perception begins.
He appeals through the senses, and you cannot appeal to the senses with
abstractions. It is a good deal easier for most people to state an abstract
idea than to describe and thus re-create some object that they actually
see" (*MM*, 67).

One of the most striking aspects of O'Connor's fiction is, in fact,
the cumulative sense of *authenticity* that resonates throughout the stories.
In a volume of celebratory essays, Andrea Hollander Budy expresses her
admiration for O'Connor's "ability to envision, to locate her stories,
detail by detail, and to deliver her characters *through* those details."[10]
Indeed, part of O'Connor's brilliance lay in her ability to encapsulate a
character, personality, object, setting, or speech in a mere word or
phrase, a skill she shared with Dickens and Dostoevsky. Her repeated
use of the word "bidnis" in her letters, to which I have already alluded,
works this way, as does the mere four-word phrase in her essay "The
King of the Birds," in which a sullen young boy epitomizes the rhythms
and the sounds of Southern colloquialism when he looks at the author
and asks, "Whut is thet thang?" (*MM*, 13). Or, to return to "The Life
You Save May Be Your Own," there is the unforgettable imagery in her
remarkable description of Mr. Shiftlet's reaction to Lucynell Crater's
crass insult: "The ugly words settled in Mr. Shiftlet's head like a group
of buzzards in the top of a tree" (*GM*, 57). Or, in "A Good Man Is Hard
to Find," there are the particularized details of the grandmother's family,
from Bailey's wife, "whose face was as broad and innocent as a cabbage"
to the grandmother's "big black valise that looked like the head of a

---

[10] Andrea Hollander Budy, "An Enduring Chill," *Flannery O'Connor: In
Celebration*, ed. Sarah Gordon (Athens: Hill Street Press, 2000) 69.

hippopotamus" (*GM*, 2). Such carefully particularized details lend precisely the credibility that O'Connor found lacking in the work of professional and amateur writers alike who filled their works with abstractions and generalizations.

II. Experience

In order to draw another perspective upon what I have been discussing, I would like to suggest a unique intellectual and spiritual kinship that reveals something particularly useful about how to read O'Connor. Nearly two hundred years earlier, William Blake, whose commitment to mystery, vision, and spirituality is equally undeniable, had made a comparable claim about the need for carefully delineated detail. Lambasting Sir Joshua Reynolds, that comfortable artistic establishment spokesman for a classicist art founded on general consensus, Blake declared in the first decade of the nineteenth century, in his annotations to Reynolds's *Discourses on Art*, that "To Generalize is to be an Idiot[.] To Particularize is the Alone Distinction of Merit—General Knowledges are those Knowledges that Idiots possess."[11] "Labour well the Minute Particulars," he advises his reader in his complex illuminated epic, *Jerusalem* (c. 1815).[12] Already in an early work, *The Marriage of Heaven and Hell* (1790), he insists upon the primacy of the senses for the visionary artist *and reader*, observing there (in the voice of a counterculture "devil") that "Man has no Body distinct from his Soul for that calld Body is a portion of the Soul discernd by the five senses[,] the chief inlets of Soul in this age."[13] O'Connor more than once expressed her admiration for what she called "analogical vision" in the sense in which that term was understood by medieval readers of (especially) religious texts, readers whose lives and reading habits were often,

---

[11] Annotations to *The Works of Sir Joshua Reynolds: The Complete Poetry and Prose of William Blake*, rev. ed., ed. David V. Erdman (Garden City NY: Anchor/Doubleday, 1982) 641. In all quotations, I have followed Blake's occasionally eccentric spelling and punctuation.

[12] Blake, *Complete Poetry and Prose*, 205.

[13] Ibid., 34.

significantly, *contemplative* in nature. This analogical quality, she wrote, "had to do with the Divine life and our participation in it" (*MM*, 72). Or, as Sarah Gordon puts it, for O'Connor "the *anagogical* vision imbues the work with Christian mystery and is also involved in our perception of this mystery."[14]

Like Blake, O'Connor understood that the avenue to this participation in the divine passed through the physical senses, an idea she would have found reiterated in the work of one of her favorite authors, St. Thomas Aquinas. Brian Abel Ragan tells us that she would have been drawn especially to Aquinas's conviction that "the spiritual senses are contained in the literal."[15] Furthermore, O'Connor's observation that "the longer you look at one object, the more of the world you see in it" (*MM*, 77) recalls the visionary *desiderata* with which Blake began his "Auguries of Innocence":

> To see a World in a Grain of Sand
> And a Heaven in a Wild Flower
> Hold Infinity in the palm of your hand
> And Eternity in an hour[.][16]

Blake and O'Connor also shared startlingly similar views regarding the prophet and prophetic art. O'Connor writes that the fiction writer's "kind of vision is prophetic vision. Prophecy, which is dependent on the imaginative and not the moral faculty, need not be a matter of predicting the future. The prophet is a realist of distances" (*MM*, 179). Blake, for his part, puts it this way: "Every honest man is a Prophet[;] he utters his opinion both of private & public matters / Thus / If you go on So / the result is So[.] / He never says such a thing shall happen let you do what you will. a Prophet is a Seer not an Arbitrary Dictator."[17] Both Blake and O'Connor envisioned a prophet in Ezekiel's mold, what Richard

---

[14] Gordon, *Obedient Imagination*, 142.

[15] Brian Abel Ragan, *A Wreck on the Road to Damascus: Innocence, Guilt, and Conversion in Flannery O'Connor* (Chicago: Loyola University Press, 1989) 15.

[16] Blake, "Auguries of Innocence," *Complete Poetry and Prose*, 490.

[17] Blake, "Annotations to *An Apology for the Bible*," *Complete Poetry and Prose*, 617.

Giannone calls a "prophet-as-watchman" who "must warn the people of judgment," serving as the "eyes for the modern world that cannot see devils for what they are."[18] Such prophets are never popular with their auditors, of course. That both Blake and O'Connor regarded themselves as cultural outcasts largely misunderstood by a complacent and (to them) imaginatively and spiritually backsliding public—the traditional situation of the prophet—further reinforces the sense of intellectual and spiritual kinship that emerges from their writings about art.

That these two artists shared so much common imaginative and philosophical ground makes particularly significant for an understanding of O'Connor's fiction Blake's reflections on one of his visual works. In 1809 Blake mounted a public exhibition of sixteen of his own paintings at the shop of his elder brother James Blake in Golden Square, London. To Blake's chagrin, the exhibition was largely a failure; it failed to attract either public approbation or—more important—the sales and commissions the artist so urgently needed. Much as O'Connor talked back to her detractors and interrogators, Blake blamed the failure of his exhibition on an unresponsive public and on the professional reviewers he regarded as its arbiters of taste, and he wrote at length about the misguided but culturally conditioned public preference for the merely fashionable over the visionary or sublime, for the easy over the difficult.

Blake's situation, as he articulated it in a number of verbal and visual works from this important period in his career, is rhetorically, intellectually, imaginatively, and spiritually (or philosophically) analogous to O'Connor's in many respects, not the least of which involves her perception of herself as a Catholic writer working within a predominantly non-Catholic culture "which doubts both fact and value" and in which "religious feeling has become, if not atrophied, at least vaporous and sentimental" (MM, 117, 161). This is precisely why, for both artists, the aim of art—or at least the sort of art that concerned them—was to teach the reader how to see, and to do so by educating that reader into a variety of intellectual, imaginative, and spiritual self-confidence that would permit an unvitiated encounter with the truth (or

---

[18] Richard Giannone, *Flannery O'Connor and the Mystery of Love* (Urbana: University of Illinois Press, 1989) 149.

vision) contained within, and disclosed by, the work of art without the interference of any external critic, commentator, facilitator, priest, or other intrusive intermediary. In this "therapeutic process" that effectively trains the reader and prepares her or him for "the passage by the dragon," Sessions reminds us, "the efficacy of the sacrament" depends finally not on the worthiness of the priest who administers it but rather "on the worthiness of the one receiving the sacrament, the reader."[19]

In "A Vision of the Last Judgment," Blake provides the key to what we may legitimately call the sacramental aspect of his art, and—looking far ahead—of O'Connor's as well. Discussing some of the figures that appear in his painting, Blake writes,

> If the Spectator could Enter into these Images in his Imagination[,] approaching them on the Fiery Chariot of his Contemplative Thought[;] if he could Enter into Noahs Rainbow or into his bosom or could make a Friend & Companion of one of these Images of wonder which always intreats him to leave mortal things as he must know[,] then would he arise from his Grave[,] then would he meet the Lord in the Air & then he would be happy[.] ...I intreat then that the Spectator will attend to the Hands & Feet[,] to the Lineaments of the Countenances[;] they are all descriptive of character & not a line is drawn without intention & that most discriminate & particular[.] [A]s poetry admits not a Letter that is Insignificant[,] so Painting admits not a Grain of Sand or a Blade of Grass Insignificant[,] much less an Insignificant Blur or Mark[.][20]

Nowhere else does Blake so fully explain for his audience the methodology of "seeing" and "knowing" that his art requires, a methodology that is rooted in enlightened and imaginatively engaged penetration of every detail, no matter how minute. The parallels with

---

[19] Sessions, "How to Read O'Connor," 213.

[20] Blake, "A Vision of the Last Judgment," *Complete Poetry and Prose*, 560.

O'Connor's art are remarkable, even if she never stated them in quite this manner.

The key element in the whole transactional scheme of reading and cognition that Blake outlines in this passage comes early on in his notion of how the "Spectator" must *enter into* the images she or he perceives, approaching them on the "Fiery Chariot" of her or his "Contemplative Thought." This is Blake's point about meeting the Lord "in the Air": the imaginative transaction literally "transports" the Spectator out of her or his empirical position and to another cognitive plateau. Note, too, that Blake is quite specific—even using capitalization to indicate emphasis—about the fact that the vehicle for this operation is *Contemplative* Thought. It is worth noting in this context that the theologians and spiritual thinkers for whom O'Connor expressed particular fondness all belong to the contemplative tradition: St. Augustine, St. Thomas Aquinas, Jacques Maritain, Pierre Teilhard de Chardin. Indeed, it was St. Thomas and his notion of art as "a virtue of the practical intellect" that she recommended to Cecil Dawkins and her students as early as 1957 (*HB*, 221). Contemplative thought is of course little regarded among the sort of readers I described earlier as unsophisticated or unprofessional. This is precisely because it is based not upon the expectation of the (relatively) instant gratification to be found in discovering the "answer," "moral," or "point" of a work of art—of solving the puzzle, so to speak—but rather upon the greater reward that is achieved by allowing the work to unfold itself to the reader who is herself or himself open to this variety of communication. As O'Connor admonished Cecil Dawkins, "don't mix up thought-knowledge with felt-knowledge" (*HB*, 491). The reader who can distinguish between the two is more likely both to discover and to appreciate—by "entering into" it—the mystery that lies at the heart of O'Connor's works and the works of all spiritually committed visionary artists.

That Blake speaks of Contemplative Thought specifically as a Fiery Chariot is no less important, for his phrase alludes directly to the experience of the prophet Elijah who was transported into heaven in a whirlwind, borne on a chariot of fire, his prophetic mantle drifting down to his successor Elisha (2 Kings 2:11–13) who returned to his people as their now acknowledged new prophet. Blake's Fiery Chariot is clearly the vehicle of God that transports (or translates) the individual "Spectator" from one "state" to another, assuming that Spectator into a heaven that is either literal (for Elijah) or figurative and symbolic (for Blake and his Spectator). In practical terms, this Chariot is the imagination, but an imagination that operates slowly (remember it is *contemplative* thought), taking the time to observe, absorb, and open itself to the mystery within the experience in which it participates. Coupled with the equally specific reference to "Noahs Rainbow," which is the visible sign of "the everlasting covenant between God and every living creature" (Genesis 9:16), Blake's reference to the Fiery Chariot cements the redemptive and sacramental relations he envisions among contemplation, "close reading," and individual salvation through participation in the divine.

Blake says that the individual who participates in this sort of transactional reading/viewing experience "arise[s] from his Grave" and "meet[s] the Lord in the Air," at which point she or he attains happiness. They meet, for all intents and purposes, in the Imagination, or in a world of pure spirit: "This world of Imagination is the World of Eternity[;] it is the Divine Bosom into which we shall all go after the death of the Vegetated body[.] This World [of Imagination] is Infinite & Eternal whereas the world of Generation or Vegetation is Finite & Temporal[.]"[21] Blake's phrase about meeting the Lord in the Air deliberately echoes St. Paul's observations on redemption, which he casts in terms of sleep and waking. The redeemed, Paul says, are already awake, but those unredeemed who are still asleep will be saved too: "For the Lord himself shall descend from heaven with a shout, with the voice of the archangel, and with the trump of God: and the dead in Christ shall rise first: Then we which are alive *and* remain shall be caught up together with them in the clouds, to *meet the Lord in the air* [my emphasis]: and so shall we ever be with the Lord" (1 Thessalonians 4:16–17). Blake's intricate fabric of references also hints at the idea of

---

[21] Ibid., 555.

transfiguration as it figures both in the Bible and in Christian doctrine. Even more important, it suggests the phenomenon of *transubstantiation* that lies at the heart of the Catholic sacrament of the Eucharist.

Blake's notion of the Last Judgment is not just religious or doctrinal, however. As I have already suggested, it is also intellectual and aesthetic, and in that sense it also has much to do with how he—and O'Connor later—views the role of art in the formation of the "redeemed" and visionary individual. For Blake, the work of art is both a model for thinking *and* an invitation to think. Put slightly differently, every work of art furnishes an occasion for its audience to "enter into" that work and in the process to enter into themselves as well, both as empirical readers perusing a "text" and as moral, ethical, and spiritual beings exploring a mystery. As we have already seen, this is very much the way O'Connor sees the matter.

Finally, I want to consider something else Blake says about entering into his images, something that bears special relevance for O'Connor's methods and aesthetic. Blake stresses that attaining Wisdom and Sense (or spiritual and imaginative consciousness) depends upon an individual's ability to "discriminate...most minutely the Manners & Intentions [and] the Characters in all their branches." It is little surprise, then, that Blake exhorts us to attend to what he calls "minute Particulars." The hands and feet of the characters in his paintings, along with the lineaments of their countenances, "are all descriptive of Character," he reminds us, and "not a line is drawn without intention and that most discriminate and particular." In short, the truth—and the vision—is to be found not in some abstracted, generalized notion the artist tries to impose upon the work of art, but rather in the detailed particulars that tie the work and what it illustrates *directly* to the physical world *at the same time* they lead the reader or viewer *away* from that physically limited mortal sphere. For her part, O'Connor put it this way: "[A]ny abstractly expressed compassion or piety or morality in a piece of fiction is only a statement added to it. ...[Y]ou can't make an inadequate dramatic action complete by putting a statement of meaning on the end of it or in the middle of it or at the beginning of it. ...[W]hen you write fiction you are speaking *with* character and action, not *about* character and action" (*MM*, 75–76).

Elsewhere, O'Connor wrote that if any novelist "is going to show the supernatural taking place, he has nowhere to do it except on the literal level of natural events, and that if he doesn't make these natural things believable in themselves, he can't make them believable in any of their spiritual extensions" (*MM*, 176). But the writer is nevertheless still concerned, ultimately, not with this surface texture of natural reality but rather with the mystery that lies behind it:

> [I]f the writer believes that our life is and will remain essentially mysterious, if he looks upon us as beings in a created order to whose laws we freely respond, then what he sees on the surface will be of interest to him only as he can go through it into an experience of mystery itself. His kind of fiction will always be pushing its own limits outward toward the limits of mystery, because for this kind of writer, the meaning of a story does not begin except at a depth where adequate motivation and adequate psychology and the various determinations have been exhausted. Such a writer will be interested in what we don't understand rather than in what we do. (*MM*, 41–42)

This is precisely the point Blake was making two centuries earlier. For Blake, as for O'Connor, this phenomenological "gateway"—this texture of particularized textual minutiae—has to engage the Spectator initially at his or her normal level of reality and consciousness. Put most simply, this level of the work must be eminently *familiar*, so that it can furnish the common ground upon which the artist-audience transaction proceeds. Indeed, in the greatest of such works—whether verbal or visual—there frequently exists a striking appearance of simplicity, even of naiveté. Blake's *Songs of Innocence and of Experience* furnish countless examples of this phenomenon; the apparently simple, naive verses of poems like "Infant Joy" or "The Lamb" or "Spring" have misled generations of unwary readers into dramatic underestimations of the depth and complexity of those poems. At the same time, however, generations of very young readers have read (or had read to them) these same poems and have delighted in a variety of "meaning" that the texts convey to them at their own early stage of mental sophistication.

III. Contemplation

While discussing the nature of the writer's art, O'Connor herself remarked on the paradoxical nature of literary texts to yield different types of meaning or signification—from the frivolous to the profound—to different varieties of readers: "We all write at our own level of understanding, but it is the peculiar characteristic of fiction that its literal surface can be made to yield entertainment on an obvious physical plane to one sort of reader while the selfsame surface can be made to yield meaning to the person equipped to experience it there" (*MM*, 95). O'Connor's stories appear to work in a fashion analogous to Blake's *Songs* for many readers, which may be one reason why so many of those readers (and critics) have historically found themselves stretching to discover more, or "deeper," signification than they seem to be able to apprehend at the level of surface detail, where O'Connor says so much of her primary information is situated. The anecdote of The Misfit's hat is instructive on this point, of course, but so is O'Connor's interesting observation to "A." about one of her seemingly most enigmatic stories: "Odd about 'The [*sic*] Temple of the Holy Ghost.' Nobody notices it. It is never anthologized, never commented upon. A few nuns have mentioned it with pleasure, but nobody else besides you" (*HB*, 487). Indeed, student readers too seem mostly to be puzzled by the story. They are vaguely embarrassed by the presence in it of the hermaphrodite (which O'Connor engagingly called "the It" [*HB*, 202]), or they are confused about just what Temple One and Temple Two have been taught by the nuns at Mount St. Scholastica (the blandness of contemporary Catholic schooling having erased the rich mythology that attended the old nuns's schools), or they cannot understand the seemingly perpetual rage that inflames the story's central character, the little girl who near the end interrupts her "ugly thoughts" and "mechanically" begins her prayers with an injunction to God to "Hep me not to be so mean" (*GM*, 96). Most of all, they are unable to penetrate the remarkable, sacramental calm that pervades the story's final paragraph: "Her mother let the conversation drop and the child's round face was lost in thought. She turned it toward the window and looked out over a stretch of pasture land that rose and fell with a gathering greenness until it touched the dark woods. The sun was a huge red ball like an elevated Host drenched in blood and when it sank out of sight, it left a line in the sky like a red clay road hanging over the trees" (*GM*, 96–97).

There is no way to "explicate" this conclusion to a reader who is not able, at an entirely conscious level, to slow down, to permit the language and the imagery to work within the contemplative mind, to meditate upon the relationships among the sharp physical descriptions (the Host drenched in blood and its parallel image, the red clay road, both of them hanging over the scene), the spiritually pregnant allusion to the bloody Eucharist (or Monstrance), and the palpable silence that accompanies the carefully cadenced and richly alliterative language.

This is precisely the sort of moment of contemplative silence that O'Connor undoubtedly had in mind when she admonished the unnamed Professor of English, as I indicated earlier, that "the meaning of a story should go on expanding for the reader the more he thinks about it." This is why it is the *contemplative* mind, in particular, that O'Connor's fiction requires, for in order for the story to go on expanding, the reader must pause, "listen," consider, reflect, and respond—usually repeatedly. When I teach O'Connor, I tell my students over and over to budget more time for the reading than they normally do, and then to *go slowly*! If I insist enough, some of them actually do so, and they usually report that the resulting reading experience is perceptibly different from that to which they are accustomed. I know that for myself, reading O'Connor, there is no substitute for a deliberately slow pace, because I have grown increasingly conscious over the years of how her words accumulate various levels of "meanings" from the resonances that this type of reading begins to make apparent. Yet I am conscious, too, always, of something of which I am also aware when reading Blake: that when the process of reading and cognition seems to be proceeding most productively for me, I gradually become aware that I am "getting it"—that I am developing an intuitive sense of what the author is trying to communicate, although I am largely incapable of spelling out in empirical fashion how or why I know this. I believe this is the result of the sort of "entering into" the text that both Blake and O'Connor advised their readers to attempt. I remain convinced that the reading process they require of us is inherently "sacramental" in the sense in which these two devoutly Christian writers understood it—that the text becomes the mediating agency in a transfigurative and transubstantiative transaction between an eternal creative genius (whether O'Connor's very Catholic "God" or Blake's "Human Imagination Divine," both operating through the artist) and a mortal, temporal reader. This reader is transfigured within the reading process by the operation upon her or his consciousness of the grace that transforms and transports that reader into an eternal realm of mystery, a realm that begins by degree to unfold itself within the space of that expanded human consciousness, which it both ennobles and redeems in the process.

"The Bottom Rail Is on the Top": Race and "Theological Whiteness" in Flannery O'Connor's Short Fiction

Timothy P. Caron

> If difference is made so vast that the civilizing process becomes indefinite—taking place across an unspecified infinite amount of time—history, as a process of becoming, is excluded from the literary encounter. Flannery O'Connor's "The Artificial Nigger" makes this point with reference to Mr. Head's triumphantly racist views in that brilliant story.
>
> —Toni Morrison, *Playing in the Dark: Whiteness and the Literary Imagination*

I have a confession, one that I should probably make here at the outset. I'm an Apostate, not a True Believer. Apostates and True Believers are the two categories into which I lump readers and critics of Flannery O'Connor's fiction. The True Believers are those readers who see the world in much the same way that O'Connor herself saw it: as a fallen world in which evil is a "mystery" that must be endured; moreover, programs of social justice will do little, if anything at all, to change significantly and substantially the fundamental evils with which the world is beset. On the other hand, there are the Apostates. I recognize that the theologically charged terms I have employed might suggest that the Apostates, as a group, hold no Christian beliefs, either Catholic or Protestant. As I am using the term, however, it might describe both those who, in fact, do not adhere to any belief system or denomination associated with the Christian faith, or it might describe those whose

Christianity is simply different from that of the True Believers, a Christianity, for instance, concerned just as much with the material conditions of the here and now as the heavenly rewards of the hereafter. Such an exercise in taxonomy is, of course, risky—the True Believers have contributed greatly to our appreciation and understanding of O'Connor, while the Apostates' position is easily dismissed as the view of the faithless "innerlekchuls" whom O'Connor loved to deride. One of the greatest difficulties I found in writing this essay was in trying to negotiate a clear middle ground that acknowledges the contributions of the True Believers while pointing out a blind spot in some of their arguments. In this essay, I would like to attempt a few things: first, I will sketch more fully a profile of these groups of O'Connor's readers, paying particular attention to the issue of race and how it is treated in representative criticism of each camp. Next, I will examine three of O'Connor's short stories, "Everything That Rises Must Converge," "Revelation," and especially "The Artificial Nigger," offering counter readings of these stories from an Apostate's perspective. Finally, I would like to take up Toni Morrison's call made in *Playing in the Dark* to examine the racialized underlying principles of much of American literature and its criticism. Applying Morrison's ideas on "literary whiteness" to O'Connor's fiction compels us to recognize that O'Connor so thoroughly replicates the dominant religiosity of the white South of the 1950s and 1960s as to construct a category I call, borrowing from Morrison, "theological whiteness."

Specifically, what is revealed in a counter reading of these stories, a reading that follows D. H. Lawrence's infamous dictum to "trust the tale, not the teller," is the white South's rising anxiety over race and changing social codes, such as segregation, and a mounting fear of "blackness." In their reading of O'Connor, the True Believers either avoid the topic of race altogether, focusing instead on the "conversions" of the central white characters, or consider African Americans only as a sort of spiritual catalyst for Southern whites who need help in understanding God's salvational plan. In my opinion, these three stories reveal a deep anxiety, perhaps even a fear, of "blackness" as manifested by the white South in the middle of the twentieth century. When racial concerns are placed at the forefront in reading these stories, they become less about salvational concerns and become more about a Southern dread of encroaching "blackness," or the erosion of social customs such as racial segregation. For me, these stories are more concerned with maintaining the various racial categories and socioeconomic levels of traditional white Southern culture. In both urban and rural settings, from Julian's mother's horror when confronted with her dark-skinned twin on a city bus, to Mrs. Ruby Turpin's unalloyed relief that she "wasn't born a nigger," to Mr. Head's journey to Atlanta to show his grandson a black person, these short stories reveal the white South's apprehension over the slow but steady dissolution of the color line.

I. "Nearly Five Decades of Repetitive Affirmations"[1] or "a Critical Language…that Conveys the Meaning More Precisely"[2]?

Common to most True Believers' critical approach is a reliance upon O'Connor's nonfiction, both her occasional addresses and her letters, to provide the key to a proper reading of her work. Often these critics are following O'Connor's explicit instructions on how her fiction is to be read. While she never told us what her stories "meant" or what her novels' "themes" were, O'Connor insisted that she was writing as a devout Christian and as a faithful member of the Catholic Church. Following the adamant statements found in *Mystery and Manners*, a critical orthodoxy has developed within O'Connor criticism, described by Michael Kreyling in his introduction to *New Essays on Wise Blood* as "nearly five decades of repetitive affirmations of the theological message believed to inform O'Connor's work, reinforced by the tacit belief that her considerable suffering crowned her word with a special truth

---

[1] Michael Kreyling, introduction, *New Essays on Wise Blood*, ed. Michael Kreyling (Cambridge: Cambridge University Press, 1995) 3.

[2] John R. May, "The Pruning Word: Flannery O'Connor's Judgment of Intellectuals," *Southern Humanities Review* 4 (1970): 335.

status."[3] Actually, it is difficult to imagine an author who has had a greater shaping influence in determining how her work will be received, read, and taught to subsequent generations of readers than Flannery O'Connor, and as a group, the True Believers follow her directions quite closely. James M. Mellard, in his "Flannery O'Connor's Others: Freud, Lacan, and the Unconscious," makes much the same point, noting that "of modern authors who have had their way with critics, Flannery O'Connor must be among the most successful." While other authors—Mellard mentions Joyce, Faulkner, and Woolf—have dictated the terms of their reception because of the difficulty of their work, "O'Connor has seemed to depend less upon the determinations effected by form than upon those achieved by instruction. O'Connor simply tells her readers—either through narrative interventions or by extra-textual exhortations—how they are to interpret her work."[4] As a result, certain phrases from her nonfiction, through their repeated appearances in critical articles and books, have begun to take on a bit of a shop-worn feel and are in danger of becoming critical commonplaces.

One doesn't have to read far in O'Connor criticism to run up against several statements taken directly from her nonfiction that form the foundation of most True Believers' approach. For example, we come to realize that her penchant for brutal conversions and hard-won spiritual insights earned through violence are what are necessary to reach "Christ-haunted," not "Christ-centered" Southern readers: "I have found that violence is strangely capable of returning my characters to reality and preparing them to accept their moment of grace" (*MM*, 122). To reach an audience that has drifted from the church, she must "shout for the hard of hearing" and "draw large startling figures for the nearly blind" (*MM*, 33–34). Furthermore, we are quickly informed that she took her Catholic faith seriously—"I am no disbeliever in spiritual purpose and no vague believer. I see from the standpoint of orthodox Christianity. This means that for me the meaning of life is centered in Redemption by Christ and what I see in the world I see in its relation to

---

[3] Kreyling, introduction, *New Essays*, 3.

[4] James M. Mellard, "Flannery O'Connor's Others: Freud, Lacan, and the Unconscious," *American Literature* 61/4 (1989): 625.

that" (*MM*, 32)—and that this focus is the source of her frequently commented upon "anagogical vision" (*MM*, 72). These insights then serve to bolster what might be the central tenet of the O'Connor critical orthodoxy: the nearly pervasive violence found within her work is to be viewed as a metaphor for the mysterious workings of Christian conversion. She writes, "I have found, in short, from reading my own writing, that my subject in fiction is the action of grace in territory held largely by the devil" (*MM*, 118). This is not to say, however, that there have not been sophisticated and nuanced readings of O'Connor's work by True Believers, such as Robert Brinkmeyer and Richard Giannone, which have greatly added to our understanding and appreciation of her work. Rather, I'm hoping to point to a growing consensus, an orthodoxy, if you will, that is slowly accreting around her work. The orthodoxy is that only a certain type of Catholic reading will generate the correct and proper reading of her work.

Among the True Believers, perhaps the most insistent voice for the orthodox religious reading of O'Connor's work is John R. May in his 1975 essay, "Flannery O'Connor: Critical Consensus and the 'Objective' Interpretation." This essay functions as a sort of self-fulfilling prophecy of the True Believers' position. Early in the essay, while theorizing about how a valid literary interpretation is crafted, May posits that "the valid interpretation is found in the community of scholars rather than in the work. 'Objectivity,' such as it is, is discovered in the shared under-standing of the community of scholars."[5] If we grant such a claim, then the Apostate O'Connor scholar has no critical ground upon which to stand, for True Believers have already fashioned the critical consensus on O'Connor's work, and no direct appeal to the stories and novels themselves to consider how the South's tortured racial history might be reflected there will be admitted into the conversation. I would maintain that such a claim works far better as a description of the state of O'Connor criticism than as a prescription for how it should proceed.

In his eagerness to make his case, May then goes on to equate the "consensus" found in O'Connor scholarship with the "consensus" he

---

[5] John R. May, "Flannery O'Connor: Critical Consensus and the 'Objective' Interpretation," *Renascence: Essays on Value in Literature* 27 (1975): 180.

sees within biblical scholarship and in the process flattens many of the distinctions between and among the various faiths found under the umbrella term "Christian." May claims that "the most obvious case of progress toward consensus and thus 'objectivity' is in the area of biblical exegesis," finding that "within the last few decades the quest for the 'objective' interpretation has often, *even in the most controversial texts of the Bible*, overcome the biases of denominational interpretation."[6] Granted, most mainline Christian denominations could agree to certain foundational principles about the divinity of Christ and his role in effecting humanity's salvation, but what then are we to make of the strong hermeneutical differences between Protestants and Catholics? Between foot-washing Baptists and high-church Anglicans? Between the Seventh Day Adventists and Pentecostals? What of the wide range of opinions on the ordaining of female clergy in some Protestant denominations? Same-sex marriages? Add to these any one of a number of questions that have sparked spirited debate both between and within these interpretive communities. I argue that the diversity of these denominations, not their similarities, is what is much needed within the narrower sphere of O'Connor criticism.

To be sure, the True Believers are not completely monolithic in their outlooks or ideas and opinions. One of the continuing debates within the ranks of O'Connor's Christian interpreters revolves around the extent to which O'Connor herself shared the views of her Protestant Southern neighbors. This is an issue O'Connor addressed, claiming that she felt a "deep underground sympathy" for the South's foot-washing, snake-handling Protestant fundamentalists, differing with them not so much in the contours of their Christian belief, but more in the nature of their church structures (*MM*, 202). However, despite these small fissures within the ranks of the True Believers, it is possible to sketch a typical True Believer's reading of an O'Connor text. As Louise Y. Gosset notes, "the hound-of-heaven paradigm describes the fundamental course of action in O'Connor's fiction," and this particular "paradigm" has been seized by the True Believers with great gusto, creating a standard

---

[6] Ibid., 183–84; my emphasis.

reading. As described by Gossett, the most accurate reading of an O'Connor text looks like this:

> The crux of the fiction is the human being's need to recognize the peril of damnation in which he lives. The religious implications of this need do not eventuate in reassurances that the characters who come to recognition will live cheerful, successsful lives. For O'Connor, the nonnegotiable, incontrovertible terms of the demand that man change constituted the drama. The human being hears, refuses to listen, persists in his own ways, attempts to escape, and is finally struck down by his conceit, which proves to have been working in the cause it has resisted.[7]

Gossett has succinctly and eloquently summed up the True Believers' findings, whether one is discussing either of O'Connor's novels, *Wise Blood* or *The Violent Bear It Away*, or virtually any one of her short stories. What Gossett has done here is give voice to May's "objective" reading of O'Connor's work.

For a test case, one need only look at a representative sampling of readings of one of the stories under consideration here, "The Artificial Nigger." In the majority of the readings of this story, considerations of race are usually deflected by theological considerations. For example, W. F. Monroe begins his essay, "Flannery O'Connor's Sacramental Icon: 'The Artificial Nigger,'" by observing how the racist slur "nigger" can make us "squirm"[8] but quickly moves to a consideration of the story's

---

[7] Louise Y. Gosset. "Flannery O'Connor." *The History of Southern Literature*, eds., Louis D. Rubin, Blyden Jackson, S. Moore Rayburn, and Lewis P. Simpson (Baton Rouge: Louisiana State University Press, 1985) 489-93.

[8] If anything, the word's power to make us "squirm" has only increased, especially on a college campus as diverse and multiethnic as the one where I teach, California State University, Long Beach. I'll always remember the conversation I had with one of our interlibrary loan staffers as to why I was ordering so many articles with the "n-word" in the title. It's easy to parody this sort of sensitivity regarding racialized language into a kind of political correctness thought police, but such a dismissal undervalues the dignity and consideration owed to my librarian colleague.

debt to Dante and O'Connor's antagonism toward "secular wisdom." For Edward Strickland, in "The Penitential Quest in 'The Artificial Nigger,'" the story is straightforward in its theological intentions and is a "sinner-come-to-salvation" story,[9] a type common enough in O'Connor's corpus. George Cheatham, in "Jesus, O'Connor's Artificial Nigger," asserts that the racist piece of lawn statuary of the story's title symbolizes nothing less than Jesus Christ.[10]

Even those True Believers who employ reading strategies other than the New Critical approaches favored by most True Believers often still come around to many of the same conclusions. Mary Neff Shaw, Doreen Fowler, and James M. Mellard give us, respectively, a Bakhtinian O'Connor, a deconstructive O'Connor, and perhaps strangest of all, a Lacanian O'Connor. In "'The Artificial Nigger': A Dialogical Narrative," Shaw sidesteps the issue of race to concentrate almost exclusively on the story's shifting narrative perspective and finds that "O'Connor ruptures the narrator's authority, alters the realistic opening paragraphs, and appends several paragraphs to the concluding section so that both the introductory and concluding passages are enclosed in a frame of *mystery*," and "only then are O'Connor's *religious* and dramatic intents concomitantly achieved."[11] Fowler, in "Deconstructing Racial Difference: O'Connor's 'The Artificial Nigger,'" almost completely avoids the theological language and assumptions common to the True Believers but nonetheless asserts in the spiritually charged language of her conclusion that the text reveals a "boundless universe" and that the story's central characters, Mr. Head and his grandson, Nelson, "glimpse the *annealing* power of the natural world to make of all one endless, seamless whole,"[12] a claim that echoes the True Believers' assertion of

---

[9] Edward Strickland, "The Penitential Quest in 'The Artificial Nigger,'" *Studies in Short Fiction* 25/4 (Fall 1988): 453.

[10] George Cheatham, "Jesus, O'Connor's Artificial Nigger," *Studies in Short Fiction* 22/4 (Fall 1985): 478.

[11] Mary Neff Shaw, "'The Artificial Nigger': A Dialogical Narrative," in *Flannery O'Connor: New Perspectives*, ed. Sura P. Rath and Mary Neff Shaw (Athens: University of Georgia Press, 1996) 150; my emphasis.

[12] Doreen Fowler, "Deconstructing Racial Difference: O'Connor's 'The Artificial Nigger,'" *The Flannery O'Connor Bulletin* 24 (1995–1996): 29; my emphasis.

O'Connor's "anagogical vision." Mellard, in what must surely be some of the densest prose ever devoted to Flannery O'Connor, concludes that a Lacanian analysis "can be fruitfully extended to just about every one of O'Connor's stories and to both of the novels as well"[13] and that such an approach will reveal, even in our postmodern world that often seems contemptuous of theology, "a vindication of sorts for O'Connor" and her avowedly Christian concerns, albeit "within a broadly defined Western cultural tradition."[14] Despite their eclectic mix of more recent theoretical paradigms, however, it is possible that these critics, and others like them, might be more enthralled by the prevailing received wisdom of O'Connor criticism than is revealed at first glance.

As I have sought to demonstrate elsewhere,[15] O'Connor's theology led her to advocate a "go-slow" policy on issues such as racial integration. She believed that the South's pre-Civil Rights "manners" were sufficient to shepherd the region through the tumultuous 1950s and 1960s and felt that racial justice would be meted out in heaven if not in her lifetime in Georgia. Some True Believers writing about "The Artificial Nigger," by so closely aligning themselves with O'Connor's worldview of half a century ago, run the risk of sounding a bit outdated or insensitive in their racial attitudes. For instance, Cheatham accounts for some of what he believes to be uncharitable readings of the story to "oversensitivity to the story's racial overtones."[16] Given the history of the American South, is it possible to be *over*sensitive to race? Like O'Connor, these True Believers value a reader's soul so highly that they sometimes look past the material conditions in which these souls are currently living. While he does not treat "The Artificial Nigger" in his essay, perhaps the most egregious example of this type of reading that uses religion to deflect racial concerns in O'Connor's work is Henry M.

---

[13] Mellard, "Flannery O'Connor's Others," 643.

[14] Ibid., 632.

[15] In *Struggles Over the Word: Race and Religion in O'Connor, Faulkner, Hurston, and Wright* (Macon: Mercer University Press, 2000), I maintain that, despite her fierce Catholic loyalties, O'Connor's theology led her to place salvational concerns over social justice, and thus she was, in one important sense, closely aligned with her Southern Protestant neighbors.

[16] Cheatham, "Jesus, O'Connor's Artificial Nigger," 475.

W. Russell's "Racial Integration in a Disintegrating Society: O'Connor and European Catholic Thought." In this essay, Russell uses Continental Catholic theologians such as Jacques Maritain and Gabriel Marcel to claim that religion will provide a "richer context" than the regional and social customs of the American South for understanding O'Connor's views on race. In a strange twist, however, Russell so completely embodies the views of the author he is studying that it is sometimes hard to tell who is talking, critic or author, Russell or O'Connor, when he makes pronouncements like, "If the manners of a country or a culture are lived on the level of sensibility (as O'Connor suggests), then those manners cannot be changed by swift, legal fiat without generating a welter of lies at the deepest core of life—a cure worse than the disease."[17] Such claims sound positively nostalgic for the good old days of social segregation, as if registering voters in Mississippi and throughout the South was somehow worse than a continued marginalized, legally segregated second-class citizenship, if not an outright betrayal of some theological principle. While few True Believers are as shrill or as reactionary as Russell, what is common among them is an insistence that the religious reading, specifically the religious reading informed by a culturally and socially conservative Catholicism, will reveal the fiction's true meaning, or as John R. May concisely states in "The Pruning Word: Flannery O'Connor's Judgment of Intellectuals," that it is not necessarily required that a reader "understand Flannery O'Connor's Christianity in order to appreciate fully the characters she has created. However, for those who are familiar with this perspective, a critical language can be employed that conveys the meaning more precisely, and this is the eschatological language of apocalypse or revelation."[18] Claiming this ground is a masterstroke for the True Believers because any other reading subsequently becomes a misreading, any other interpretation a misinterpretation.

---

[17] Henry M. W. Russell, "Racial Integration in a Disintegrating Society: O'Connor and European Catholic Thought," *The Flannery O'Connor Bulletin* 24 (1995–1996): 34.

[18] May, "The Pruning Word," 335.

Considerations of race are unavoidable in discussing O'Connor's work, and the True Believers were long sensitive to charges that O'Connor was less than enlightened on issues of race. To put it simply, they felt that charges of racism "threaten to undermine our esteem for the most important Southern writer since Faulkner."[19] Melvin Williams, in "Black and White: A Study in Flannery O'Connor's Characters," and Claire Kahane, in "The Artificial Niggers," were among the first to criticize O'Connor's writing from the perspective of race. A generation after the original publication of these essays, the True Believers are still scrambling to answer the arguments posed by Williams and Kahane. *The Habit of Being*, the collection of O'Connor's letters published in 1979, then proved to be something of a mixed blessing to the True Believers, for it provides plenty of support for their foundational premise that the religious reading is the right reading, but it also pointedly reveals that O'Connor passed along racist jokes in her letters and often used the slur term "nigger" when writing about African Americans. Of those among the O'Connor faithful who seek to account for the many uncharitable statements in O'Connor's letters, Ralph C. Wood's "Where Is the Voice Coming From? Flannery O'Connor on Race" is the most balanced of the True Believers' responses to the claims initially leveled by Williams and Kahane. Wood grants that, indeed, O'Connor "often sounds like an unabashed racist in her privately expressed opinions"[20]; however, he brackets the fiction from the nonfiction, arguing that the fiction embodies her "convictions," that is her unshakeable, bedrock beliefs, while the letters show her "opinions," those messy, day-to-day attitudes and ideas of an imperfect person. Implicit in this treatment by Wood is an unequal valuation of the two forms of writing, with the fiction far outweighing the letters. Rather than using the letters to illuminate the fiction, and thereby perhaps knocking O'Connor off of her pedestal, it is vital to Wood's argument that the two types of writing are kept separate, so he claims that she was able to "keep her instinctive dislike for Negroes

---

[19] Ralph C. Wood, "Where Is the Voice Coming From?: Flannery O'Connor on Race," *The Flannery O'Connor Bulletin* 22 (1993–1994): 90.
[20] Ibid., 92.

from corrupting her work."[21] This bifurcation should sound familiar to anyone familiar with the white Protestant South's dictum to "hate the sin but love the sinner." Wood has just performed a similar rhetorical move: in one deft gesture, he is able to sever O'Connor's holy and sacramental fiction cleanly from its impure source, thereby allowing him to venerate the fiction for its spiritual importance while cordoning off the author's personal shortcomings as revealed in the letters. To be fair, at no point does Wood excuse or condone O'Connor's objectionable racial attitudes. Wood concedes, "O'Connor's gradualist solution for remedying racial injustice, if it had won the day, would surely have slowed our progress toward racial equality during the last thirty years. Far more stringent measures were required than she was willing to sanction."[22] Throughout the entire essay, Wood maintains that the sentiments expressed in the letters do not "infect" (my metaphor, not Wood's) the fiction, but he does seem to understand the limits of his own argument. Here, for example, is one of the most stinging criticisms made by either True Believers or Apostates of O'Connor's racial views:

> It is true that [Christians] are commanded to love rather than to like our neighbors, but it is also surpassingly difficult to love those, black or white, whom we do not like. Nor is it legitimate to deny the evils that lie at our own feet while training our eyes on eternity. And so it must be said, not in accusation but in contrition, that neither the suffering of Southern blacks nor the sins of Southern whites sufficiently stung Flannery O'Connor's Christian conscience. She never criticized, in open and angry and unequivocal terms, the racial abominations committed in her own native territory.[23]

Eventually, Wood seems unable to reconcile the huge contradiction within such an argument: how is that while O'Connor might not have liked African Americans, she is allegedly able to write about them in a

---

[21] Ibid., 109.
[22] Ibid., 103.
[23] Ibid., 97.

manner that is free of racial bias? The question is never fully addressed but is instead deflected by an appeal to the Christian encomium, oft times more honored in the breach than in the keeping by white Southern believers, of a common humanity found in all of us being God's children, or as Wood puts it, "the most profound commonalit[y] shared by blacks and whites, chiefly our common dependence on the grace and judgment of God."[24] If one grants the starting premise of the True Believers, that O'Connor's salvational concerns should be at the center of our readings of the fiction, then the occasional impolite term or the unenlightened joke can be gotten past because the concern for her readers' immortal souls far outweighs the intermittent racial *faux pas*. The True Believers are anxious that O'Connor's readers come to share her opinion that the "long-run efficacy of love"[25] is to be more highly cherished than a federally mandated end to the humiliations of living a second-class citizenship in the Jim Crow South.

II. "The Signifiers through which
White Southern Identity Was Constructed"[26]

What happens, though, if we begin with different foundational assumptions, if our starting premises are different from those of the True Believers? Recently, Jon Lance Bacon and Katherine Hemple Prown have authored two of the most groundbreaking book-length Apostate investigations of O'Connor's fiction. Bacon, in his *Flannery O'Connor and Cold War Culture*, demonstrates that O'Connor was not only looking toward the great beyond but also had her gaze leveled upon her contemporaneous American Cold War consumer culture, while Prown's feminist investigation, *Revising Flannery O'Connor: Southern*

---

[24] Ibid., 90.

[25] The phrase comes from a review by Wood. See Ralph C. Wood, "The Long-run Efficacy of Love: Four Books on Flannery O'Connor," *The Flannery O'Connor Bulletin* 18 (1989): 99–105.

[26] Katherine Hemple Prown, *Revising Flannery O'Connor: Southern Literary Culture and the Problem of Female Authorship* (Charlottesville: University of Virginia Press, 2001) 4.

Literary Culture and the Problem of Female Authorship, reveals the degree to which O'Connor's finished manuscripts thoroughly replicate the dominant cultural values of the patriarchal South in an effort to win approval for her writing. While race is not central to Bacon's or Prown's works, both make provocative observations on the subject that, if explored more fully, could greatly help to overthrow the hegemony of the True Believers. Bacon, while discussing the role of the farm as a setting for O'Connor's fiction, observes that her rural landscapes allow O'Connor an imaginative space that serves as a counterpoint to the nation's values. For Bacon, settings like the McIntyre farm in "The Displaced Person" represent a distinctively Southern space, a space in which the region's "racial hierarchy" must be maintained in order to retain its "regional distinctiveness."[27] In this respect, Prown's comments on race in the short stories likewise draw attention to the ways in which O'Connor draws upon the South's legacy of racial exclusion. Prown's feminist methodology lends itself to speculations on the intersection of race and gender in the construction of O'Connor's critical reception. Her findings, when speaking specifically of "The Artificial Nigger," differ drastically from the received wisdom of the True Believers as she concludes, much like Melvin Williams, that "O'Connor viewed blacks primarily as the signifiers through which white southern identity was constructed and embraced the Agrarians' nostalgic view of the authentic southern past."[28]

The collision between this "nostalgic view of the...southern past" and the reality of the South's rapidly changing social codes is rendered in the typically violent terms common to O'Connor's fiction in her short story "Everything That Rises Must Converge." When race is placed at the center of this story, which is not exactly a forced reading considering that the story's principal action involves a ride on a recently integrated bus, "Everything That Rises Must Converge" becomes quite a different story than the one we have previously encountered in most True Believers' readings, orthodox readings that maintain that "the racial

---

[27] Jon Lance Bacon, *Flannery O'Connor and Cold War Culture* (Cambridge: Cambridge University Press, 1993) 87–88.

[28] Prown, *Revising Flannery O'Connor*, 4.

issue," though prominent, "should not be construed as the story's shaping principle."[29] Race, in fact, is central to the story. Julian is on the bus with his mother because she will not ride alone after dark now that they have been integrated. Then, throughout the entirety of the bus journey itself, white characters discuss the galling move of African Americans from the back of the bus and jockey for seats so that they will not have to sit next to blacks. Finally, in the story's conclusion, Julian's mother's condescending racism provokes the justifiable anger of her black narrative twin. "Everything That Rises Must Converge" is a type of story common to O'Connor's oeuvre: intellectuals are revealed to be not quite as smart as they think they are, and the more sympathetic character proves to be Julian's mother, principally because, despite her flaws, her "manners" provide her with a genteel means of dealing with life's difficulties. On the contrary, I would maintain that her gentility, her "manners," are her greatest vice, not her redeeming virtues that are to be passed on to Julian as he makes his way through "the world of guilt and sorrow" (CS, 404). Julian's mother dies secure in the knowledge that she "knows" who she is, and like the grandmother from "A Good Man Is Hard to Find," this knowledge cannot be feigned because she is facing the prospect of her own mortality. As Julian's mother faces death, she calls out for Caroline, "the old darky who was [her] nurse" (CS, 409), and retreats back into a "moonlight and magnolias" version of the South, characterized by faithful black servants waiting on benevolent whites in large family manors. After Julian's mother has her stroke, Julian tells her that the South's changed social dynamics, so vividly played out on the bus and on the street corner, will not prove to be fatal to her: "'From now on you've got to live in a new world and face a few realities for a change. Buck up,' he said, 'it won't kill you'" (CS, 419). Of course, Julian is wrong; his mother does die when faced with the incontrovertible fact of the South's shifting racial relations.

In the logic of O'Connor's stories, however, death is often a sweet release, a return to God or the divine, as in "The River," and is

---

[29] Robert D. Denham. "The World of Guilt and Sorrow: Flannery O'Connor's 'Everything That Rises Must Converge.'" *The Flannery O'Connor Bulletin* 4 (1975): 42-51.

frequently the more palatable option when faced with living in a fallen world. Julian's mother's death then has the added benefit of not only allowing her to shake off this mortal coil, but it is also literally a return to her ancestral home, the mansion owned by her ancestors, the tellingly named Godhigh family. As is the case in so many of O'Connor's stories, her characters are usually better off dead, and Julian's mother is returned to a heaven of clear-cut racial categories, leaving Julian to make his way through a world made strange by integration, where, as Julian's mother puts it, "the bottom rail is on the top" (*CS*, 407). In an interesting detail that is perhaps more telling than O'Connor might have intended, the old Godhigh family mansion has fallen into disrepair, and the once proud family has been displaced: "Negroes were living in it" (*CS*, 408). Indeed, the bottom rail *is* on top.

As Laurel Nesbitt reminds us in her essay, "Reading Place in and Around Flannery O'Connor's Texts," we should pay particular attention to the physical spaces, the settings, of O'Connor's work: "O'Connor not only comments on place, but...she stands on and defends particular ground herself."[30] The ground upon which O'Connor stands and defends is, of course, the South, but with Nesbitt's reminder before us, we see that it is more precisely the white South of the 1950s and 1960s, a region that was anxious over its crumbling social codes of racial exclusion. This anxiety is reflected both in the urban and rural landscapes of O'Connor's fiction; in fact, "Revelation," a story often lauded by the True Believers because of its ending in which Ruby Turpin glimpses an integrated heaven, with its farm setting is just as much concerned with the unsettling prospect of integration as "Everything That Rises Must Converge." Like Julian's mother, Ruby is dismayed over the possibility that the "bottom rail" might be placed "on top" (*CS*, 507). As is the case with many of O'Connor's characters, Ruby's fatal flaw, the sin for which she must be brought low, is that she suffers from an overabundance of pride. Ruby's elaborate hierarchies of race and class are intended by O'Connor to be funny, and they would be humorous if they were not such a picture-perfect representation of the

---

[30] Laurel Nesbitt, "Reading Place in and around Flannery O'Connor's Texts," *Post Identity* 1/1 (1997): 145.

white South's fear of change. The thing to be most feared by the region, according to its own internal logic, is racially tainted members of the community who carry no outward marker of their inner conditions, what Ruby's husband, Claud, calls the "white-faced niggers" (*CS*, 496). This racial apprehension finds its corollary in the theological readings often supplied for "Revelation"; Ruby worries over her standing before God, longing for some outward sign of the redeemed state of her immortal soul. O'Connor provides this confirmation in the story's final two paragraphs when Ruby sees the celestial staircase ascending to heaven.[31] "Revelation" provides one of the clearest statements of O'Connor's racial politics—indeed, Ruby Turpin will have to share her heaven with those whom she previously considered to be unworthy of inclusion, but what are the terms of that inclusion? Those most like Ruby in her smug self-reckoning—those solid citizens who, "like herself and Claud, had always had a little of everything and the God-given wit to use it right. …marching behind the others with great dignity, accountable as they had always been for good order and common sense and respectable behavior"—are bringing up the rear of this divine procession, and their "virtues," that is, their self-satisfaction, are "burned away" (*CS*, 508).

From an Apostate perspective, however, the conclusion to "Revelation" does not hold hope for racial reconciliation to the extent claimed by the True Believers. Ruby's vision, a vision that both O'Connor and the True Believers who follow her steadfastly desire for the reader to adopt, directs our attention toward infinity, "into the starry field" (*CS*, 509), to a time and place far removed even from the realm of human comprehension. The story's "turn or burn" theology is apparent: fix your gaze upon redemption while it is still available, and racism is a "mystery" to be remedied in the next world. Furthermore, Ruby's vision

---

[31] *HB*, 549. In a letter to her friend, "A.," now known to be Elizabeth Hester (1922–1998), O'Connor reveals that Ruby's vision was not originally in the story but was added as she revised the story: "I did not finish a draft of this ["Revelation"] before I got sick but I am more or less anesthetized to it and have no idea if it works or not, particularly the last paragraph. I started to let it end where the hogs pant with a secret life, but I thought something else was needed." For O'Connor, what was clearly needed was a less theologically ambiguous ending, one in which the action of grace was made apparent in the life of her central character.

Is still freighted with the offensively racist language of the white South. she sees "a vast horde of souls...rumbling toward heaven. There were whole companies of white-trash, clean for the first time in their lives, and bands of black niggers in white robes, and battalions of freaks and lunatics shouting and clapping and leaping like frogs" (CS, 508). In an interesting turn of phrase, O'Connor describes African Americans in this procession as "*black* niggers in *white* robes" (my emphasis), underscoring their racial difference from those who are truly and thoroughly white, not just cloaked in the whiteness of their robes. And even though O'Connor's murky syntax makes it unclear as to whether or not the "white-trash" and the "black niggers" or just the "freaks and lunatics" are indecorously ascending the stairs, an Apostate reading of the passage suggests that not even the occasion of entering into heaven can cause these black characters to desist from their racially inflected antics and capers. In other words, this is not a procession of equals ascending toward heaven.

Of course, the True Believers are quick to point out that what we are seeing in this passage is seen through the eyes of Ruby Turpin, a woman who, despite the "action of grace" in her life, is still comfortable in assigning these class and race markers to her fellow Southerners. In Ruby's mouth, the word "nigger" and its uses, in fact, would be one of the telltale indications of her own refinement and good breeding. For instance, she would never use the term in racially mixed company, nor would she use it to describe every single member of the black race, only those who fit within the racially coded outlines of the term: either a man or a woman who lives in an abject state of reduced economic circumstances. In Ruby Turpin's world, a "nigger" then is someone in whom she cannot recognize herself. Interestingly enough, when she is playing the parlor game of ranking the South's population within its clearly demarcated lines of race and class, she imagines what she would say to Jesus if she had to choose between being black or "white-trash." She would choose to be a "neat clean respectable Negro woman, herself but black" (CS, 491).

Contemplating O'Connor's use of the term "nigger" has greatly occupied the True Believers, and there is no escaping the word—and its

considerable power—when discussing the story "The Artificial Nigger."
Joyce Carol Oates, in a brief introductory essay that precedes the story
in its recent reprint in the *Kenyon Review*, seeks to gloss over O'Connor's
use of the term, saying that the offensive word

> would appear to have been a usage common to her, as to
> her fellow Caucasian Georgians. Forty years after the
> composition of "The Artificial Nigger," the very word "nigger"
> has become so highly charged with political significance that any
> work of art containing it, especially by a white Southerner, is
> unwittingly abrasive, even provocative. O'Connor could not
> have foreseen how the word "nigger" would have come to seem,
> in some quarters of America, an actual obscenity of the nature of
> those sexual obscenities she would not have wished to include in
> her fiction.[32]

Despite her clear eagerness to excuse O'Connor for her complicity
in the South's racism, Oates points out an inconsistency in O'Connor's
and the True Believers' logic. They are so firmly oriented along a
vertical theological axis that languishes over the soul's status before a
morally requiring God that they fail to see the network of horizontal
relationships between and among Southern blacks and whites. In "A
Good Man Is Hard to Find," for instance, the grandmother recognizes
The Misfit, and Bailey lets fly with an expletive that makes even a cold-
blooded killer blush, presumably the word "fuck," but O'Connor's
sensibilities, as Oates points out, are too refined actually to write out the
word on the page. Katherine Hemple Prown, in *Revising Flannery
O'Connor*, makes the provocative assertion that O'Connor appropriated
many of the Fugitive/Agrarian views on race and gender and that she
distanced herself from many, if not most, feminine concerns in an
attempt to win critical approval for her writing. Based on her
unwillingness or inability to pepper her fiction with "four-letter words,"
however, O'Connor might have been more of a Southern "lady" who

---

[32] Joyce Carol Oates, "The Action of Mercy," *The Kenyon Review* 20/1 (1998):
160.

was influenced by the region's ideas regarding "decorous" behavior for women than Prown supposes. In order to make a theological point, however, she is not squeamish at all in coolly describing a talkative old lady who takes three slugs in the chest.

In a movement of similar discursive violence, O'Connor did not flinch in titling her story "The Artificial Nigger," refusing to give the story a new title, even though John Crowe Ransom, just prior to the story's publication in the spring 1955 issue of the *Kenyon Review*, asked her to change it. Subtler racialized language, primarily comprised of racially coded terms and stereotypes, runs throughout the story, revealing in O'Connor's treatment of her black characters a regional insistence upon monitoring "blackness" and policing the color line. It is crucial to remember that the entire story revolves around Mr. Head taking his grandson, Nelson, to Atlanta because the boy has never seen a "nigger"—the foundational premise of the story is predicated on the principle of racial categorization and exclusion. As Mr. Head tells Nelson, this journey into Atlanta's "heart of darkness," so to speak, is necessary because "There hasn't been a nigger in this county since we run that one out twelve years ago and that was before you were born" (*CS*, 252). Once on the train, however, they quickly encounter many black characters, including a dining car waiter and a man traveling with two young women who are presumably his daughters. The waiter stops the Heads, in their ignorance, from simply barging into the train's kitchen and serves as nothing more than a comic stock character, a two-dimensional racial stereotype: he is the self-important black figure who orders, bosses, and cajoles whites because of his occupation.

The successful looking black traveler and his daughters, however, are a different story. Their function, rather than comic relief, is to demonstrate the completely constructed nature of the South's conception of race. Nelson, in fact, does not even recognize the man's "blackness" because he isn't literally black but is "coffee-colored" instead (*CS*, 254). Nelson's confusion reveals that there is nothing "natural" or intrinsic about the category "nigger" but that it is socially constructed. In O'Connor's description of him, the business traveler is portrayed as wealthy, elegant, even stately:

> A huge coffee-colored man was coming slowly forward. He had on a light suit and a yellow satin tie with a ruby pin in it. One of his hands rested on his stomach which rode majestically under his buttoned coat, and in the other he held the head of a black walking stick that he picked up and set down with a deliberate outward motion each time he took a step. He was proceeding very slowly, his large brown eyes gazing over the heads of the passengers. He had a small white mustache and white crinkly hair. Behind him there were two young women, both coffee-colored, one in a yellow dress and one in green. Their progress was kept at the rate of his and they chatted in low throaty voices as they followed him. (*CS*, 254–55)

Despite the outward signs of his material success, which must be infuriating to Mr. Head, in the white South's eyes, he will always be a "nigger." In fact, the ability to label the black businessman a "nigger" is precisely one of the things that gives a poor "cracker" like Mr. Head a sense of dignity and self-worth: no matter how bad things are for him, his white skin guarantees him greater mobility and opportunity in the Jim Crow South. Just as African Americans have been run out of the Heads' county back home, so must this man be banished from the train car reserved for whites. He is again segregated from the rest of the white passengers while in the dining car. The train is the logical setting for Nelson's first lessons in racial exclusion, considering its importance in the creation and development of Jim Crow legislation. As a symbolic representation of greater freedom and movement, trains were one of the primary battlegrounds as the white South policed the color line.

Erasing the color line on trains could lead to further erosion of the South's segregated society; therefore, the story's lessons regarding race must continue to be reinforced even after the young man and his grandfather get off the train. As described in the terms of the story, a simple walk through the segregated streets of Atlanta for these two is actually an entry into a realm of darkness that threatens to consume them. In a standard True Believer reading of "The Artificial Nigger,"

O'Connor has her two country bumpkins wander on a Dantean journey through the black residential section of Atlanta, moving inexorably toward their climactic encounter with grace. If one reads the story, however, from an Apostate's perspective, a considerable distance emerges between the story and its conclusion. In other words, once we become attuned to racial considerations in the story, its theologically charged ending seems increasingly out of place and heavy-handed. Following his wanderings through black Atlanta, in which he renounces his grandson after a strange encounter with a woman (I will have more to say about this scene shortly), and his safe return to the county that has literally "exorcised" its blackness, Mr. Head is ready to have the standard O'Connor moment of grace:

> Mr. Head stood very still and felt the action of mercy touch him again but this time he knew that there were no words in the world that could name it. ...He stood appalled, judging himself with the thoroughness of God, while the action of mercy covered his pride like a flame and consumed it. ...He realized that he was forgiven for sins from the beginning of time, when he had conceived in his own heart the sin of Adam, until the present, when he had denied poor Nelson. He saw that no sin was too monstrous for him to claim as his own, and since God loved in proportion as He forgave, he felt ready at that instant to enter Paradise. (CS, 269–70)

A reader unaccustomed to O'Connor's "hound-of-heaven" paradigm would surely be startled by such a conclusion, an ending whose efficacy at conveying her theological point the author herself questioned. In a letter to Ben Griffith, she stated, "I wrote ["The Artificial Nigger"] a good many times, having a lot of trouble with the end." In order to "gain some altitude and get a larger view," O'Connor followed the suggestions of Caroline Gordon,[33] admitting that "the end of 'The

---

[33] See Thomas F. Haddux's excellent essay, "Contextualizing Flannery O'Connor: Allen Tate, Caroline Gordon, and the Catholic Turn in Southern

Artificial Nigger' was a very definite attempt to do just that and in those last two paragraphs I have practically gone from the Garden of Eden to the Gates of Paradise." She concludes her discussion of this story with her firm proclamation "to keep trying [this approach] with other things" (*HB*, 78). What exactly has propelled Mr. Head from the "Garden of Eden to the Gates of Paradise," a journey whose trajectory, in Christian terms, covers the entire span of time? A lawn jockey, for O'Connor writes elsewhere in this same letter, "What I had in mind to suggest with the artificial nigger was the redemptive quality of the Negro's suffering for us all." Even if one grants that such a lowly object can bear up under the theological weight that O'Connor is eager to invest in it, how can one remove this racist curio from its cultural context? It is a statue whose cultural work is to convey the message of white superiority, but for O'Connor and the True Believers, it is miraculously transformed into an icon of equal weight and value as the burning bush of the Old Testament.

Curiously, the figuration of blackness that receives the most attention in this letter is not the story's spiritual catalyst but a black woman the Heads encounter in the city. As Nesbitt argues, O'Connor relies upon exaggerated racial stereotyping in her presentation of this character, blending maternal depictions with a kind of earthy sensuality.[34] The woman who gives Nelson directions is described as wearing a "pink dress that showed her exact shape" (*CS*, 261). This woman captivates Nelson in explicitly sexual terms: he "drink[s] in every detail of her," noticing her "tremendous bosom." During their brief encounter, Nelson "wanted her to reach down and pick him up and draw him against her and then he wanted to feel her breath on his face. He wanted to look down and down into her eyes while she held him tighter and tighter. He felt as if he were reeling down through a pitchblack tunnel" (*CS*, 262). This encounter, much more than the Heads' standing slack-jawed before the racist statuary, I would argue, is the true heart of the story. Here is the culmination of young Nelson's journey, the

---

Literature," *Southern Quarterly* 38/1 (Fall 1999): 173–90, for an insightful exploration of the relationship between O'Connor and Gordon.

[34] Nesbitt, "Reading Place in and around Flannery O'Connor's Texts," 166.

moment at which he begins to understand how the white South constructs its contradictory notions of blackness. Blackness is both maternal—comforting and nurturing—*and* sexual—alluring and threatening. In the same letter to Ben Griffith, O'Connor discusses this character: "You may be right that Nelson's reaction to the colored woman is too pronounced, but I meant for her in an almost physical way to suggest the mystery of existence to him—he not only has never seen a nigger but he didn't know any women and I felt that such a black mountain of maternity would give him the required shock to start those black forms moving up from his unconscious" (*HB*, 78). O'Connor's letter reveals precisely what is so disturbing to a boy like Nelson, someone who has not yet learned the intricate mechanisms that separate whites and blacks in the American South: he has within himself those "black forms" that must be exorcised.

III. "When Criticism Remains Too Polite or Too Fearful to Notice a Disrupting Darkness before Its Eyes"[35]

In the introduction to *Playing in the Dark: Whiteness and the Literary Imagination*, Toni Morrison writes of the genesis of her investigation into the Africanist presence in American literature. She describes the experience of reading Marie Cardinal's *The Words to Say It*, an autobiographical exploration of the author's mental illness and recovery through language. In particular, Morrison is drawn to Cardinal's response to a Louis Armstrong performance. While listening to Armstrong's music, Cardinal experiences her first anxiety attack: "My heart began to accelerate, becoming more important than the music, shaking the bars of my rib cage, compressing my lungs so the air could no longer enter them. Gripped by panic at the idea of dying there in the middle of spasms, stomping feet, and the crowd howling, I ran into the streets like someone possessed." Cardinal's vivid description provokes

---

[35] Toni Morrison, *Playing in the Dark: Whiteness and the Literary Imagination*, (New York: Vintage, 1993) 91.

Morrison to wonder, "What on earth was Louie playing that night?"[36] After quickly adopting a more serious tone, Morrison uses this moment from Cardinal's text to establish the parameters of her investigation for *Playing in the Dark*, namely "the way black people ignite critical moments of discovery or change or emphasis in literature not written by them."[37] While the majority of *Playing in the Dark* is devoted to examining works by Willa Cather, Edgar Allan Poe, and Ernest Hemingway, Morrison's observations prove to be just as provocative when considering the extraordinary lengths to which O'Connor went textually and imaginatively in order to segregate her fiction along racial lines.

Morrison clearly hopes that her ideas will be applied to O'Connor's fiction as she mentions O'Connor on two different occasions in *Playing in the Dark*: once when she is generally mentioning the trend common among the True Believers of reading the religious dimension in her stories to the exclusion of racial considerations,[38] and once when she specifically mentions "The Artificial Nigger" while discussing the various "common linguistic strategies employed in fiction to engage the serious consequences of blacks."[39] This second mention is the most suggestive because it serves as an example of one of the most common responses to "blackness" in American literature, what Morrison calls the practice of employing a "dehistoricizing allegory" to read our nation's fiction.[40] The phrase "dehistoricizing allegory" perfectly encapsulates the main True Believer strategy, a strategy vindicated by repeated appeals to O'Connor's nonfiction. When O'Connor tells us that she meant for a piece of racist lawn statuary to suggest "the redemptive quality of the Negro's suffering for us all" (*HB*, 78), then we are free to displace the messy topic of race from our readings and firmly fix our gaze upon heaven, for it is there that race will cease to matter. This "allegory" of inclusion is never truly manifested in the fiction, however, and is found

---

[36] Ibid., vii.
[37] Ibid., viii.
[38] Ibid., 14.
[39] Ibid., 67.
[40] Ibid., 68.

only in the subsequent readings and interpretations of the fiction. Instead, what we see in O'Connor's stories are African Americans whose function is to point the way to heaven for her white characters. Readers of O'Connor's fiction, directed by the author's pronouncements, can easily dismiss racial considerations because O'Connor's black characters are rendered only through what Morrison calls "metonymic displacement." In other words, they are only roughly drawn figures of blackness in which "color coding and other physical traits become metonyms that displace rather than signify the Africanist character."[41] This "color coding" is evidenced throughout O'Connor's fiction but is perhaps nowhere more remarkable than in her description of the black woman in "The Artificial Nigger." In a few broad strokes, O'Connor renders a stereotype of black femininity that is both maternal and sexual. Indeed, the racial stereotypes O'Connor leaned upon in her fictional depiction of African Americans helps to promote the religious readings favored by the True Believers, for these depictions confirm what the white South supposedly "knows" about African Americans: that they are nurturing and sexual, cunning and childlike, inscrutable and obvious. In this sense, O'Connor's fiction then promotes a sort of "theological whiteness," not merely "literary whiteness," as so much of her work and its attendant criticism is predicated upon exclusionary principles: her black characters are little more than spiritual Step-n-fetchits, ushering her white characters toward their salvational moment, while the readers of her work loudly proclaim the inclusive spirit that supposedly informs her fiction.

In writing of Hemingway, Morrison states that much of her interest in his work lies in considering "how much apart his work is from African Americans. That is, he has no need, desire, or awareness of them either as readers of his work or as people existing anywhere other than in his imaginative (and imaginatively lived) world."[42] Much the same could be said of O'Connor. She lived in a small Southern town for most of her professional life, during some of the most turbulent times of the preceding century, when considerations of her region's troubled

---

[41] Ibid.
[42] Ibid., 69.

social/racial structure must have been one of the most common topics of everyday conversation. In her fiction, however, there is a willful blindness toward race in favor of a domineering theology. When black characters do appear, as they inevitably must if she is going to write about the modern South, they are relegated to a kind of second-class citizenship not unlike the treatment that they fought so heroically to overturn. Morrison concludes *Playing in the Dark* with an admonition that those of us who read, write about, and teach Flannery O'Connor should take to heart: "All of us, readers and writers, are bereft when criticism remains too polite or too fearful to notice a disrupting darkness before its eyes."[43] O'Connor criticism will remain impoverished and far too narrow in its orthodoxy until we place the issue of race at the center of our discussions.

---

[43] Ibid., 91.

III.

The Word:
Denominational Doctrine in
O'Connor's Fiction

Christian but Not Catholic: Baptism in Flannery O'Connor's "The River"

Joanne Halleran McMullen

In a 1956 letter to "A.," Flannery O'Connor mentions she was soon to "entertain a man who wants to make a movie out of 'The River'" because he envisioned her 1952 story as "a kind of documentary" (*HB*, 171). Her question to "A."—"How to document the sacrament of Baptism???????"—suggests her belief that this story does indeed embody the essence of this sacrament. Her concern in posing this question seems to revolve around her doubt that film would be the proper medium. But did O'Connor actually document the Catholic sacrament of Baptism in "The River"? I believe she did not.

Many of O'Connor's readers may not be cognizant of the restrictions placed upon members of the Catholic Church in the pre-Vatican II era. Further, readers are often confronted with literary criticism that portrays O'Connor's work as the embodiment of Catholicism. She reinforced that impression repeatedly to friends and literary correspondents; one only need read her letters published in *The Habit of Being*. But does O'Connor succeed in presenting a credible Catholic view, as opposed to a Christian one, in her fiction? Investigating whether O'Connor's work embraces Catholic views, beliefs, values, and traditions, or Protestant ones is important because the divergence of these two Christian branches was critical to O'Connor as she indicated in her personal correspondences. It is also important because a religious "uncovering" will explain why so many readers do not recognize O'Connor's stated intent until schooled by her "faithful" critics. It is important because mainstream O'Connor critics unrelentingly insist that the religious context of O'Connor's fiction is traditionally Catholic and available as such. My assertion: their arguments are in need of revision.

Critics who claim that O'Connor's work is Catholic in perspective are numerous. In *Flannery O'Connor: A Memorial*, J. J. Quinn, S.J., includes a collection of tributes to O'Connor as a Catholic writer. Many of these testimonials praising her Catholicism are even by Catholic clerics. Two examples quoted here demonstrate the overriding theme of this text. Sr. Mariella Gable, O.S.B., writes, "[O'Connor] elicited from her fiction some of the profoundest Catholic truths ever concretized in fiction."[1] Rev. Leonard F. X. Mayhew states, "In a real and special sense, however, she was precisely a 'Catholic' novelist. She was very much aware of the presently effective currents in the Church."[2] Even these two believers, however, admit that O'Connor does blur the distinction between Catholicism and Protestantism in her fiction. For example, Gable also writes, "But more than being a committed *Christian* she was the first great writer of ecumenical fiction anywhere in the world."[3] Mayhew states, "Her writing is profoundly marked by a highly individual synthesis of her Catholic philosophy with sympathy for the sometimes bizarre evangelism of the rural South."[4] Apparently Mayhew does not see this as posing a problem to believing that O'Connor was "precisely a 'Catholic' novelist," yet this very ecumenicism and individual syntheses are at the root of the problem for readers looking to O'Connor's work for a Catholicism they know. Ecumenicism was not a concept embraced by the Catholic Church until the Second Vatican Council held shortly before O'Connor's death, so a synthesis that accepted Protestant evangelism would move O'Connor decidedly away from Catholic doctrine. Those trying to derive Catholic concepts from O'Connor's works relying on a pre-Vatican II perspective would be disinclined to

---

[1] J. J. Quinn, S.J., ed., *Flannery O'Connor: A Memorial* (Scranton PA: University of Scranton Press, 1964, 1995) 44.

[2] Ibid., 63.

[3] Ibid., 44; my emphasis.

[4] Ibid., 63.

believe that "sympathy for the sometimes bizarre evangelism of the rural South" would or could elicit a Roman Catholic endorsement.

The Catholic Church, in the time of O'Connor, was insistently specific on the separateness between other Christian offshoots termed "Protestant" and what faithful Catholics identified as "the Church." O'Connor wrote to "A." in 1955 that "Dogma can in no way limit a limitless God. The person outside the Church attaches a different meaning to it than the person in" (*HB*, 92). She talks about her creative writing in this same letter and tells "A." that "the direction it has taken has been because of the Church in me or the effect of the Church's teaching" (*HB*, 92). In a 1962 letter to Brainard Cheney, O'Connor discusses the importance of her *Catholic* affiliation: "For those who come into it, the Catholic Church is not a preference but a necessity; but you still don't have to say Catholic Church. You need just say the Church. …In other words, when you say the Church, you can mean only one, and the reader will get the point without thinking that what he's been reading is a piece of Catholic propaganda."[5] O'Connor's letters and essays advise readers of what she believes to be appropriate behavior for a faithful Catholic. In them they learn of her strict adherence to the Catholic religion in practice, yet her personal *Catholic* religious fervor does not translate intact into her fiction. Before looking at O'Connor's "The River" as an illustration of how Catholicism seems to take a back seat to Protestant fundamentalism in this short story, it is important to examine several points: (1) O'Connor's awareness of the religious divergence of these two branches of Christianity, (2) her philosophical approach to writing, and (3) church history detailing the dogma of the Catholic Church of her day.

The books catalogued in *Flannery O'Connor's Library: Resources of Being* indicate that she had at her disposal precise knowledge of the distinctions between the two branches of Christianity she so liked to fuse in her fiction but that were such distinct entities in her mind and in Catholic teachings. Her personal library included the following:

---

[5] C. Ralph Stephens, ed., *The Correspondence of Flannery O'Connor and the Brainard Cheneys* (Jackson: University Press of Mississippi, 1986) 147–48.

Modern Catholic Thinkers: An Anthology, by A. Robert Caponigri (ed.)
The Catholic Companion to the Bible, by Ralph L. Woods (ed.)
Christianity Divided: Protestant and Roman Catholic Theological Issues by
    Daniel J. Callahan et al.
The Spirit and Forms of Protestantism, by Rev. Louis Bouyer
The Teaching of the Catholic Church: A Summary of Catholic Doctrine
    (vols. 1–2), by Canon George D. Smith (ed.)
Catholic Theology in Dialogue, by Gustave Weigel, S.J.
Early Christian Baptism and the Creed, by Joseph Crehan, S.J.
History of the Variations of the Protestant Churches, by James Benign
    Bossuet
A Popular History of the Reformation, by Philip Hughes
The Reformation in England, by Philip Hughes
*Letters from Vatican City: Vatican Council II (First Session): Background
    and Debates*, by Xavier Rynne
Protestant Hopes and the Catholic Responsibility, by George Tavard
The Catholic in America: From Colonial Times to the Present Day, by
    Peter J. Rahill
Frontiers in American Catholicism, by Walter J. Ong, S.J.
Patterns in Comparative Religion, by Mircea Eliade
Zen Catholicism: A Suggestion, by Dom Aelred Graham
Parish Holy Week Missal, by Leonard J. Doyle (ed.)

O'Connor's underlinings and notes in some of these books, as well as her book reviews, assure us of her intimate knowledge of Catholic and Protestant theology and of her awareness of the vital differences between Catholic and Protestant Christianity. In O'Connor's book review of *Faith and Understanding in America* by Gustave Weigel, S.J., she notes, "The Catholic who wishes to understand the intellectual problems of his time cannot afford to be ignorant of modern Protestant theology."[6] Additionally, she marked the following passage in her copy of *In Soft Garments: A Collection of Oxford Conferences*, by Ronald Knox: "The Protestant only feels his religion to be true as long as he goes on

---

[6] Leo J. Zuber and Carter W. Marter, eds., *The Presence of Grace and Other Book Reviews by Flannery O'Connor* (Athens: University of Georgia Press, 1983) 76.

practising it; the Catholic feels the truth of his religion as something independent of himself, which does not cease to be valid when he, personally, fails to live up to its precepts."[7] Personally committed to Catholicism, O'Connor, however, felt no compulsion to impose her religion upon her characters. Her characters could fail to live up to the precepts of the Catholic Church, yet their doing so would have no adverse implications on her own religious worthiness. O'Connor displayed this sentiment through other marginal notes in her library holdings and emphasized this attitude repeatedly in her letters. With various correspondents such as Ted Spivey and Cecil Dawkins, she insisted that the validity of the Catholic religion was independent of its practice. She acknowledged the existence of discernable differences between Catholic and Protestant doctrines to them and others, but she believed that separating her private religious beliefs from her creative expressions was the purview of a scholarly writer.

Even though she mocked academic misreadings of her work, O'Connor many times mentioned that she loved being read by scholars. She constantly sought validation as a serious literary figure, an accomplishment she believed could only be achieved through exercising her independence from restrictions that would pigeonhole her into a regional and/or religious niche. O'Connor marked the following passage in the *Introduction to Saint Thomas Aquinas*: "The very hiding of truth in figures is useful for the exercise of thoughtful minds, and as a defense against the ridicule of the unbelievers, according to the words, *Give not that which is holy to dogs (Matt.* vii [7:6])." She also marked "*On the contrary*, Gregory says: *Holy Scripture by the manner of its speech transcends every science, because in one and the same sentence, while it describes a fact, it reveals a mystery.*"[8] O'Connor's marginal notations single out this passage from *Modern Catholic Thinkers* edited by A. Robert Caponigri: "The life of the Catholic student and scholar is commanded by two principles. There is, on the one hand, the ideal 'sentire cum ecclesia,' to think and feel with the Church, as the basis of his identity as a Catholic; on the

---

[7] Arthur F. Kinney, *Flannery O'Connor's Library: Resources of Being* (Athens: University of Georgia Press, 1985) 57.

[8] Ibid., 72.

other, there is the ideal of free intellectual activity which he shares with every genuine student and scholar, without regard to other commitments and which, he knows, is the sole basis for authentic achievement in the intellectual order."[9]

O'Connor's belief that she could be independent from strict Catholic doctrine in her fiction, juxtaposed with a quest for scholarship through "free thinking," empowered her, nay commanded her, to avoid doctrinaire presentations of Catholic beliefs. She believed that her license as a creative writer allowed such liberties as folding Catholic ideas into a broader more Christian-centered ideology. O'Connor, therefore, saw dissemination of a *Christian*, as opposed to a *Catholic*, message as giving her authenticity as an artist. By drawing upon the people and places she knew and disseminating her religious message in the guise of the religion of the region, she could hope to attract a larger reading public, garner a more receptive critical response, and find deliverance from literary obscurity.

However, this artistic freedom draws readers decidedly away from perceiving O'Connor's fiction as Catholic. As Joseph Martos writes, "Catholics [in the days before the Second Vatican Council] officially regarded Protestants as heretics even if unofficially they respected their freedom of conscience."[10] The certainty that Protestant sects were heretical was strong and long-standing and directly attributed to the Reformation that began in 1517 with Martin Luther's posting of the ninety-five theses on the door of Castle Church in Wittenberg, Germany. The Reformation sparked the need for response within the Catholic Church culminating in the Council of Trent (1545–1563), which vigorously worked at "combating the Protestant heresies" while it "summarized Catholic doctrine and excommunicated those who believed otherwise."[11] In O'Connor's day, the Church's requirement on remaining true to Catholic doctrine and practices was a harsh and

---

[9] Ibid., 35.

[10] Joseph Martos, *Doors to the Sacred: A Historical Introduction to Sacraments in the Catholic Church* (Garden City NY: Image Books [Doubleday & Company, Inc.], 1982) 133.

[11] Ibid., 114.

unbending reality imposed upon the faithful under pain of mortal sin. There was no "free intellectual activity" when it came to the average cradle Catholic in the 1950s and 1960s. In addition, Catholics did not think of themselves as belonging to a Christian religion; they belonged to the Church of Rome, founded by Christ, the "one true Church." Denouncing this church in any way would amount to the damnation of their eternal souls—a prospect not to be taken lightly.

Critics often gloss over O'Connor's departure from Catholic dogma in her fiction because she continued to announce support for a Catholicism that mirrored the traditional Catholic mindset demanded from the pulpit. For example, in her essay "The Church and the Fiction Writer," she writes, "The Catholic sacramental view of life is one that sustains and supports at every turn the vision that the storyteller must have if he is going to write fiction of any depth" (*MM*, 152). O'Connor is adamantly mindful of the importance of the *Catholic* version of Christianity. In her essay "In the Protestant South," she stresses the need for "future Catholics [to have] a literature" that will be separate and distinct and "undeniably theirs, but which will also be understood and cherished by the rest of our countrymen.... You may ask, why not simply call this literature Christian? Unfortunately, the word Christian is no longer reliable. It has come to mean anyone with a golden heart. And a golden heart would be a positive interference in the writing of fiction" (*MM*, 192). Yet O'Connor's fiction does not provide Catholics with a literature "undeniably theirs," nor can it be "understood and cherished" as being Catholic. O'Connor's concern that "every given circumstance of the writer is ignored except his Faith" placed literary demands on her text that caused her to wrap her religious convictions in mystery (*MM*, 195).

To understand how O'Connor's fiction diverges so dramatically from what was Catholic theology in her day, we must review the 1992 text *Roman Catholicism Yesterday and Today* by Robert A. Burns, O.P. This Catholic priest discusses Catholic beliefs before, during, and after O'Connor's life and writes that "[U]ntil the Protestant Reformation of the sixteenth century, Catholicism was capable of permitting many theologies (short of heresy) and various liturgies without feeling the need for total uniformity."[12] Tolerant pre-Reformation Catholicism was not the Catholicism of O'Connor's contemporaries. Instead they would know a religion shaped by the Council of Trent (1545–1563) and unquestioned until the Second Vatican Council (1962–1965). In fact, the Council of Trent was the vehicle the Church used to refute Protestant deviations from Catholic dogma and doctrine. As Burns explains, this council

> was held to present the authoritative answers of the Catholic Church to the objections of the Protestant reformers. In order to promote Catholic unity, clear definitions were given concerning Catholic dogma. ...Because of the narrowness of this definition, Catholicism tended to become exclusivistic in its thinking and static in its world view. The Council of Trent also issued a number of regulations to promote unity. ...[T]he liturgy of the Mass was standardized and the *Index of Forbidden Books* was issued. These edicts helped maintain Catholic uniformity for the four hundred years after Trent. Great stress was placed on Church authority to maintain this post-Tridentine Catholic oneness.[13]

After the Council of Trent, but before the Second Vatican Council, "lay people were subject to their pastors, pastors were subject to their bishops, and all were subject to the pope."[14] O'Connor obviously recognized and complied with this hierarchical jurisdiction as evidenced by her request in a 1957 letter to Father J. H. McCown to grant her permission to read a book listed on the *Index of Forbidden Books*, a decision, as a pre-Vatican II Catholic, she shouldn't make for herself (*HB*, 259). However true and faithful she was as a Catholic in practice, her fiction does not observe the same religious rigidity imposed upon her and Catholics of the time.

---

[12] Robert A. Burns, *Roman Catholicism Yesterday and Today* (Chicago: Loyola University Press, 1992) 7.

[13] Ibid., 8.

[14] Martos, *Doors to the Sacred*, 133.

Burns also notes that "the chief instrument of Catholic education during the latter part of the nineteenth century and continuing into the 1960s was *The Baltimore Catechism*," which contains within its pages "the theology of the Council of Trent."[15] This Catholic substitute for the Bible presented the doctrines of the Church in question/answer format. As Burns states, "Little room was given to question what the catechism taught and any expression of doubt was often treated as though it were an attack upon the faith."[16] This inflexible attitude toward upholding dogma and the formulaic severity in the expression of one's faith was the instruction Catholics of that time, O'Connor's time, received.

"Because of the strong conservatism of the Church, most Catholics knew very little about either biblical or theological innovations."[17] Catholic scholars, however, unlike the faithful, were encouraged to "make use of discoveries in archaeology and linguistic analysis" by Pope Pius XII through his 1943 encyclical letter *Divino Afflante Spiritu*.[18] But in 1950, the Pope published the encyclical *Humani Generis* "that effectively reversed the openness of *Divino Afflante Spiritu* and plunged the Church into another period of deep conservatism that lasted until the beginning of Vatican II."[19] So, while lay scholars like O'Connor may have felt free to analyze Catholic dogma, the faithful not only *did* not—they *could* not.

The hold of the Council of Trent over Catholic practice and thought was to change when Pope John XXIII opened the Second Vatican Council on 11 October 1962. The council continued until early December 1965 (the year after O'Connor's death). After Vatican II, changes in Catholic customs and terminology came about, the use of the vernacular in liturgical ceremonies was allowed, and rules such as fasting during Lent were relaxed. However, neither Catholic doctrine nor dogma changed because of it. The Catholic Church in O'Connor's time continued to be the conservative, static, traditional institution that had

---

[15] Burns, *Roman Catholicism Yesterday and Today*, 28.
[16] Ibid., 29.
[17] Ibid., 31.
[18] Ibid.
[19] Ibid.

risen out of the Council of Trent. Catholic and non-Catholic readers familiar with the Church of O'Connor's era may discover a pervasive Christianity informing her work, but they cannot easily identify within her fiction the Tridentine Catholic Church of her day and theirs—the Catholic Church that embraced the long-standing conservatism firmly in place and unquestioned for four hundred years.

I. Is "The River" Catholic?

Utilizing the above discussion of Church history as a starting place, and with our focus specifically on O'Connor's short story "The River," it is possible to determine its adherence, or lack thereof, to the traditional Catholic dogma of her day. While "The River" does afford a fundamentalist Christian view of baptism without question, it does not give any indication to its readers that the author intended to "document" a Catholic interpretation. If this story were to yield a version of the sacrament easily accessed as Catholic, readers might properly expect the story to contain images that comply with pre-Vatican II Catholic baptismal doctrine and ceremony. They might also reasonably expect the behavior of the fictional characters engaged in conferring and receiving the sacrament to mirror that of faithful Catholic parishioners in like pursuits. However, O'Connor does not provide this religious framework.

"The River" begins with the description of an unnamed child "glum and limp" who "ain't fixed right" (CS, 157). The young child of O'Connor's focus is "four or five," a neglected, pitiful, pitiable creature. He leaves the house with a runny nose and eyes, pushed out of the door by his father. We are soon to learn that the child's spiritual well-being has been as neglected by his parents as has his physical and emotional welfare. The child is unceremoniously given into the care of a babysitter who doesn't even know his first name.

As O'Connor was wont to do, some of her characters in "The River" begin their existence as disembodiments. In this story's beginning the child is shoved "toward a pale spotted *hand*." A loud *voice* says, "He ain't fixed right." O'Connor connects the hand and voice that belong to the child's only real caregiver to pronouns and inanimate objects when she writes that the young boy's father "found *her* looming in [the door], a speckled *skeleton* in a long pea-green coat and felt helmet" (*CS*, 157; my emphasis). When O'Connor does identify this woman, she is referenced as Mrs. Connin only—first name then and forever unknown. This familiar O'Connor technique of depersonalizing a character is overtly present in the opening pages of the story and serves to distance Mrs. Connin from the child. The babysitter's mention, shrouded in terms of death (for Mrs. Connin is not a person but a skeleton with a focus on body parts), leads readers astray. Mrs. Connin seems to be paramount to the everlasting life of the soul of this child. She will be the person who introduces the child to his first knowledge of Jesus; she is to be the instrument that will try to "fix him right." In Catholic terms, Mrs. Connin will assume the role of Catholic sponsor for the child's baptismal rite. Because a Catholic baptismal sponsor must vow to take on the role of spiritual guardian, agreeing to raise the child in the Catholic faith should disaster befall the parents, this is not a role taken or given lightly. Catholics believe baptism infuses sacramental and, therefore, spiritual life into the soul of the baptized. Does O'Connor intend for Mrs. Connin to be the child's sponsor as required for a Catholic baptism? If so, should she not be connected to images of joy and life? Additionally, O'Connor introduces another impediment to readers' believing that Mrs. Connin could act as a Catholic sponsor for a Catholic baptism. In the 1950s and 1960s, the Catholic Church imposed strict conditions for the selection of a proper pre-Vatican II Catholic sponsor. We can believe that Mrs. Connin would be an acceptable sponsor for a *Christian* ceremony but not for a *Catholic* one, for while Mrs. Connin is a person of faith, certainly, she is not a practicing Catholic, a requirement for such duty in O'Connor's day.

The child's given name is "Harry." When Mrs. Connin asks Harry his name, he reports it as "Bevel," the name of the baptizing preacher to whom he, and we, will soon be introduced. This name, if we believe O'Connor was using a naming technique to reinforce her symbolism as she often did, could mean that Harry's "new" name would symbolize that he is ripe for "belief" and a rebirth into Christ through the baptism she will arrange for him. We have two reasons to believe this might have been her intention: *Bevel* connects him to Bevel the preacher, and the letters of Harry's new name can be rearranged to construct a phonetic pronunciation of "believe" [bē•lēv]. Catholics do confer names on their children during the baptismal ceremony, but the usual practice as mentioned in the *Baltimore Catechism* and practiced by the faithful in the 1950s and 1960s was to name children for the saints or for the Virgin Mary. Harry announces his name long before the baptismal ceremony, and Bevel (to my knowledge) is not a saint's name, nor would it be connected with one canonized in the Catholic Church by the ordinary practicing Catholic familiar with the Church in O'Connor's time. Critics and readers alike must rely on the genuineness of O'Connor's words: "I write the way I do because and only because I am a Catholic" (*HB*, 114), and could, therefore, agree that "The River" is a story mirroring a sacramental rebirth. And it can be seen so. But the question that surfaces is: Can it be viewed as a *Catholic* mirroring?

It is important to refer here to the *Baltimore Catechism* to ground us in the Catholic interpretation of faith and the sacraments as believed by the traditional faithful in O'Connor's time and now. The Catholic Information Center (www.catholic.net) indicates that the catechism has not changed since it was written in 1891: "[The] *Baltimore Catechism* is a timeless classic. The only changes that have been made in the Church, since it was written, are those in the area of discipline. No changes have been made in the area of doctrine and morality. The same Faith that was believed when the *Baltimore Catechism* was written, is the same Faith that is believed today."[20]

The sacrament of baptism itself, as defined by the *Baltimore Catechism*, has undergone no evolution from 1891 through O'Connor's day to the present. The definition and explanation of the Catholic sacrament as defined in the catechism remains as follows:

---

[20] Online at http://www.catholic.net/rcc/Catechism/Doit.html Benziger Brothers 1891 and 1921. HTML translation by Catholic Information Center on Internet, Inc., 1995.

152 Q. What is Baptism?

A. Baptism is a Sacrament which cleanses us from Original
    Sin, makes us Christians, children of God, and heirs of
    Heaven.

154 Q. Is Baptism necessary to salvation?

A. Baptism is necessary to salvation, because without it we
    cannot enter into the kingdom of Heaven.

155 Q. Who can administer Baptism?

A. The priest is the ordinary minister of Baptism; but in case
    of necessity anyone who has the use of reason may
    baptize.[21]

The river baptism of Harry/Bevel, though not orthodoxly Catholic
in ceremony, would be valid in the eyes of the Church because it was
performed by a minister with the intent to baptize a child into
Christianity. While the teenage preacher Bevel, wearing khaki trousers,
a blue shirt, a red scarf, and singing in a "high twangy voice," is not the
usual black-cassock-frocked priest, he could carry out a valid Catholic
baptism. As Bernard Hassan in *The American Catholic Catalog* states, "So
important is baptism that the Roman Catholic Church will accept as
valid a baptism performed by non-Catholics."[22] This sacrament, as *A
Catholic Dictionary* reports, is conferred "as a result of washing with water
accompanied by the words 'I baptize thee in the name of the Father and
of the Son and of the Holy Ghost.'"[23] Additionally those familiar with
Catholic doctrine and dogma would know that only through this
sacrament can a person be "spiritually regenerated, and made capable of

---

[21] Thomas L. Kinkead, *An Explanation of the Baltimore Catechism of Christian
Doctrine* (Rockford IL: Tan Books and Publishers, Inc., 1891, 1988) 140–43.

[22] Bernard Hassan, *The American Catholic Catalog* (San Francisco: Harper & Row,
1980) 4.

[23] Donald Attwater, ed., *A Catholic Dictionary*, 3rd ed. (New York: Macmillan
Company, 1958) 45.

receiving the other sacraments."[24] So the baptism of this child by a non-Catholic preacher through immersion in a river would be considered a *bona fide* baptism in the eyes of the Church despite the lack of overt resemblance to Catholic ceremony, custom, or ritual.

As readers, we have two options here. We can consider that O'Connor intended Harry/Bevel's baptism at the river to be valid in the eyes of the Church (as O'Connor refers to the *Catholic* Church), or that she did not. If we consider Harry/Bevel's baptism by the preacher valid in Catholic terms, why would O'Connor introduce another baptism by the child himself at the end of the story? In addition, since the Catholic Church recognizes three types of baptism (water, blood, and desire) and receiving one of these "is necessary to salvation" as *A Catholic Dictionary* states,[25] which type does the young child receive either *at* the river or *in* the river at the story's end?

To determine which type of baptism O'Connor intended the child to receive, an examination of the types of baptisms possible in the Catholic Church as explained by the *Baltimore Catechism* is necessary:

158 Q. What is Baptism of water?

A. Baptism of water is that which is given by pouring water on the head of the person to be baptized, and saying at the same time, I baptize thee in the name of the Father, and of the son, and of the Holy Ghost.

159 Q. What is Baptism of desire?

A. Baptism of desire is an ardent wish to receive Baptism, and to do all that God has ordained for our salvation.

160 Q. What is Baptism of blood?

A. Baptism of blood is the shedding of one's blood for the faith of Christ.[26]

---

[24] Ibid.

[25] Ibid.

[26] Kinkead, *An Explanation of the Baltimore Catechism*, 145–47.

With Mrs. Connin in attendance, Harry/Bevel appears to be baptized through a baptism of water at the river by a preacher, but he later seeks baptism by his own hand at the end of the story. If this is a *Catholic* story, the reader must wonder what O'Connor is suggesting. Is Harry/Bevel's river baptism by a preacher, which appears to be "of water," insufficient in some way so that he must seek baptism himself at the end of the story? O'Connor has the first baptism performed as an immersion in a river (not traditionally Catholic in the 1950s and 1960s); however, this preacher-conferred sacrament does seem to meet Catholic requirements as there is "a minister to perform the ceremony, a sponsor to stand in for the child who is younger than the age of reason as are Catholic infants, and a preacher who '[says] the words of baptism.'" It is unclear in this story whether the "words of baptism," as indicated in the *Baltimore Catechism* question 158 (see above), are uttered verbatim during the ceremony performed at the river, but O'Connor does seem to intend their utterance as this passage featuring the preacher insinuates: "'All right, I'm going to Baptize you now,' and without more warning, he tightened his hold and swung him [the child] upside down and plunged his head into the water. He held him under while he said the words of Baptism" (*CS*, 168). There is little doubt, then, that to a reader familiar with the rules of the Church, this river baptism complies with Catholic rules and meets the criteria of a valid Catholic baptism of water.

If this river baptism, though not orthodoxly Catholic, is "of water" and is valid in Catholic terms, readers must be legitimately puzzled when O'Connor seeks another baptism for the child at the end of the story. The receiving of baptism a second time conflicts with Catholic dogma. The Church expressly forbids receiving baptism, confirmation, or Holy Orders more than once "because they imprint a character in the soul."[27] However, it is true that the Catholic Church does allow for a second "conditional" baptism should the first be invalid because

> The Church wishes to be certain that all its children are
> baptized; so when there is any doubt about the first Baptism, it

---

[27] Ibid., 139.

baptizes again conditionally, that is, the priest says in giving the Baptism over again: If you are not baptized already, I baptize you now. Therefore if the person was rightly baptized the first time, the second ceremony has no effect, because the priest does not intend to give Baptism a second time. But if the first Baptism was not rightly given, then the second takes effect. In either case Baptism is given only once; for if the first was valid, the second is not given; and if the first was invalid, the second is given.[28]

By all appearances, the child's first baptism appears valid.

O'Connor was familiar with the *Baltimore Catechism*, yet it appears that she must have intended the child's second baptism to be the one that imprinted a character in his soul because she writes that the young child "intended not to fool with preachers any more but to Baptize himself and to keep on going this time until he found the Kingdom of Christ in the river" (*CS*, 173). The text leads us to assume that this second baptism was the baptism O'Connor believed necessary for the child's salvation, and that she considered the first baptism by the river performed by the preacher to be insufficient for some reason known to her. O'Connor certainly emphasizes this second baptism for the child, his attempt "to Baptize himself," when she writes that this baptism will be the "one that makes him count."

Converts to Catholicism are always "conditionally" baptized into the Church to ensure not a re-baptism, but a first valid baptism. For this reason, as mentioned above, persons baptized in a non-Catholic ceremony would have their Catholic rites begin with the words "If you are not baptized, I baptize you." So readers of "The River" expecting O'Connor to afford the young child a Catholic sacramental baptism could accept the need for Harry/Bevel to be conditionally baptized. However, the young child's second baptism still does not conform with the rules surrounding baptism of water. There is no priest or minister to administer the sacrament, no words are said, and the baptism is performed *by* the child *for* the child at the river. As the *Baltimore Catechism*

---

[28] Ibid.

states (and Catholics or those familiar with Catholicism would know), "no one can baptize himself."[29] Harry/Bevel, therefore, despite all of his efforts to "count" in the waters of the river at the end of the story, cannot transform this action of a second baptism into a valid *Catholic* baptism of water even if we were to consider his first riverside baptism tainted. Clearly this second baptism is not "of water" and is not Catholic.

O'Connor undoubtedly makes two baptisms available to Harry/Bevel. If O'Connor does intend to nullify the validity of the first baptism at the river then according to Catholic doctrine the child would need the second baptism she offers him to achieve salvation. However, this second baptism, the child's self-drowning in the river, is not performed by a minister of God nor is it accompanied with the proper discourse of baptism. The second baptism, therefore, cannot be "of water." And we must be concerned with the type of baptism O'Connor intended, for a Catholic must receive one of the three types of baptism to enter the kingdom of heaven. Does O'Connor mean for Harry/Bevel to receive a valid baptism in the form of a Catholic baptism of blood in his attempt to count at the end of the story? *A Catholic Dictionary* defines this type of baptism as consisting of "suffering martyrdom for the Faith or for some Christian virtue, which infuses sanctifying grace into the soul and forgives sin. Martyrdom produces this effect by a special privilege, as being a supreme act of love in imitation of the passion of our Lord, but the martyr must have had attrition for his sins. Baptism of blood extends to infants."[30]

O'Connor makes a point of telling us that Harry/Bevel is "four or five." "The age of reason, with its capacities and obligations, is assumed to begin about the end of the seventh year."[31] So, for purposes of this sacrament, if we consider the child a religious "infant" in Catholic terms, he could be eligible to receive the sacrament in this form. However, the child does not endure martyrdom for Christ as he is not drowned by someone else in defense of his faith; he drowns himself in search of faith. O'Connor, then, has effectively eliminated both "water" and "blood" as

---

[29] Ibid., 145.

[30] Attwater, *A Catholic Dictionary*, 59.

[31] Ibid., 12.

baptismal types for Harry/Bevel's initiation into Christianity, leaving only baptism of desire as the remaining valid Catholic option for his second attempt at seeking everlasting salvation through the Church.

One could think, perhaps, that baptism of desire most appropriately fits the second baptism Harry/Bevel undergoes and is what O'Connor intended the child to receive. Catholic doctrine allows for this baptismal type to substitute for either water or blood as a means to enter heaven. Indeed, O'Connor makes clear that Harry/Bevel desperately desires the kingdom of Christ. She writes that as he plunges himself under the water "he knew that he was getting somewhere, all his fury and fear left him" (*CS*, 174). The *Baltimore Catechism* substantiates that baptism of desire must be achieved through an "ardent wish." Harry/Bevel certainly meets this criterion. However, the catechism is explicit that this type of baptism must be desired "by one who has no opportunity of being baptized—for no one can baptize himself."[32] The definition of this version of baptism is clarified by Kinkead: "When it is not possible thus to be baptized, an act of perfect contrition or pure love of God will supply the omission...and at least implicitly include a desire and intention to receive Baptism of water should occasion offer. Infants are not capable of Baptism of desire. An [sic] heathen, believing, even though in a confused way, in a God whose will should be done and desiring to do that will whatever it may be, probably has Baptism of desire."[33]

For baptism of desire, as for baptism of blood, age is a factor. We must decide if Harry/Bevel, at age "four or five," is a religious "infant" in Catholic theological terms or not; O'Connor surely mentions his age for a reason. If he is theologically an infant, he is "not capable" of receiving this type of baptism. But Harry/Bevel does certainly fit the criterion of "believing, even though in a confused way." His attempt to count at the end of the story could be construed as an act of pure love. Baptism of desire does allow the act of desiring itself to become the catalyst initiating this baptismal type. The impediments confronting Harry/Bevel, though, hinge on several Catholic restrictions captured in two phrases of the above definition (my emphasis): "*When it is not possible*

---

[32] Kinkead, *An Explanation of the Baltimore Catechism*, 145.

[33] Attwater, *A Catholic Dictionary*, 144.

thus to be baptized, and [receiving it should] *at least implicitly include a desire and intention to receive Baptism of water should occasion offer."*

This child *had* the possibility of being baptized at the river by the preacher, and in fact the ceremony was performed. O'Connor, though, has the child blatantly reject his first baptism when she writes that he "intended not to fool with preachers any more but to Baptize himself and to keep on going this time until he found the Kingdom of Christ in the river" (*CS,* 173). All Catholics explicitly know, as stated above and repeated here for clarity, the *Baltimore Catechism* admonition: *no one can baptize himself.*[34] This child obviously desired baptism to achieve salvation, but we must still question whether O'Connor provides him with a Catholic sacrament in his desperate search for his savior.

The *Manual of Christian Doctrine,* authorized as a "Course of Religious Instruction" for novitiates and Catholic clerics for use in Catholic high schools and colleges, states in answer to the question "What is baptism?" that "Baptism is a sacrament which cleanses us from original sin and actual sin, and makes us children of God and of the Church."[35] The manual continues: "Baptism is not absolutely necessary, since it may be supplied by two means: perfect love of God and martyrdom."[36] These are not contradictory statements; "baptism" in the first quotation means restrictively "baptism of water." The manual states unequivocally that of the three kinds of baptism (water, blood, desire), only baptism of water "is a sacrament."[37] The manual also answers the question of whether baptism of desire produces the same benefits as baptism of water with an emphatic "No; it does not imprint a character, it does not confer sacramental grace, it does not remit all the temporal punishment due to sin."[38] So while it is possible to gain entrance into heaven through an intense desire to seek God or through martyrdom for God, only baptism of water imparts the benefits of a sacrament.

---

[34] Kinkead, *An Explanation of the Baltimore Catechism,* 145.

[35] No stated author, *Manual of Christian Doctrine* (Philadelphia: John Joseph McVey, 1926) 397.

[36] Ibid., 400.

[37] Ibid.

[38] Ibid.

If baptism of desire is what O'Connor really intended for young Harry/Bevel, then readers would be correct in believing that this type of baptism would be acceptable to the Catholic faith and sufficient for entry into heaven. However, the child's drowning does not constitute baptism of desire as defined by the *Baltimore Catechism*; and even if we refute this fact, and believe that desire is the baptism the child received, baptism of desire is not a sacrament; the child was not martyred, nullifying his reception of baptism of blood; and O'Connor seems to negate the child's receiving baptism of water by positing the second river immersion as the baptism that will make him count. O'Connor has compromised the soul of this child by denying him the baptismal imprint of this sacrament.

Additionally, the *Baltimore Catechism* admonishes: "[N]ever under any circumstance repeat the Baptism on the same person. It is a sin to try to baptize more than once when you know Baptism can be given only once."[39] O'Connor, as a practicing Catholic, would know of this Church warning. Therefore, while we can easily believe that Harry/Bevel desires God with a perfect love, we still must wrestle to make sense of the information O'Connor presents us. Are there two baptisms? Does O'Connor intend the child to receive baptism of desire despite the fact that he did have the occasion to receive baptism of water? Why isn't the child afforded the sacramental form of baptism? In searching "The River" in an attempt to map O'Connor's textual rendering of the sacrament of baptism onto a baptism declared Catholic and sacramental by the Catholic Church and as delineated for the faithful in the *Baltimore Catechism*, readers find a distorted, incomprehensible rendering of a religious rite that does not coincide with their experiences either as Catholics or with their observations of rituals performed by Catholics.

II. Into the Christian River

Readers endeavoring to derive a shared connotation and internal consistency with what they believe to be Catholic doctrine continue to encounter extraordinary complications in perceiving "The River" as a

---

[39] Kinkead, *An Explanation of the Baltimore Catechism*, 146.

documentation of the *Catholic sacrament* of baptism. O'Connor's portrayal of this sacrament at the river and the relentless pursuit of a second baptism by the child when the first was sufficient both run counter to expectations and defy explanation if we are searching for believable *Catholic* literature. In *Semantic Theory: A Linguistic Perspective*, Don L. F. Nilsen and Alleen Pace Nilsen state, "The primary purpose of language is to establish for the communicators a particular relationship with the real world in terms of reference. When the audience knows some but not all of the qualities of the referent, then an incomplete relationship exists and it is the purpose of communication to provide additional qualities of the referent for the audience."[40] Because O'Connor's language has not established a connection with the real world of the Roman Catholic Church, traditional Catholicism becomes clouded in her fiction, blurring itself into all that is Christian. Despite O'Connor's communication through lectures and letters to convince her correspondents (and later her critics) that the "qualities" of her fiction indeed reflect the "qualities" of traditional Catholicism, readers unfamiliar with O'Connor's explanations of her work, unless taught otherwise, are unable to glean from her fiction the message of the *Baltimore Catechism*. Her stories do not provide a glimpse of pre-Vatican II Catholic ritual and ceremony. "The River" does not reduce to a *Catholic* essence.

O'Connor as a writer spent much time constructing her own meaning and much time imposing it upon the literary community. Traditional critics privy to and believers of O'Connor's own explications of her text have fallen victim to O'Connor's "spin control" and refuse to acknowledge the text she lays before them. Her treatment of baptism is foreign to the teachings of the *Baltimore Catechism* and the Council of Trent, both of which defined all that was Catholic in O'Connor's day, yet traditional O'Connor critics repeatedly ignore the nuances in her text that assign contradictions with orthodox pre-ecumenical Catholicism. They are content to believe that the Christian beliefs O'Connor focuses on in her fictional works are equivalent to the

---

[40] Don L. F. Nilsen and Alleen Pace Nilson, *Semantic Theory: A Linguistic Perspective* (Rowley MA: Newbury House, 1975) 9.

Catholic beliefs she discusses in her letters and essays; they continue to believe that there exists a Catholic presence in O'Connor's fictional work because O'Connor has said there is one. Those supporters seem consistently and patently to ignore Northrop Frye's argument in *The Double Vision: Language and Meaning in Religion*, that readers expect to find within their books "a satisfactory verbal replica" of the world known to them.[41] These critics seem also to dismiss O'Connor herself, who echoes Frye's sentiment in her essay "Novelist and Believer" by cautioning that readers will be hindered in accepting a writer's vision "in direct proportion as [their] beliefs depart from his" (*MM*, 162).

Has O'Connor succeeded in infusing her work with mystery and with *Christian* revelation? She most undoubtedly has. Has O'Connor brought forth dogma espoused by the Roman Catholic Church into her fiction as she so staunchly insists in her letters and essays? She most definitely has not. Instead "The River" becomes another in a stream of O'Connor's fictional works where language and linguistic portrayals artfully and self-consciously challenge an overtly *Catholic* sacramental interpretation. Despite critical statements to the contrary, O'Connor actively avoids evidence of the traditional Catholic Church in her fiction while adroitly shaping the way she was critically perceived. "The River" is not a traditional Catholic rendition of the *Catholic* sacrament of baptism as it was practiced then or now. O'Connor has violated our conventional knowledge of any of the forms of a Catholic baptism in this short story. Harry/Bevel does not receive a Catholic baptism of water, of blood, or of desire. This young child who had the benefit of sacramental salvation at the river abandons O'Connor's Church and drowns himself in search of a God he barely knows. Not to recognize this fact is to ignore the printed page.

---

[41] Northrop Frye, *The Double Vision: Language and Meaning in Religion* (Toronto: University of Toronto Press, 1991) 14.

The Scandalous Baptism of Harry Ashfield: Flannery O'Connor's "The River"

Ralph C. Wood

Several years ago when I taught Flannery O'Connor's "The River" to an undergraduate class, a student brought me up short by asserting that the parents of Harry Ashfield should have filed charges against Bevel Summers and Mrs. Connin for child abuse. Summers is the river preacher who baptizes young Harry Ashfield, and Mrs. Connin is the Christian woman who brings the boy both to hear and to heed the evangelist's invitation for him to be baptized. Since little Harry drowns himself in a mistaken attempt to gain yet more of the same significance that he had first found in baptism, the story's real miscreants and malefactors are Summers and Connin—so the student argued with considerable cogency. Rather than leading the child to new and greater life, the fundamentalist preacher and fellow believer have practiced the ultimate deceit upon little Harry: they have made him believe that his life's significance lies beyond life. Thus have they engendered the child's needless, indeed his meaningless death.

In this reading of the story, O'Connor's river preacher and lay evangelist are not well-meant but benighted creatures: they are examples of the Christian treason against the fundamental premise upon which modern existence is built—namely, that physical life itself is the ultimate good, since nothing either precedes or follows it. Such mortalism insists, as Bertrand Russell famously declared, that when we die we rot. With a great cosmic void surrounding us—with literally nothing coming before or following after us—human life has its only justification within its own terms. Since human existence has value in relation to nothing transcending itself, its only worth is found either in the pleasures we can manage to enjoy (in the case of hedonists) or in the good deeds we can manage to accomplish (in the case of moralists). Hence the stark conclusion: death is the ultimate enemy and remaining alive at all costs is the ultimate good, whether to enjoy more pleasures or else to do more good deeds. To die in devotion to a nonexistent kingdom of a nonexistent God is thus the ultimate lie.

In "The River," as with all of her stories, O'Connor presses her readers to drastic conclusions. Either Preacher Summers and Mrs. Connin have done Harry a terrible and final violence, or else they have given him the most important of all gifts—eternal life. There is no humanistic way of avoiding such a drastic either/or. The story's dire outcome cannot be justified by insisting that the child unfortunately literalized the preacher's message and thus mistakenly ended his own life. The story would thus become a trite exercise in the sentimentality that O'Connor despised. She likened sentimentality in both morality and religion to pornography in art: it is a cheap and easy way of achieving a bogus effect. Yet neither does O'Connor encourage any quick and conveniently Christian verdict. As we have seen, there are good reasons for concluding that Harry Ashfield's baptism is an instance of what Nietzsche called Christian nihilism: a flight from the one and only world into unreality and delusion, into nothingness. "The River" focuses, in fact, on the single act requiring the sharpest moral and religious assessment: the rite of initiation into Christian existence as either the ultimate reality or the ultimate delusion. As the public event that incorporates believers into the visible church, baptism is the sacrament of transferred citizenship from the *civitas terrena* to the *civitas dei*: from a realm that is perishing to another that is eternal. Or else it is a snare and a cheat that leads to spiritual and, in this case quite literally, to physical death.

This essay seeks to show that O'Connor makes Harry Ashfield's altered allegiance as scandalous and objectionable as possible, so the readers will be compelled to make a dire decision about the boy's baptism and death—whether they are fraudulent and enslaving or else truthful and freeing. In fact, the narrator conducts little Harry through all of the essential steps of Christian initiation, but not in the sweet and pretty fashion that turns the baptism of most children into an empty rite of entrance to bourgeois existence. Rather O'Connor makes the boy's entry to eternal life both violent and uncouth: from a succinct catechumenate under the unschooled Mrs. Connin, to the proclamation of the divine word via the boy evangelist Bevel Summers, to an exorcism of a real and present devil, to the monosyllabic confession of faith made by young Harry himself, to his own triune baptism by the river preacher, to a verbal anointing that seals the significance of his immersion, to the confirmation of his baptism in the decision he makes to put himself under the water permanently, and finally to his refusal of a wholly negative eucharist when he rejects the candy stick proffered by Mr. Paradise. Thus is Harry Ashfield scandalously—or else mistakenly—incorporated into the only universal community, the church catholic, the single community comprised of all the baptized. To make sure Ashfield's baptism is not some sort of fundamentalist fluke, O'Connor has it conform to every aspect of her own Roman Catholic tradition. Thus are all readers, whether Roman or Protestant or Orthodox, whether hedonist or humanist or atheist, faced with their own crisis of decision: whether to regard Harry's thoroughly Christian baptism as a huge mistake or a wondrous gift.

Flannery O'Connor sets the rural and uncultured world of the Connins in stark contrast to the urban and sophisticated life of the Ashfields, the better to lure readers into believing the latter superior to the former. The two-room Connin house is a flimsy structure whose pseudo-brick covering is belied by the family dogs that bed beneath it. The floorboards are so widely spaced that the dogs' tails protrude through the cracks. The walls of the Connin home contain forbidding pictures of elderly relatives, annual calendars no doubt acquired without cost, and an amateurish depiction of Christ as a carpenter. Though there may be others, we learn of only a single book in the Connin library, a nineteenth-century work titled *The Life of Jesus Christ for Readers Under Twelve*. Mrs. Connin herself is a woman with sparse and lengthy teeth, a skeletal body, a helmet-like hat, and a fundamentalist faith. She is an unattractive reflection of her unattractive environs.

Her family is even less winsome. Mr. Connin has been hospitalized with a cancerous colon after failing to be healed by the ministrations of the Reverend Bevel Summer. He has become an embittered unbeliever. Rather than heeding his wife's injunction to praise God for the life he still has, Mr. Connin declares stubbornly that "he ain't thanking nobody" (*CW*, 156). The four Connin children are equally loathsome in both their demeanor and their deportment. Sarah Mildred has "her hair up in so many curlers that it glared like the [tin] roof" on the house (*CW*, 157). Taking advantage of the city kid who has never seen a hog other than Porky Pig in a comic book, the Connin children connive to make sure that naïve little Harry is trampled by the stinking family swine. Thus is the Connin world revealed to be so mean and narrow, so backward and ugly, that it seems to justify Karl Marx's celebrated denunciation of "the idiocy of rural life."[1]

The urbane life of the Ashfields, on the other hand, is characterized by its up-to-date beliefs and habits. Abstract art adorns the Ashfield apartment. When Harry steals the book about Jesus from Mrs. Connin, the Ashfields' sophisticated friends instantly recognize its value as a collector's item. The Ashfields themselves are both partygoers and party-givers. They stay out late and sleep in late, often hungover. Their refrigerator is filled with leftover cocktail snacks, and their tables are littered with over-full ashtrays. They are also philosophical materialists, having taught their son that he is the product of mere natural causes. Harry thus believes that he was "made...by a doctor named Sladewall" (*CW*, 160). As a mere accident of nature, the child is a bother and a burden to his parents. They attempt to purchase his love by buying him new toys as soon as he breaks the old ones. When Mrs. Connin comes to collect Harry in the morning, his father gruffly stuffs the boy's arms into his coat. When Mrs. Ashfield puts him to bed at night, she exhibits little motherly care herself. Her erotic gait is as revealing as her uncaring kiss: "She hung over him for an instant and brushed her lips against his forehead. Then she got up and moved away, swaying her hips lightly"

---

[1] Karl Marx and Frederick Engels, "Manifesto of the Communist Party," in *Marx and Engels: Basic Writings on Politics and Philosophy* (Garden City, New York: Doubleday Anchor, 1959) 11.

(*CW*, 68). The world of the Ashfields is marked by mockery above all else. In a house where everything is a joke, Harry himself has learned to treat everything risibly. Hence his assumption that Bevel Summers is yet another jester, and thus also his mimicry of the evangelist by declaring that he shares the preacher's name.

It is evident that O'Connor presents her readers with two antithetical worlds, both of them noxious. Yet they are far from equal in value, as the story's action makes clear. The cultured Ashfield world is one-dimensional; it is sealed off in a self-satisfaction that virtually nothing can penetrate. It is not life giving; it is indeed a burned-out realm, a wasteland, a field of ashes. The Connin world, by contrast, is richly complicated and full of surprising promise. Mrs. Connin, for instance, is imbued with a religiosity that fills her with charity, even if her children remain wantonly mean-spirited and her husband bitterly atheistic. Hers is a faith that does not depend on easy and obvious rewards. While the Ashfields live for trivial satisfactions, Mrs. Connin makes heroic sacrifices for her family. She takes care of other folks' children in her own home during the day, after doing cleaning work elsewhere at night. Yet never do we hear Mrs. Connin complaining about her hard lot. We learn, on the contrary, that she cares deeply for others, especially young Harry. When she embraces the boy with the love he has never known at home, he responds in kind. He clings tightly to her and the things he associates with her, even if it means stealing her handkerchief and her book.

Though her regard for young Ashfield is manifestly authentic, Mrs. Connin knows that human love alone will not finally suffice for a boy so bereft as Harry Ashfield. She discerns—perhaps because she does not depend on the world's material benefits—that the child hungers for spiritual satisfaction, that he yearns in some inchoate way for the love of God, that he needs not generic love or vague philanthropy, therefore, but the quite particular and incarnate love of God. Thus does Mrs. Connin teach Harry the most rudimentary of lessons—that he is not the accidental product of an unsponsored and undirected natural process, but that the figure whose portrait Harry hadn't recognized is in fact his creator. "He had been made by a carpenter," she tells him, "named Jesus

Christ" (*CW*, 160). She also teaches him that this carpenter is his redeemer, for the picture book shows Jesus salvaging the Gadarene demoniac, driving "a crowd of pigs out of a man" (*CW*, 160). Having learned what horrible creatures pigs can be, Harry is at once fixated on this good news about his ultimate origin, finding that it renders him strangely tranquil: "His mind was dreamy and serene as they walked" (*CW*, 160).

Mrs. Connin is walking Harry through the woods to the river where Bevel Summers preaches. She knows Harry needs not merely to be taught the rudiments of the faith but also to receive the proclaimed Word and to be baptized, if her brief catechizing of him is to be efficacious—though of course she would never put the matter in such terms. Mrs. Connin knows, in sum, that Harry Ashfield needs to be marked with the outward and visible sign of the faith. He needs to be incorporated into Christ's body called the church. This rustic Protestant's obsession with baptism reveals that Mrs. Connin would likely belong to the Churches of Christ, the American denomination founded in the nineteenth century by Alexander Campbell.[2] For one of their central tenets is that baptism is not an empty ritual meant for the socializing of teenagers: it is an act that is utterly essential for salvation, a doctrine the boy-preacher named Bevel Summers clearly espouses.

O'Connor does not make the eighteen-year-old river preacher a figure easily to be credited, even as she does not make Harry's baptism an event easily to be affirmed. Summers evokes an almost instantly negative response from most of my students. This is yet another shyster evangelist, they say, akin to those whom they have seen on television always asking for money, if only via the crawler across the bottom of the screen. Bevel Summers has in fact won fame as a preacher who both sings and heals, and who thus would likely have received generous gifts from the beneficiaries of his curative charismatic gifts. He draws large crowds, as desperate souls gather at the river in the hope that he will perform miracles on their sick and lame. Yet on this occasion Summers

---

[2] "Restoration Movement," in *Concise Dictionary of Christianity in America*, ed. Reid, Linder, Shelley, Stout and Noll (Downers Grove IL: InterVarsity Press, 1993) 293.

frustrates their desire. He has come to teach them that there is not one kind of pain but two, even as there are two rivers of two different kinds.

There is indeed the terrible physical pain that requires natural and perhaps even supernatural healing.[3] Yet human pain is amenable to human cure. The second kind of pain does not submit to such therapy. This other disease has origins and agonies that are not merely human, and it requires a second kind of river for its healing. Martin Luther referred to this latter pain as the bruised human conscience. It is the essential human illness. It is the pain of sin and guilt and alienation from God and thus also from man. It is the source of all moral evils that plague the world—whether the self-abandoning pleasures sought by hedonists or the self-centered injustices fought by humanists. Its cure, therefore, lies in another stream than the clay-draining river in which the preacher stands. When Bevel Summers announces this second cure, he does not speak for himself, therefore, but for the God of the gospel. Though apparently untutored in formal theology, much less in Roman Catholic thought, Summers performs the first act of Christian initiation by purifying the baptismal waters through a proclamation of the true Word.[4]

> Listen to what I got to say, you people! There ain't but one river and that's the River of Life, made out of Jesus's blood. That's the river you have to lay your pain in, in the River of

---

[3] As a woman who would herself die at thirty-nine of acute lupus erythmatosus, Flannery O'Connor knew the terror of such pain. She even took baths at Lourdes, the celebrated Marian healing center in France. Later O'Connor would confess that she prayed more for her crippled novel-in-progress, *The Violent Bear It Away*, than for her crippled legs. "I am the kind of Christian," she added, "who had rather die for his religion than take a bath for it." She also confessed that the main miracle of Lourdes is that so little disease is communicated in its filthy waters.

[4] Though Summers is a fundamentalist Protestant evangelist, he performs the rite of baptism in utter consistency with Roman Catholic teaching. See, for example, the entries on baptism in Ludwig Ott, *Fundamentals of Catholic Dogma*, first published in German in 1952 and translated into English by Patrick Lynch (Rockford IL: Tan Books, 1955); and in *Catechism of the Catholic Church* (Mahwah NJ: Paulist Press, 1994).

Faith, in the River of Life, in the River of Love, in the rich red river of Jesus' blood, you people! ...All the rivers come from that one River and go back to it like it was the ocean sea and if you believe, you can lay your pain in that River and get rid of it because that's the River that was made to carry sin. It's a River full of pain itself, pain itself, moving toward the Kingdom of Christ, to be washed away, slow, you people, slow as this here old red water river around my feet." (*CW*, 162)

Bevel Summers has a rich analogical imagination because he discerns the essential link between the human and the holy that has been joined in the incarnate Lord whom he proclaims. He thus likens Jesus' atoning blood to the muddy river that is his liquid pulpit. Nothing would seem to be healed or cleansed by a washing in waters either so muddy or so bloody. Yet Summers perhaps knows William Cowper's eighteenth-century hymn, much beloved by Southern Protestants for its emphasis on the sanguinary character of the atonement: "There Is a Fountain Filled with Blood." The river whose healing powers Summers proclaims flows not from any natural source. It is drawn, as Cowper says, "from Emmanuel's veins; / And sinners plunged beneath that flood, / Lose all their guilty stains."

That Bevel Summers's preaching is universally Christian and not provincially fundamentalist is readily evident. Martin Luther and John Calvin both regarded themselves as Catholics who had been driven from the Church, not as willful rebels against Rome. Thus did they both seek to recover what they held to be authentic Catholic teaching—namely, the twin doctrines of *sola gratia* and *sola fide*.[5] Salvation comes solely by

---

[5] The seeming antithesis of Catholic and Protestant Christianity results not from the work of the magisterial Reformers, therefore, but from two subsequent events: on the one hand, the decrees of the Council of Trent (1445–1463) that made salvation seem to be a matter largely of good works and, on the other hand, the nineteenth-century American revivalism that insisted on punctiliar salvation—a single and instantaneous conversion experience of saving grace that requires no consequent life of faithful works, though of course it often produces such a life. Among many books demonstrating the thoroughly Catholic character of the Protestant doctrine of justification by faith alone, none is more helpful than Hans

grace and solely through faith, both of them enabling and neither of them being separable from the other. Thus does the once-accomplished justification by grace alone through Christ's cross issue in a lifelong sanctification of believers through faith alone, as guilty souls are gradually cleansed and redeemed by living in and through the Spirit's abiding presence. Yet the saving result is neither instant nor painless. It often proceeds at the pace of the languid river meandering muddily past Bevel Summers's feet, and it often entails radical self-denials—even death. O'Connor is both catholic and Catholic, therefore, in her insistence that salvation is no instantaneous emotional cure but rather a painful yet joyful conformity—always by means of grace through faith—of sinful human wills to the sinless sacred will. The dread illness of sin, her story reveals, can be healed only as Christians are immersed in the baptismal waters of holy dying and as they are fed, when possible, on the hearing of the Word as well as the eucharistic life that enables holy living.

Satanic evil being the chief obstacle to such living and dying, it must receive an initial purgation before sinners are baptized: "Since Baptism signifies liberation from sin and from its instigator the devil, one or more *exorcisms* are pronounced over the candidate."[6] O'Connor famously confessed that, when the devil appears in her work, he does not indicate "this or that psychological tendency, but an evil power bent on its own supremacy." O'Connor has this devil show up at Harry's baptism in the person of Mr. Paradise. Having failed to be healed of a cancerous growth that still bulges at his temple, this cynical denier of divine grace is a sort of resentful Satan who had rather reign in hell than serve in heaven. That Mr. Paradise is in fact a Luciferian and nihilistic figure is made evident in his manner of fishing: he dangles his line in the water without a hook, convinced that there is nothing to be caught and nothing worth catching. He is also a scoffer, accusing Summers of

---

Küng's *Justification: The Doctrine of Karl Barth and a Catholic Reflection* (Philadelphia: Westminster, 1964).

   [6] "The celebrant then anoints [the baptized] with the oil of catechumens or lays hands on him, and he explicitly renounces Satan" (*Catechism of the Catholic Church*, 317).

having greedy financial motives for his preaching: "Pass the hat and give this kid his money. That's what he's here for" (*CW*, 163). Knowing, on the contrary, that Mr. Paradise has come both to prevent and to destroy faith, Preacher Summers rightly calls for his audience to make a total act of belief, whether in fealty to the demonic or else in the faith that is also an exorcism: "Believe in Jesus or the devil!" he cries. "Testify to one or the other!" (*CW*, 163).

At first Harry Ashfield had found the preacher's name so ludicrous that he mocked it to his face: "My name is Bevvvuuuuul" (*CW*, 164). But he soon discovers that, unlike his parents, Summers is no joker. He is a man who wrestles with realities both holy and demonic, both seen and unseen. For when Summers pulls the boy into the water, Mr. Paradise lets out a loud derisory laugh. Harry instantly recognizes this satanic presence and renounces him in a desperate gesture if not by explicit word: he "grasped the back of the preacher's collar and held it tightly" (*CW*, 165). Discerning what is truly evil, the boy is ready to embrace the good. "Thus prepared," declares the *Catechism of the Catholic Church*, the baptized "is able to *confess the faith of the Church*, to which he will be 'entrusted' by Baptism."[7] So Harry makes his clear monosyllabic confession once the preacher has summoned him to eternal life, as the uppercase spelling of the operative word indicates:

> "If I Baptize you," the preacher said, "you'll be able to go to the Kingdom of Christ. You'll be washed in the river of suffering, son, and you'll go by the deep river of life. Do you want that?"
>
> "Yes," the child said, and thought I won't go to the apartment then, I'll go under the river.
>
> "You won't be the same again," the preacher said. "You'll count." ...Suddenly the preacher said, "All right, I'm going to Baptize you now," and without more warning, he tightened his hold and swung him upside down and plunged his head into the water. He held him under while he said the words of Baptism

---

[7] *Catechism of the Catholic Church*, 317.

and then he jerked him up again and looked sternly at the gasping child. [The child's] eyes were dark and dilated. "You count now," the preacher said. "You didn't even count before." (*CW*, 165)

The charge that Connin and Summers have abused naïve little Harry hinges on the preacher's question and the child's positive response to it. How could a mere four-year-old possibly comprehend the significance of so momentous a matter? Haven't these two fundamentalist Christians taken cynical and selfish advantage of the impressionable child? The answer lies in discerning what it means to *count*. I contend that the preaching of Bevel Summers is at once so richly suggestive and so starkly simple that the children whom Jesus insisted on being brought to him (Mark 10:14; Luke 8:16) can comprehend it.[8] Even a small child—especially a small child—can detect whether he really matters to his mother and father. Harry has eagerly embraced Mrs. Connin's love because he knows that his parents regard him, like everything else, as a joke. He discerns that, in giving him everything he wants, they have given him nothing. In his own childish way, therefore, Harry desires to have real significance, to be *somebody*, to experience real importance in life. He wants to *count*, not just momentarily but absolutely and permanently.

Young Harry has yet to fathom the implications of his life-altering "Yes," and thus of Summers's sealing claim that he will not remain as he

---

[8] The preeminent theologian of the twentieth century, Karl Barth, agrees: "At this point [the utterance of "I believe in Jesus Christ" in the Apostles' Creed] everything becomes clear or unclear, bright or dark. For here we are standing at the centre. And however high and mysterious and difficult everything we want to know might seem to us, yet we may also say that this is just where everything becomes quite simple, quite straightforward, quite childlike. Right here in this centre, in which as Professor of Systematic Theology I must call to you, 'Look! This is the point now! Either knowledge, or the greatest folly!'—here I am in front of you, like a teacher in a Sunday school facing his kiddies, who has something to say which a mere four-year old can understand. 'The world was lost, but Christ was born, rejoice, O Christendom!'" (*Dogmatics in Outline* [New York: Harper & Row, 1959] 66–67).

once was, now that he truly "counts."[9] This saving truth becomes
evident to him when, back at his city dwelling place, the child is
confronted with his parents' mockery of his fledgling faith. His father
ridicules the prayers of intercession that Summers had offered for Mrs.
Ashfield's "affliction," and she herself—leaning over him with her
alcohol-and-cigarette ladened breath—seems to be unbaptizing him:
"She pulled him into a sitting position and he felt as if he had been
drawn up from under the river" (CW, 168). Though Harry sleeps late
the next morning, his parents have not yet risen when he gets up. No
doubt remembering the new life that he had encountered the previous
day in baptism, the boy passes severe judgment on the wasteland world
of his parents: he empties ashtrays onto the floor and rubs their contents
into the carpet. But defiant rejection of parental evils will not suffice if
young Ashfield is truly to "count." He must also "work out his salvation
in fear and trembling" (Philippians 2:12), for baptism issues in a
transformed life. In a quiet but typically dramatic "moment of grace," as
O'Connor called it—a transcendent discernment of the truth and thus a
total turning of the will from self-interest to self-surrender—Harry lies
on his back, looking at his damp shoes: "Very slowly, his expression
changed as if he were gradually seeing appear what he didn't know he'd
been looking for. Then all of a sudden he knew what he wanted to do"
(CW, 169). With excellent untutored logic, he reasons that he won't
have to return to the deadly lovelessness of his parents' apartment if he
plunges himself into the waters wherein, as Summers told him, there is
life. So he strikes out for the river, taking nothing other than "half a
package of Life Savers" from his mother's purse. This telling gesture

---

[9] Roman Catholic teaching holds that, while a baptized person can achieve
eternal salvation even without confirmation, this second sacrament nonetheless
perfects baptism through "an increase of Sanctifying Grace." Harry receives no
sacramental laying on of hands nor any anointing with consecrated oil, but he does
learn what confirmation signifies—the necessity of making his witness, if only in a
death witnessed by but a single person, Mr. Paradise: "[confirmation] too imprints
on the soul an *indelible spiritual mark*, the 'character,' which is a sign that Jesus Christ
has marked a Christian with the seal of his Spirit by clothing him with power on high
so that he may be his witness" (*Catechism of the Catholic Church*, 330).

reveals that, in the deadly place Harry is leaving, cheap candy is the nearest equivalent of salvation.

What the Ashfield boy does at the river may appear to be a pathetic act of suicide, a final despairing escape from his parental world. On the contrary, the narrator explicitly declares that Harry seeks lasting life and not quick death: "He intended not to fool with preachers any more but to Baptize himself and to keep on going this time until he found the Kingdom of Christ in the river" (*CW*, 170). Reasoning with the splendid consistency of a four-year-old, he concludes that, because he has been made to count for so very much by staying under the water so little, he will count absolutely if he stays under the water permanently. In theological terms, Harry Ashfield desires not partial but full salvation, not only baptismal grace but also confirming grace. He also knows, at least instinctively, that to be reared by his parents would be to experience a living hell.

Since baptism is an indelible sacrament, it can be performed only once and never by oneself. It's important thus to note that Harry does not, in fact, baptize himself again. He does not utter the triune baptismal formula at all. Indeed, he almost fails to keep himself under the water, so resistant is the natural buoyancy of his body. The boy himself fears, in fact, that the entire baptismal business may be a deceit, that there may be no radical newness of life, that the world of salvation may be no better than the hellish world of his parents—so near are faith and doubt, so close are salvation and damnation, in O'Connor's world as in life itself.

Young Harry is able to perform his final act of faith only when he sees Mr. Paradise coming after him with a striped candy cane. Here the child is offered, albeit in an entirely negative way, the third and culminating act of Christian initiation: the Eucharist, the partaking of Christ's own redeeming death through the consecrated bread and wine. In Harry's radically compressed commencement in Christian existence, there is no time for a positive performance of this third act. Yet the child instinctively recognizes and refuses an anti-eucharistic offering when the demonic Mr. Paradise wields it as a phallic candy-stick of sexual seduction. Though humanistic readers may want to see the old man as seeking to save the boy from drowning, O'Connor's symbolism is unmistakable—if only by way of nearly what every schoolchild is taught: "Do not accept offers of candy from strangers." In flight from this Luciferian seducer, Harry finally is able to remain beneath the water. No longer angrily fighting it, he yields graciously to the river's gentle pull: "For an instant he was overcome with surprise; then since he was moving quickly and knew that he was getting somewhere, all his fury and his fear left him" (*CW*, 171).

It was a popular medieval belief that the soul—the *homunculus*, the little human-shaped spiritual being that literally informs the *corpus*—exits the body at the time of death, and that devils and angels rush to the death-scene to fight for its final possession. Only the devil appears when young Harry dies, perhaps because the boy's salvation is so secure. In the story's final paragraph, we are shown the defeated and frustrated Mr. Paradise bobbing on the surface of the water, as Harry might see him from beneath the river: "Finally, far downstream, the old man rose like some ancient water monster and stood empty-handed, staring with his dull eyes as far down the river line as he could see" (*CW*, 171). So firmly has the boy's baptism brought him into the only undying life that he is able to perform the ultimate *imitatio Christi*, as he finds the kingdom of Christ not in a figurative but a literal death.

* * *

My students who insisted that Mrs. Connin and Bevel Summers should be arrested and charged with child abuse were thoroughgoing inhabitants of the late-modern age—an age wherein, as we have noticed, survival has become the ultimate good and death thus the ultimate evil. With such an elevation of bodily existence as the prime virtue, bodily pain also becomes the final enemy, especially when it involves the suffering of children. As O'Connor observed, a sentimental age such as ours makes the suffering of children the supreme criterion for establishing one's moral bona fides. Not for a moment does she seek to justify the suffering and death of children. Such horrors are not problems to be scientifically solved, as she said, but mysteries to be faithfully endured.

Yet O'Connor also worried about our almost maniacal dread of pain as well as our even more obsessive concern with the suffering of children. Such seeming goods become abstract and dangerous virtues, she argued, when they are severed from the source of pity and compassion. Their advocates tend, as in the case of my students, to regard suffering and death as direst of all enemies and to believe that, if only we could conquer or at least prevent such evils, life then would be supremely happy. Happiness, in turn, becomes defined largely in terms of the various creature comforts and pleasures. The moral conclusion is ludicrous: the purpose of life is to stay alive, indeed never to die. O'Connor's answer to such noxious notions, rather like the ending of "The River," has caused considerable consternation:

> One of the tendencies of our age is to use the suffering of children to discredit the goodness of God, and once you have discredited his goodness, you are done with him. The Alymers whom Hawthorne saw as a menace have multiplied. Busy cutting down human imperfection, they are making headway also on the raw material of good.... In this popular pity, we mark our gain in sensibility and our loss in vision. If other ages felt less, they saw more, even though they saw with the blind, prophetical, unsentimental eye of acceptance, which is to say, of faith. In the absence of this faith now, we govern by tenderness. It is a tenderness which, long since cut off from the person of Christ, is wrapped in theory. When tenderness is detached from the source of tenderness, its logical outcome is terror. It ends in forced labor camps and in the fumes of the gas chambers. (*CW*, 830–31)

Since there seems to be little connection between the advocacy of tenderness and the burning of Jews at Auschwitz and Dachau, many humanists and even some Christians have objected to O'Connor's assertion that secular pity is likely to turn into mass murder. Yet for O'Connor there is a subtle link between them. Just as Hawthorne's Aylmer sought to eradicate his wife's birthmark with a chemical procedure but killed her in the process, so does our culture seek to heal every ailment, whether mental or physical, with an appropriate therapy. That we may cure bodies while killing souls was O'Connor's great worry. She knew that the mass exterminations committed by the Nazis were justified, at least in part, by the already established German practice of ridding society of its "undesirables," including people whose pain could not be relieved.[10]

Not for O'Connor alone, but for much of Western culture as well, the chief guard against the genocide that is produced, ironically, by this deadly desire to end all suffering and death has been the conviction that the triune and incarnate God himself has endured the ultimate suffering and death. Faith in this crucified Lord, by embracing the suffering and death that lead to eternal life, is thus the antidote to our "culture of death," as Pope John Paul II called it. There are things that are worthy of suffering and dying for—the chief of them being a right relation with both God and man. Mrs. Connin and Bevel Summers both possess this saving relation that comes by baptismal faith. Rather than being arrested and prosecuted for child abuse, therefore, they are to be commended for giving little Harry Ashfield the one gift that cannot be taken away: both temporal and eternal salvation. His death thus makes for a supremely happy ending to a supremely happy story.

---

[10] See Robert Jay Lifton, *The Nazi Doctors: Medical Killing and the Psychology of Genocide* (New York: Basic Books, 1986) and especially Walker Percy's "Unpublished Letter to the *Times*" in Patrick Samway, ed., *Signposts in a Strange Land* (New York: Farrar, Straus and Giroux, 1991) 348–51.

Flannery O'Connor and the Discernment of Catholic Fiction

John R. May

The question of the Catholic dimension of American fiction continues to be a matter of considerable critical interest. Why it is unresolved is due, I think, in significant measure to a failure on the part of scholars to focus the question on the fiction itself—and to ways in which religious faith insinuates itself subtly into story—as opposed to the acknowledged faith of the writer, the writer's expressed intentions, and the broad issue of doctrinal expectations. Without a doubt, biography and the demand for clear theological references cause considerable confusion when we try to discern what makes fiction Catholic and especially—it is my contention in this essay—what makes Flannery O'Connor's fiction Catholic.

Flannery O'Connor has been called a Catholic writer mainly because she made her adherence to Catholicism abundantly clear. But what of the stories she wrote? How or in what sense is her fiction *Catholic* since, on the surface at least, it has so little to do with things specifically Catholic? I insist in this essay on focusing on the fiction itself, and the discernment of whether or not *it* is Catholic or, more precisely, open to a Catholic interpretation, as being the surest way of deciding who is or is not a Catholic fiction writer. The matter of deciding whether the *author* is Catholic is best, if not exclusively, determined by the writer's confession of faith, whether in essays, interviews, or letters, and in documented religious practice.

Three works on American Catholics and their art, published within the past fifteen years, all take their start from biography but narrow its implications; nevertheless, they demonstrate in varying degrees why biography as such is perhaps the weakest link in the complicated process of discerning who is or is not a Catholic author. The works are Paul

Giles's *American Catholic Arts and Fictions: Culture, Ideology, Aesthetics* (1992); Anita Gandolfo's *Testing the Faith: The New Catholic Fiction in America* (1992); and Ross Labrie's *The Catholic Imagination in American Literature* (1997).

Labrie's book "considers only authors who were practicing Roman Catholics, and it focuses only on literary works that center on Catholic belief and spirituality."[1] Gandolfo ignores the biographical "except [and this is of course a major exception] when the writers themselves have publicly discussed the relationship between life and fiction." She calls fiction Catholic principally "insofar as it is informed by a concern for the experience of being a Catholic in the United States."[2] The demand for explicit appeals to religious experience or clear Catholic theological references also causes considerable confusion when we try to decide what makes fiction Catholic, and this has been a stumbling block for many who want to call O'Connor's works Catholic for explicit reasons.

O'Connor writes almost exclusively about rural fundamentalist *Protestants*; Catholic priests function briefly as antagonists in only two of her stories, "The Enduring Chill" and "The Displaced Person." "A Temple of the Holy Ghost" takes its title from the sex education at a Catholic girls' school, introduced by teenage cousins visiting the child and her mother, and ends with Benediction of the Blessed Sacrament in the school's chapel. The only explicit appeal to a sacrament of Christianity is to baptism in "The River" and *The Violent Bear It Away*, and they are backwoods, fundamentalist rituals of immersion. Immersion was not permitted by the Roman Church during O'Connor's life, though it is becoming more widely practiced in American Catholic churches today in the aftermath of the liturgical reforms of the Second Vatican Council; the Trinitarian baptismal formula itself, however, is still rigidly prescribed.

Of the three books, Paul Giles's work is clearly the most helpful in this context precisely because he not only provides a transition from

---

[1] Ross Labrie, *The Catholic Imagination in American Literature* (Columbia: University of Missouri Press, 1997) ix.

[2] Anita Gandolfo, *Testing the Faith: The New Catholic Fiction in America* (New York: Greenwood Press, 1992) xii.

biography, strictly conceived, but also favors implicit, even unconscious, appeals to Catholicism over the explicit. He begins with as forthright a statement of purpose as any reader could possibly want: "to examine the continuing significance of religion, and specifically Roman Catholicism, as an ideological force within modern American literature, film, and photography."[3] First of all, he limits himself to born or converted Catholics (without concern for whether they continued "practicing" or not), but he rejects "that old fashioned kind of biographical approach that seeks to domesticate texts through relating them to the events of one author's individual life" in favor of analyzing texts "in terms of a wider cultural pattern, to indicate how cultural materials affect artistic composition in ways the author would probably not recognize, and hence to elaborate the *unconscious sediments* of artistic production."[4]

Therefore, Giles is helpful in discerning what *is* or *is not* Catholic fiction precisely because he moves beyond the need for explicit Catholic references. Catholic "arts and fictions," he writes, provide significant "insight into how Catholicism has operated in modern times as an *implicit* ideological aesthetic that continues to have psychological and cultural relevance."[5] Because, for Giles, cultural influences shape the artistic product, we can avoid neither the narrow assumption that biography may be helpful in the discovery of the religious sensibility of a work of art nor the broader implication that, insofar as religious cultures exceed the confines of formal belief, one ought conceivably to be able to perceive the sediments of Catholicism, for example, in the works of born Protestants or Jews, or even nonbelievers, since religious cultural influences operate below the level of consciousness. As an obvious case in point, consider the complex question of the authorship of a motion picture, where director, scriptwriter, cinematographer, editor, and producer may all have a hand in the final cut.

In determining what is or is not Catholic fiction, we are on far safer grounds—and this is the wisdom of more than a half century of

---

[3] Paul Giles, *American Catholic Arts and Fictions: Culture, Ideology, Aesthetics* (New York: Cambridge University Press, 1992) 1.

[4] Ibid., 30; my emphasis.

[5] Ibid., 27; my emphasis.

theorizing about the relationship between theology and literature—when we pursue the cultural sediments of faith or, as R. W. B. Lewis suggested forty years ago, the *literary* analogues of theological issues. There is a clear connection, therefore, between Giles's approach and Lewis's in "Hold on Hard to the Huckleberry Bushes," which many consider to be the seminal essay on the autonomy of the literary text in its interaction with religion. Lewis's title is an image Emerson attributed to an elderly Boston woman who was talking about the struggle of earlier Puritan generations to persevere in the faith. For Lewis, "hold[ing] on hard to the huckleberry bushes" becomes the central image for his recommendation that theological literary critics not look for evidence of explicit religious language in fiction, but rather stick to the language of the text and try to discover the literary analogues of religious belief. "The issue," in Lewis's words, "is whether one scrutinizes literature for its univocal formulations of particular historical doctrines one cherishes or whether one submits for a while to the actual ingredients and the inner movement and growth of a work to see what attitude and insight, including religious attitude and insight, the work itself brings into being."[6]

That fiction itself can be a vehicle of religious truth is clear from Jesus' use of parables. That he taught in parables is evident from the Gospels themselves, and that many are stories in the strict sense has long since been demonstrated by a number of scholars. The great wedding feast, the prodigal son, the talents, the ten maidens, the unforgiving servant, the unjust steward, the wedding garment, the wicked tenants, and the workers in the vineyard are freely invented dramatic narratives involving conflicts between human beings that symbolize rather than describe our relationship with God. Surely a story's appeal to the whole person is one of the implicit reasons Jesus used parables to instill a feeling for the new order of God's kingdom that he was instituting, and the implications for our understanding of the Catholic novel or short story are significant.

---

[6] R. W. B. Lewis, "Hold on Hard to the Huckleberry Bushes," in *Trials of the Word: Essays in American Literature and the Humanistic Tradition* (New Haven: Yale University Press, 1965) 99.

Flannery O'Connor, as we are constantly reminded in reading the criticism of her works if we aren't familiar with the primary sources themselves, spoke often about the shape of fiction informed by faith, and in notable instances late in her all-too-brief career she provided us with clear evidence of her attempts to speak in terms of the literary analogues of belief. In an essay composed of relatively late material from her public lectures, based principally on a talk at Georgetown University in 1963 and titled "The Catholic Novelist in the Protestant South," O'Connor addresses what she considers the specific truths of Catholicism, providing what seems to be an apologia for her own fiction, set as it is almost exclusively in the rural Protestant South. "The Catholic novel," she writes,

> can't be categorized by subject matter, but only by what it assumes about human and divine reality. It cannot see man as determined; it cannot see him as totally depraved. It will see him as incomplete in himself, as prone to evil, but as redeemable when his own efforts are assisted by grace. And it will see this grace as working through nature, but as entirely transcending it, so that a door is always open to possibility and the unexpected in the human soul. Its center of meaning will be Christ; its center of destruction will be the devil. No matter how this view of life may be fleshed out, these assumptions form its skeleton. (*MM*, 196–97)

O'Connor's fellow Southerner Walker Percy, who was haunted by persistent references to his being a Catholic writer, specifically by questions about what made his novels Catholic, insisted also on speaking in terms of the literary analogues of belief; and on the most notable occasion of his addressing the issue, he seemed to be building upon O'Connor's elaboration twenty years earlier on fiction's assumptions about "human and divine reality." In his 1984 Flora Levy Lecture at the University of Southwestern Louisiana (now the University of Louisiana at Lafayette), titled "How to Be an American Novelist in Spite of Being Southern and Catholic," Percy said,

The Christian ethos sustains the narrative enterprise in ways so familiar to us that they can be overlooked. It underwrites those very properties of the novel without which there is no novel: I am speaking of the mystery of human life, its sense of predicament, of something having gone wrong, of life as a wayfaring and a pilgrimage, of the density and linearity of time and the sacramental reality of things. ...[A]ny novelist who does not believe that his character finds himself in a predicament not entirely of his own making or of society's making is in trouble as a novelist. And any novelist who begins his novel with his character in a life predicament which is a profound mystery to which he devotes his entire life to unraveling...is a closet Jew or Christian whether he likes it or not.[7]

Percy could just as easily have added Catholic to his list of "closet" believers, except that his interests on this occasion were ecumenical, speaking broadly about our American Jewish-Christian heritage, since Flora Levy in whose honor the lecture series was named was a Jewish benefactor of ULL.

A prominent American theologian, writing about Catholicism's key theological images, identifies three notes or marks that he considers distinctively characteristic of the Catholic faith. Richard P. McBrien, in the concluding summary essay to his popular two-volume work *Catholicism*, lists sacramentality, mediation, and communion as the significant dimensions of the Catholic worldview—these are, in his words, "the theological foci of Catholicism." Because of the principle of *sacramentality*, writes McBrien, "the Catholic vision sees God in and through all things: other people, communities, movements, events, places, objects, the world at large, the whole cosmos. The visible, the tangible, the finite, the historical—all these are actual or potential carriers of the divine presence."[8] McBrien's explanation of

---

[7] Walker Percy, *Signposts in a Strange Land*, ed. Patrick Samway (New York: Farrar, Straus and Giroux, 1991) 178.

[8] Richard P. McBrien, *Catholicism* (Minneapolis: Winston Press, 1980) 1180.

sacramentality, broad and encompassing as it is, best exemplifies the sense of world that we find in O'Connor's fiction. There is scarcely a story of O'Connor's, especially among her truly great short stories, that is not permeated with this sense of sacramentality. Among the grotesque figures, con artists, and demonic characters who are paradoxically sources of grace are The Misfit for the grandmother in "A Good Man Is Hard to Find," Manley Pointer for Joy/Hulga in "Good Country People," the hermaphrodite for the child in "A Temple of the Holy Ghost," Powell Boyd and his companions for Mrs. Cope in "A Circle in the Fire," Rufus for Sheppard in "The Lame Shall Enter First," and Mary Grace for Ruby Turpin in "Revelation." Objects and creatures that function in the same way are the lawn statue for Mr. Head in "The Artificial Nigger," the peacock for Mrs. McIntyre in "The Displaced Person," the Greenleaf bull for Mrs. May in "Greenleaf," the ceiling water stain for Asbury in "The Enduring Chill," and the tattoo of the Byzantine Christ for Parker in "Parker's Back."

As a corollary to sacramentality, *mediation*, according to McBrien, reminds us that "created realities not only contain, reflect, or embody the presence of God, they make that presence *effective* for those who avail themselves of these realities."[9] Significant and obvious examples of mediation among the sacramental experiences just mentioned would include the demonstrable effect of the "artificial nigger" on Mr. Head, of the grandmother's gesture of recognition of The Misfit in "A Good Man Is Hard to Find," and of the circus freak and the host in the monstrance on the child in "A Temple of the Holy Ghost." The third mark, *communion*, that is to say *union with* others, is a necessary condition and effect of our encounter with the divine presence. "Even when the divine-human encounter is most personal and individual, it is still communal in that the encounter is made possible by the mediation of the community."[10] Communion links belief that one is saved with and through others to the image of the goal of sanctification—community of faith becomes the communion of saints. Ruby Turpin's final "vision" in "Revelation" is an ideal fictional representation of the characteristic

---

[9] Ibid.; my emphasis.
[10] Ibid., 1181.

mark of *communion*, as well as Tarwater's vision of the hillside, unacceptable for him, where the multitudes share the loaves and fishes. In the final analysis, the literary analogues of McBrien's three principal foci of Catholicism suggest that the encounter with mystery and its potential for effecting change in us comes invariably through others, even despite others, as is apparently the case with some of O'Connor's protagonists.

Building on these sources, then, I suggest that Catholic fiction—or more precisely fiction that is open to a Catholic interpretation—ought to provide us with some or all of the following literary analogues of Catholic belief (some of which are shared with Judaism and Protestant Christianity), while not negating the possibility of any one of them: the sense of a created world, providentially designed, yet everywhere and at all times impaired by human sin and negligence; a world nonetheless characterized by revelation and mystery, signs and countersigns, unprovoked trials and unexpected mercy; a sense of human nature as deprived or incomplete rather than depraved (uniquely Catholic); a sense of a world so radically altered by the Incarnation that grace is forever embodied in people and things, suggesting continuity rather than discontinuity between the visible world and the transcendent (distinguishes Catholicism from most forms of Protestantism and obviously from Judaism); a world in which human subjects are capable of genuine transformation and growth, always in and through interaction with other human beings, so that progress toward community and away from alienation signals the presence of saving grace (also uniquely Anglo-Catholic and Catholic); and, finally, a sense of human life as shaped by a hopeful orientation toward a future of promise and possibility. The short story, because of its length and dramatic focus usually on a single significant incident, can hardly be expected to exemplify all of these literary analogues of faith; in most instances, it will make one or another the center of dramatic attention.

In turning to O'Connor's fiction to address those troublesome passages that seem to touch directly upon the explicitly Catholic, I will limit myself to the three theological foci that Richard McBrien sees as fundamental characteristics of Catholicism; the constraints of space would seem to demand this. The sense of evil or sin present in the world and its structures, deeply affecting human nature—the assumption really that all religions, especially the major Western religions, seek to address—is clearly present in O'Connor's fiction; if we believe Walker Percy, and I do, it is an essential ingredient of any fiction worth the name. In O'Connor's scheme of theological analogues, I am referring to the Fall, evidence of which is in ample supply in her fiction, as well as to the experience of judgment in the stories, which calls our attention to the presence of evil. Sacramentality, mediation, and communion are McBrien's amplification of what O'Connor referred to as redemption—namely, the offer and acceptance of grace "working through nature" that makes incomplete, or specifically sinful, humans redeemable (*MM*, 185, 196–97).

Concerning the two works of O'Connor's that refer to the sacrament of baptism ("The River" and *The Violent Bear It Away*), I think we ask the wrong question if we inquire whether the baptisms, so prominent in the works mentioned, are valid Catholic sacramental rites. For O'Connor to have attempted that would have violated any semblance of realism in the stories; moreover, she is careful to avoid any indication of what baptismal formula is used. There would seem to be none in "The River" except for the meaning the preacher attaches to the river and its waters. The fact of Tarwater's actual baptism/drowning of Bishop is described indirectly from Rayber's perspective ("he knew with an instinct as sure as the dull mechanical beat of his heart that [Tarwater] had baptized the child even as he drowned him," [*VBIA*, 203]); later, the narrator has Tarwater recall the event for the truck driver in these vague words: "The words just come out of themselves but it don't mean nothing"—the words of baptism, of course, that Mason had sown in his soul (*VBIA*, 209).

The precise question that should be asked, since we are dealing with fiction, is this: are the stories open to a Catholic sensibility, broadly conceived (as Giles proposes), and how, if at all, do the rites contribute to our sense of the distinctively Catholic, remembering Lewis's suggestion that we hold on hard to the language of the text? Even though I have dealt extensively elsewhere with the significance of

Tarwater's baptism/drowning of Bishop,[11] I would like to offer a few summary comments, especially for those who expect the presentation of a valid Catholic ritual for the stories to be considered Catholic. At the end of the novel, it is clear that Tarwater comes to realize that he has failed in both of his efforts to thwart Mason's plan for him—by cremating Mason and drowning rather than baptizing Bishop. In the perspective of the novel, he *has* baptized Bishop and he discovers finally that Buford gave Mason a proper Christian burial. This latter discovery follows his horrifying experience of pure evil at the hands of the homosexual rapist. It is then that he knows Mason was right and that he must follow the path of prophecy for which Mason prepared him, providing the basis for his ritual purification of the spot overlooking Powderhead where he last hears the sibilant tones of the enemy attacking the inner core of his spirit.

In the whole context of the "The River," the denominational character of the rite of baptism is irrelevant, especially, it seems to me, whether or not it is a *valid* Catholic rite. That it is an outward sign instituted implicitly by Christ to give "grace"—to make an ironic, qualified appeal to the classic Catholic definition of a sacrament from the *Baltimore Catechism*—is obvious in the world of the story. (Jesus insists on our being born again of water and the Spirit; it is highly unlikely that he would have used the Trinitarian formula attributed to him at the end of Matthew's Gospel that has been codified by the institutional Church.) One thing the rite in "The River" is not is magic, and this is clear from the catechesis offered by the Reverend Bevel Summers. In fact, I take it as both appropriate and significant that the story is called "The River" and not "The Baptism."

The river and the rite performed in it are unequivocally symbolic, as are the dying and rising with Christ associated with the rite of baptism in the letters of St. Paul. "Listen to what I got to say, you people," Reverend Bevel Summers shouts, "there ain't but one river and that's the River of Life, made out of Jesus' Blood. That's the river you have to lay your pain in, in the river of Faith, in the River of Life, in the River of

---

[11]John R. May, *Toward a New Earth: Apocalypse in the American Novel* (Notre Dame: University of Notre Dame Press, 1972) 134–38.

Love, in the rich red river of Jesus' Blood, you people!" (*CS*, 165). Then, speaking personally to Harry, and in language presumably he can understand, the preacher says, "You won't be the same again.... You'll count," which is something of course that Harry has never experienced at home with his parents, whose dissolute urban lifestyle is effectively lifeless, loveless, and faithless (*CS*, 168). What Harry experiences is the pain of neglect, without being able to express it, but a pain nonetheless that he would instinctively like to leave in "the River of Life." The community of shared belief provided by Mrs. Connin and the Reverend Summers offers Harry a whole new feeling about life—namely, a sense of belonging. It is hard to imagine a more precise literary analogue to the theological explanation of the effects of the sacrament of baptism than to say that through the rite we *both* "count," especially in the eyes of God, and "belong" to and within a community of believers. The desire to "count" permanently—as Harry never has in the "ashfield" of his parents' apartment—ultimately shapes his decision to return to the river of life; and even though he awakens to the understanding that the river alone "wouldn't have him," his efforts to flee the frightening Mr. Paradise, "like a giant pig bounding after him," lead ironically to an implicitly fortunate conclusion. Literal acceptance by the river for Harry's pre-symbolic imagination is of course his ultimate goal (*CS*, 173–74).

The literary sediments of specifically Catholic belief in the efficacy of the sacrament of baptism are unmistakably present in the story. The world of "The River" is a richly interwoven tapestry of the principal theological foci of *sacramentality, mediation,* and *communion.* The river not only reflects the bountiful presence of God's mercy—it is "the River of Life, made out of Jesus' blood"—but also confers the grace of acceptance, of Harry's entrance into the kingdom where he truly "counts." These redemptive riches come to him through the communion of faith represented by Mrs. Connin and the Reverend Bevel Summers and his followers.

That O'Connor considered Harry and Bishop effectively saved by the grace of the sacrament and expected an astute reader to draw this conclusion, I have no doubt. In terms of McBrien's foci, in the narrow theological sense, they were rites performed in the name of a community of belief, and the ritual, at least I feel confident in asserting, mediated the redemptive grace of Jesus Christ. Keep in mind that even the Roman Catholic Church, which controls its own institutional rites for *ordinary* circumstances, acknowledges two extraordinary modes of baptism—baptism of desire and of blood—a fortunately modest way of admitting that we have no control over God's merciful disposition of the grace of his Son's redemption.

As for the two works that make obvious appeals to the sacramental bread of communion (the recurring image of the bread of life in *The Violent Bear It Away* and the Benediction service in "A Temple of the Holy Ghost"), the former has a backwoods fundamentalist setting, the latter a specifically Catholic one and arguably O'Connor's only explicitly Catholic setting from beginning to end. The eucharistic sensibility of the novel—Tarwater's being programmed by Mason to yearn for the bread of life, and finally freely accepting it as the goal of his life—stems directly from O'Connor's profound faith in the sacrament, but it is equally clear that she had not attempted to create a specifically Catholic setting or to make the accumulated eucharistic imagery sacramental in the technical sense. That the world of *The Violent Bear It Away* is one of *sacramentality, mediation,* and *communion* seems to me unequivocally true, and in another context I have attempted to demonstrate that.[12] That the eucharistic host in the monstrance during the Benediction ceremony in "A Temple of the Holy Ghost" is genuinely Catholic in intention and execution there can be no question (Benediction is of course technically a sacramental not a sacrament). However, whether the authenticity of this Catholic sacramental is what makes the story Catholic is beside the point because it ignores the heart of the story's concerns, which is whether the child will, through her experience with the circus hermaphrodite and the Benediction host, learn to accept herself for what she is, with all of her personal shortcomings, and what she can accomplish despite them. What O'Connor achieves through the association of physical deformity with God's willing reduction of himself

---

[12] John R. May, *The Pruning Word: The Parables of Flannery O'Connor* (Notre Dame: University of Notre Dame Press, 1976) 137–50.

to the lowly dimensions of everyday food is a world in which the child's transformation is effected by the grace incarnate in visible human experiences, and with and through others, even despite them, insofar as the benediction host is linked sacramentally with the inspiration of the hermaphrodite. The child's final prayer is pure, though modest, hope, reflecting the transformation that *sacramentality, mediation*, and *communion* have effected in her. "Hep me," she prays, "not to be so mean. ...Hep me not to give her [her mother] so much sass. Hep me not to talk like I do" (*CS*, 247).

By way of a conclusion, I am urged to offer a brief reflection on the sort of sectarian analysis in which we are engaged. At the beginning of this new millennium and in an age that has seen remarkable advances in ecumenical dialogue among religious groups, it is reasonable to wonder why critics interested in religion continue to insist on the denominational labels. Labels are of course easy to apply and readily available, yet they inevitably circumvent the analytical process. They are especially regrettable when we note that, after a solid half century of interdisciplinary scholarship in the area of literature and religion, many continue to fall for the biographical fallacy, the assumption that if writers are Jewish or Catholic, they necessarily write Jewish or Catholic novels. That these labels can mean something—or should mean something—that must also be subjected to literary critical scrutiny, Kieran Quinlan has unwittingly brought to our attention in his book about Walker Percy, which regrettably calls him *The Last Catholic Novelist*. Neither Percy nor O'Connor ever effectively dodged the Catholic tag, any more than Saul Bellow or Philip Roth have been able to avoid the Jewish label. Jews and Catholics continue to be notable minorities in this dominantly Protestant Christian country, and minorities for better or worse always attract attention. But the truth of the matter is that novels by and about Jews or Catholics are not necessarily Jewish or Catholic novels.

We ought to take a hint from Walker Percy's apparent preference for talking about what is implicitly Christian and/or Jewish, referred to previously in this essay. Note that in the context of his discussion of his own work as Catholic, he refers to "closet" Jews and Christians—when it comes to our Western religious view of human beings as confused, if not confounded, yet hopeful pilgrims. In a thoroughgoing ecumenical age, we ought perhaps to be satisfied with discerning what fiction is open to a Jewish-Christian interpretation. It would clearly broaden our appreciation of many of our great living writers—such as John Updike and Toni Morrison—whose works are profoundly Jewish-Christian in worldview, and even at times I think more Catholic than some of the so-called great "Catholic" writers from the mid-twentieth century such as Graham Greene and François Mauriac, whose works were sufficiently infected with Jansenism to render their fictional worldviews antithetical to genuine Christianity and Catholicism. Nonetheless, I am fully aware that there will always be a reasonable, though at times unnecessarily parochial, desire on the part of critics to deal with the specifically Jewish or Protestant or Catholic in arts and fiction; on those occasions, we must take a cue from the Puritan woman Emerson referred to and "hold on hard to the huckleberry bushes," so that our discernment of Judaism, Protestantism, and Catholicism begins not from biography and explicit creedal or sacramental references but from the evidence of a particular faith's literary and artistic analogues or, as Paul Giles puts it, from the unconscious sediments of belief.

To end where I began, namely declaring Giles's work *American Catholic Arts and Fictions* to be most helpful in steering us clear of biography and *explicit* Catholic references in fiction in our quest for what makes a novel Catholic, I must note some reservations that I have about his explanation of the "unconscious sediments of belief" in O'Connor's fiction. With his general assumptions about "unconscious sediments" and his specific conclusion that O'Connor's fiction is indeed Catholic, I have no difficulty. He places, however, too much emphasis on the often-quoted passage from O'Connor's first letter to Betty Hester ("A.") where she declares herself "a Catholic peculiarly possessed of the modern consciousness, that thing Jung describes as unhistorical, solitary and guilty" (*HB*, 90).

In a far too brief summary of what is necessarily a complicated assessment of her theological "development,"[13] Giles moves O'Connor from her confession in her essays and letters of being a "hillbilly" Thomist, through becoming as well a neo-scholastic, to realizing effectively in her fiction what would become the modernist and postmodernist theological assumptions of David Tracy, "reading Aquinas through Rahner and Derrida,"[14] which leaves O'Connor's Catholic fiction in a state of far greater theological ambiguity than I, for one, feel comfortable with. Following Tracy especially, Giles says, "it is just this creative tension between analogy and difference that fires O'Connor's fiction."[15] He goes on to add, "It is this paradoxical sense of incompleteness and displacement in O'Connor that ensures her fiction comes to carry a larger aesthetic complexity and significance than the rigidity of the new-scholastic dogma professed in her letters and essays might imply."[16] The tension Giles finds in O'Connor's fiction is between the "untroubled certainties" of the scholastic concept of analogy ("an excessively domesticated sense of philosophical coherence") and "the absences and discontinuities of postmodernism, predicated as it is upon a world of philosophical fragmentation and difference."[17] Does one, however, have to go so far afield to find theological justification for the tension between ambiguity and certainty, displacement and coherence, by appealing anachronistically to theological developments well beyond O'Connor's reach? The answer, of course, is no.

Simply as a *literary* category, there is more than enough ambiguity in O'Connor's fiction, especially the short stories, to supply critics with continuing opportunities for serious scholarship. One can, I think, declare with assurance, if not with certainty, that the sacramental rites of baptism in "The River" and *The Violent Bear It Away* are open to a Catholic interpretation, as well as by implication the fictional narratives as a whole. If I have chosen the literary analogues of Richard McBrien's

---

[13] Giles, *American Catholic Arts and Fictions*, 358–67.
[14] Ibid., 366.
[15] Ibid.
[16] Ibid.
[17] Ibid.

key theological foci of Catholicism, it is not because I think he is a better theologian than David Tracy, or more orthodox, but rather because his mode of theological reflection is closer in tone and implication to the world of faith O'Connor knew.

Contributors

HELEN R. ANDRETTA is professor of English at York College, The City University of New York, and a mentor in the McNair Scholars Program. Primarily a medievalist but interested in interdisciplinary studies, her research and publications are in the areas of philosophical, theological, and psychological influences on literature. Andretta's publications include *Chaucer's "Troilus and Criseyde": A Poet's Response to Ockhamism* (1997); "A Thomist's Letters to 'A.,'" volumes 26 and 27 of *The Flannery O'Connor Bulletin*; and proceedings papers from *Christianity and Literature* conferences and general literature conferences. Andretta holds a Ph.D. from The City University of New York—Graduate School/University Center, and her recent research studies are for a book project on a hylomorphic approach to Flannery O'Connor and her works.

JILL PELÁEZ BAUMGAERTNER is the author of three collections of poetry: *Finding Cuba* (Chimney Hill Press, 2001), *Leaving Eden* (White Eagle Coffee Store Press, 1995), and *Namings* (Franciscan University Press, 1999); a textbook/anthology, *Poetry* (1990); and *Flannery O'Connor: A Proper Scaring* (1998). She edited the spring 2001 issue of *Christianity and Literature*, devoted to the poetry that appeared in the journal over the past fifty years. She was nominated for a Pushcart Prize and is the winner of the White Eagle Coffee Store Press's poetry chapbook contest, the Goodman Award, an Illinois Arts Council Award, the Illinois Prize of the Rock River Poetry Contest, and the CCL Midwest Poetry Contest. Baumgaertner received her BA from Emory, her MA from Drake, and her Ph.D. from Emory. She serves as poetry editor of *The Christian Century*, is president of CCL, and is a professor of

English and dean of Humanities and Theological Studies at Wheaton College.

STEPHEN C. BEHRENDT is the George Holmes Distinguished University Professor of English at the University of Nebraska, where his primary research and teaching interests lie in eighteenth- and nineteenth-century British literature, art, and culture, and women writers of the Romantic era. His current research project involves Irish women poets of the Romantic period. Behrendt's books include *Royal Mourning and Regency Culture: Elegies and Memorials of Princess Charlotte* (1997), *Reading William Blake* (1992), *Shelley and His Audiences* (1989), and three books of original poetry: *History* (forthcoming), *A Step in the Dark* (1996), and *Instruments of the Bones* (1992), all from Mid-List Press, Minneapolis. He also has edited several collections of essays on British Romantic culture and is an advisory editor to the literary journal *Prairie Schooner*. Behrendt received his Ph.D. from the University of Wisconsin, and his interest in Flannery O'Connor and the literature of the South is a long-standing and strong avocation.

TIMOTHY P. CARON is an associate professor of American literature and assistant chair of the English department at California State University, Long Beach. He teaches a wide range of courses, both to undergraduate majors and MA students, in nineteenth- and twentieth-century American literature, including seminars on William Faulkner, Toni Morrison, and Ralph Ellison. Since receiving his Ph.D. from Louisiana State University in 1994, he has published essays on Zora Neale Hurston, Richard Wright, and Cormac McCarthy. Caron has also published *Struggles Over the Word: Race and Religion in O'Connor, Faulkner, Hurston, and Wright* with Mercer University Press (2000). He is working on two book manuscripts: *"We're Brothers All": Selected Civil War Writings from* Century *Magazine*, and a study of Faulkner's critical reception.

JOHN F. DESMOND is the Mary A. Denny Professor of Literature at Whitman College. He is the author of *Walker Percy's Search for*

Community (2004) and *Risen Sons: Flannery O'Connor's Vision of History* (1987). Desmond, who received his Ph.D. from the University of Oklahoma, has published widely on Flannery O'Connor, William Faulkner, Walker Percy, Bernard Malamud, Graham Greene, Mark Twain, and Eudora Welty in *The Southern Review, Louisiana Literature, Logos, Renascence, The Mississippi Quarterly, Modern Age,* and *The Southern Literary Journal.* Desmond is the founder and president of the Walker Percy Society and serves on the editorial boards of *Literature and Belief* and *The Flannery O'Connor Review* (formerly *The Flannery O'Connor Bulletin*).

ROBERT DONAHOO is professor of English at Sam Houston State University and the current editor of *Cheers!* the Flannery O'Connor Society newsletter. He received his Ph.D. from Duke University and has published previous articles on O'Connor in the *Flannery O'Connor Review, The CEA Critic, Journal of Contemporary Thought, Literature and Belief,* and *Journal of the Short Story in English,* as well as an essay in the collection *"On the Subject of the Feminist Business": Re-reading Flannery O'Connor.* He has also published essays on postmodern American fiction, Tolstoy's novel *Resurrection,* the dramas of Horton Foote, and Larry Brown's novel *Dirty Work.*

JOHN R. MAY, whose doctorate in theology and literature is from Emory University's Institute of Liberal Arts, is the Donald and Norma Nash McClure Alumni Professor of English and Religious Studies at Louisiana State University, where he teaches courses on religion, film, and literature, especially American film and Southern literature. May is the author of *Toward a New Earth: Apocalypse in the American Novel* (1972) and *The Pruning Word: The Parables of Flannery O'Connor* (1976); the editor of *The Bent World: Essays on Religion and Culture* (1981), *Image and Likeness: Religious Visions in American Film Classics* (1992), and *New Image of Religious Film* (1997); the coauthor of *Film Odyssey: The Art of Film as Search for Meaning* (1976) and *The Parables of Lina Wertmuller* (1977); and the coeditor of *Religion in Film* (1982). His most recent book is *Nourishing Faith Through Fiction: Reflections of the Apostles' Creed in*

Literature and Film (2001). May serves on the advisory board of *The Flannery O'Connor Review*, and in October 2003 he chaired a panel discussion at the Flannery O'Connor Symposium titled *REVELATIONS*, which took place at Georgia College and State University in Milledgeville.

JOANNE HALLERAN MCMULLEN is an assistant dean of continuing education at Louisiana State University and director of LSU Extended Learning. She received her BA from the University of Kansas, her MA from Ohio University, and her Ph.D. from the University of Nebraska-Lincoln. McMullen has presented conference papers and published several articles on O'Connor including "The Verbal Structure of Infinity," in *Language, Style, and Literary Response: The Role of Stylistics in Literary and Cultural Studies*, a special issue of *Language and Literature*. She is also the author of *Writing against God: Language as Message in the Literature of Flannery O'Connor* (Mercer University Press, 1996). After the publication of her book, McMullen received correspondence from Elizabeth (Betty) Hester who revealed herself as "A.," and they established a friendship through correspondence. McMullen continues to be intrigued by O'Connor's writings and Catholicism as perceived by contemporary readers.

JON PARRISH PEEDE is counselor to the chairman of the National Endowment of the Arts, Dana Gioia. He is also director of the NEA's *Operation Homecoming: Writing the Wartime Experience* program, for which he led a team of thirty-five distinguished writers to help troops and their families share their stories. Peede previously served as director of communications at Millsaps College, where he won several national writing awards. He is the founder of Parrish House Books, a small press focused on American poets, and served as editor at Mercer University Press. He received his BA in English from Vanderbilt University and his MA in Southern Studies from the University of Mississippi. He has published stories, poems, and reviews in journals and encyclopedias.

W. A. SESSIONS, Regents' Professor of English Emeritus at Georgia State University, received his AB from the University of North Carolina at Chapel Hill and his MA and Ph.D. from Columbia. He is a poet, a critic, a writer, a playwright, and a lecturer and has garnered numerous honors and awards for his scholarship. Sessions has written numerous books and articles on Henry Howard (Earl of Surrey), Francis Bacon, and Flannery O'Connor, and he continues his active literary career as a lecturer at national and international conferences. In addition to his prolific writings and presentations, Sessions, a personal friend of O'Connor and her family, is her authorized biographer. He was also selected by Elizabeth (Betty) Hester (recently revealed to be O'Connor's longtime correspondent "A.") to serve as her literary executor.

RALPH C. WOOD, University Professor of Theology and Literature at Baylor University in Waco, Texas, holds BA and MA degrees from Texas A&M University at Commerce, as well as MA and Ph.D. degrees from the University of Chicago. Wood teaches in the departments of English and Religion at Baylor and at the Truett Theological Seminary. His major book, first published in 1988 and still in print from the University of Notre Dame Press, is titled *The Comedy of Redemption: Christian Faith and Comic Vision in Four American Novelists* (Flannery O'Connor, Walker Percy, John Updike, and Peter De Vries). He serves as an editor-at-large for *The Christian Century* and on the editorial board of the *Flannery O'Connor Review*. He is also the author *of Contending for the Faith: The Church's Engagement with Culture* (2003), *The Gospel According to Tolkien* (2003), and *Flannery O'Connor and the Christ-Haunted South* (2004).

Index